UNDER CONTRACT

UNDER CONTRACT

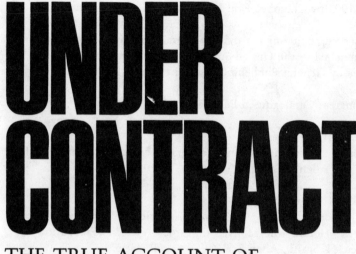

THE TRUE ACCOUNT OF
A COP HIRED TO KILL

CHEROKEE PAUL McDONALD
and ALLEN E. SMITH

DONALD I. FINE, INC.
NEW YORK

Library of Congress Cataloging-in-Publication Data

McDonald, Cherokee Paul.
   Under contract : the true account of a cop hired to kill / by Cherokee Paul McDonald and Allen E. Smith.
      p.   cm.
   ISBN 1-55611-322-6
   1. Smith, Allen E., 1949–   2. Police—Florida—Biography.
3. Detectives—Florida—Biography.   4. Murder—Florida—Prevention—
Case studies.   I. Smith, Allen E., 1949–   . II. Title.
HV7911.S564M33   1992
364.1'523'092—dc20
   [B]   91-55604
                                                                      CIP

Manufactured in the United States of America

10 9 8 7 6 5 4 3 2 1

Designed by Irving Perkins Associates

For Brian McCoy and Dennis Stefanini, we have turned our partnership into a brotherhood . . . and Amanda and Carolyn, my daughters, whom I love very much.

A.E.S.

For all undercover cops who go out into the darkness wearing only that invisible badge wrapped around their heart.

C.P.M.

Florida State Statute 777.04 (2)
Attempts, solicitation, conspiracy, generally—

Whoever solicits another to commit an offense prohibited by law and in the course of such solicitation commands, encourages, hires, or requests another person to engage in specific conduct which would constitute such offense or attempt to commit such an offense commits the offense of criminal solicitation.

Florida State Statute 782.04 (1) (a)
Murder—

The unlawful killing of a human being:
1. When perpetrated from a premeditated design to effect the death of the person killed or any human being.

With the exception of Allen E. Smith, all of the officers' names used in these stories have been changed. Most of the officers involved are still assigned to sensitive undercover roles, and the use of pseudonyms is at their request.

In addition, all of the names of the victims, witnesses, informants, and perpetrators have been changed in each of the described incidents. This was done to protect the innocent, and because several of these cases are still in the appeals process.

Each of these cases is a matter of public record, contained in police files and court documents. Quoted dialogue is taken from transcripts of formal statements, transcripts of covertly recorded conversations taped during actual operations, or the detailed recollection of Allen E. Smith. Statements and tape transcripts have been edited for length and continuity, but the editing has remained faithful to content.

A.E.S./C.P.McD.

HORSESHOES AND HAND GRENADES

"I'M TELLING YOU right now, the opening at the end of the barrel of a forty-five looks about that big." He held his two big hands up in front of his face and made a rough circle eight inches across with his open fingers. "Like the friggin' black hole of death when you're starin' into it from an inch away. I took my eyes away from the barrel and made myself look into the eyes of the guy who held that forty-five up to my face. The sonofabitch only needed to twitch that trigger to blow my brains all over the walls of the small office we stood in. I watched the way he was looking at me, like he was searching my eyes for some sign that would convince him of who I was or something. I could see a weird light in there, like he was feeling a rush of power and some kind of twisted fear. Right at that moment I didn't know which was worse." He paused for a second, his face grim. Then, "When they look at you like that, really try to look into your skull, man, you've got to *know* you are what you're telling them you are. You've got to believe it yourself, or you're a dead man."

I watched the man who sat leaning toward me as he spoke. Fort Lauderdale Police Det. (Organized Crime, Intelligence) Allen E. Smith had agreed to tell me some of his stories, and as he spoke I could feel an edge to his words. He is open and intelligent, and his soft, almost quiet voice is a surprise. His knuckles don't drag on the ground, and he doesn't speak in a series of grunted one-syllable words. He *does* have an overall look of tough about him, and you get the immediate impression that he comes not from an office or classroom, but from a world where the resolution of conflict is much more intense and absolute. I watch him talk, feel the intensity in his words, and see a glimpse of what those in his world see. He sits near me wearing tight black jeans and boots, a short-sleeved polo knit, also black, and lots of heavy gold jewelry. He looks perfect for either of the parts he has played for so long: undercover cop . . . and hired killer.

"I was standing in that office with one of our informants at the back of this place called Kenny C's Bar. It was over in North Fork, next to our city limits. You know it, CP, it's one of those satellite towns around here that never seems to change, like Davie with its cowboy look, or old Hacienda Village with its shit-kicking bar and just enough highway to run a speed trap. North Fork has managed to keep the southern attitudes and city offices, even its own little police department." His eyes change briefly. "Had some rot, too.

"It was just after nine at night when we walked into the place. It was in a tired-looking strip shopping center where the main road curved through town. There were no friggin' lights out back on the parking area, which was mostly unpaved. Huge potholes everywhere, with that fine powdery dust in the bottom of them. Kenny C's was supposed to be a rustic country-western bar, with wood paneling and cowboy stuff hung on the walls, but it was dingy and had a musty smell, like the inside of one of those adult bookstores, you know? There was hardly anybody there when we walked in, just some older rundown types with teeth missing and some chew in their lips. They were being serenaded by a big-breasted bleached blonde." He smiled then, remembering. "She sounded pretty good to me as we went past her to the office.

"The guy with the gun owned the place. He had put the word out he needed a hitman. The informant, one of those hairballs always wheeling and dealing with the cops because of his own screwups, heard the word on the street, figured he could bank some Brownie points with us and set it up for me. He had the work name 'Aries,' and was in his late forties. Drove an old pickup truck, wore pearl-buttoned shirts with the sleeves up, and had one of those belt buckles about the size of a license plate. He was tall and skinny in his snakeskin boots, and believed himself to be a real crafty dude. Shit, I could feel him trembling beside me in that office. He knew me as Al Sanetti, which is my undercover name. I was there to let the bar owner hire me as his killer, but first we had to play this little power and control bullshit."

I watched as Al Smith bunched one fist and softly pounded it into the other, his big forearms resting across the tops of his knees. I could tell he still felt the anger as he told me the story, even though years had gone by. I guess when you put yourself that far out front on a deal, out in a cop's no-man's land, the feelings leave scar tissue across your memories.

"This clown's name was Ken Cippaloni," Al said quietly, and his cop's memory for detail in personal descriptions kicked in, "He was tall and slender, early forties, pale skin and almost too-black hair, if you know what I mean. Had it all blow-dried and puffy. He had a deep voice with one of those real northern accents." Al looked at me with a quick grin and snorted a laugh, "With his bogus cowboy-style clothes, his up-North voice, his alligator shoes, pinky ring, and big cigar he came across like some guy from Little Italy playing Festus. He must have come into the place from the front door or changed his pants, because I remember noticing that he didn't have any of that damned parking lot dust on him like the rest of us. Anyway, he's got the cigar in his teeth and he says, 'If you are who you say you are, I'll apologize to you. If you turn out to be something else, I'll blow your fucking head off.' I guess he was feeling pretty good with that forty-five in his hand, but he made a mistake then, leaning in to search me.

"He got close enough for me to take that big hunk of gun away from him. I already didn't like the puke—he wanted someone killed but he didn't have the balls to do it himself. I should have taken that gun and shoved it up his ass, but hell, I had to make a case on him. I mean, I was comfortable being *undercover*. Hell, you know I've played the game plenty of times as a narc, but this was the first time for *this* game, murder for hire. I just had to go along with the scene, so I stood there while his hands found the gun at my waist. Sure I had a gun. What hitman wouldn't? I had Al Sanetti ID in my wallet, but no badge. Well, he had already formed his opinion just looking at me."

Al Smith is a big man, over six feet and two hundred pounds, lots of bone and muscle. He gives off raw physical power even when relaxed. His hands are big and knuckly, his arm, shoulder, and back muscles well-developed in a purposeful, functional way, not pretty like some body-builder on the cover of a fitness magazine. He has a warrior's face, and many of his past conflicts have left their mark. His eyes are dark but not brooding, big and full of expression and exploration. His nose juts confidently over his wide mouth, and he wears a trimmed black beard. Women *and* men size him up visually when he enters a room. He is a man both attractive and formidable. He grins at me.

"People see what they want to see, right? I've been told that with this face maybe I shouldn't ever try to hide among a group of Vienna Choir Boys. So this guy had put the word out for a hitman, and he saw one standing there. Man, I was surprised he was buying it. I always thought I look like a *cop*, you know, that 'cop look' stuff . . . around the eyes and all that. He pulled the forty-five back slightly and looked over at Aries. I had taped a wire to the informant's bony chest, and if Cippaloni found it, this deal was going down the tubes real fast. But he didn't check Aries, because right then the damned office door opened and the big-breasted blonde singer stuck her head in, saw us all standing there, and closed it again with an 'oops.'

"For a couple of seconds I could see my two partners, Stanley and McBride, leaning against the bar a few feet away. I managed to smile at them, which was the only way I could think of to signal them that everything was cool. Otherwise those two crazies would have come right through that door and *onto* Cippaloni's sorry ass. They told me later they felt like somebody pulled their pants down when we were all staring at each other like that. After the door closed, Cippaloni just grunted and went behind his desk and put the gun down. I felt my nerves tingle all the way down my spine. I told him that one was free, but if he crossed me or pulled a gun on me again, he'd better use it, because I'd hurt him so bad he'd beg me to kill him. He gave like a nervous little laugh, swallowed hard, and got down to business.

"He told me he owned the place, but not the building. I could tell he was getting his confidence back as he told me he was already paying too much rent, and now the lease was up and the guy wanted more rent *and* cash under the table. The old guy was squeezing him too hard now, and he had to get out from under. He needed the old guy *dead*, then he could make some progress with his business. He says, 'I'm only sorry I can't kill the bastard more than once, Al.'

"I told him it would be five grand, half up front, nonnegotiable. He just shrugged, like he expected it, so I asked him how's his problem gonna be solved with the old guy's death. Wouldn't there be family, or a partner, or the widow or somethin'? Cippaloni smiled then, stood, and pulled open that damned office door again. A different woman stepped in this time, like she had been waiting outside, and he introduced her as Ruth. He tells her my name and says I'm the guy who's gonna get rid of her husband.

"We looked each other over, me and the woman. She was late thirties with frosted blonde hair. She looked fit, like she exercised. Nice clothes, black slacks and a silk print blouse. She wore some good jewelry and was easy on the makeup. Not a bad piece of work, and my first impression was that she was too good for Cippaloni. Then she says, 'How *soon* do you think you'll be able to get rid of that asshole?' It didn't sound like she meant it, though, and she was looking at Cippaloni as she said it. I had the feeling her cowboy stud might be pushing her into this deal but maybe I was trying to like her. She told me her husband's name was Abe Silver, and handed me a photo of a gray-haired old man in a plain white shirt. On the back was their home address and a description of a Cadillac with the tag number. Then she stood there chewing her lip.

"I pocketed the photo. Cippaloni opened a drawer, hesitated, then pulled out a wad of cash. He threw it down on the desk in front of me and said it was twenty-five, the half up front. I nodded and picked it up, and me and Aries turned to get out of there. Cippaloni got all worried lookin' and asks me if I don't want to count the cash first. I just stared at him, then her, and told them I was sure I didn't have to count it because *they* knew and *I* knew they didn't want to start this deal off by fucking with me. They just blinked at me and I got out of the office, my skin crawling. I remember wondering how the hell I had gone from cop to hitman in the first place."

ALLEN E. SMITH was born in Detroit, but was raised in a small house surrounded by other working-class homes in Hollywood, Florida, from the time he was four-years-old. While his father was out working at various jobs, his mother labored at home, raising six kids and trying to keep things livable around the house. Al was a rough-and-tumble kid, and by the time he was sixteen he had the build and street knowledge to back it up. He says he doesn't know if it's the Cherokee Indian or Italian in his blood, but he grew up burdened by a very short temper and occasionally "went berserk" when angered. During his last year of high school he shot up another guy's prized '62 Ford because the guy had made some moves on Al's girl. Bad idea. The local cops nailed him and he was thrown into the judicial system as a juvenile offender. The judge made him one of those offers he couldn't refuse: jail, or the U.S. Army for the next three years.

"I guess I was just a bunch of hormones straining to do *something*, and I really took to the army. I mean, I *liked* it . . . well, most of it. I remember one of my favorite instructors was a sergeant who had been a sniper in Vietnam. He told me a story that stuck with me all these years. He was in a sniper position deep in the jungle, alone, and began dozing. He woke up with a start, you know how your head snaps back? He realized he wasn't alone. Four North Vietnamese regulars had set up their night position a few feet away. He stayed still until *they* finally fell asleep. Then he carefully brought his weapon up and blew away all four before they could react. I remember feeling his fear as he told me the story, then the rush he felt when he came out of it alive. I guess it formed a seed in me that would serve me years later as an undercover cop: You blend in with the jungle, become *part* of it, camouflage yourself with the shadows, and let your enemy look at you but not see you. Then kill him."

Al served in Vietnam, ironically assigned to a Military Police unit. To his surprise he found police work was something he enjoyed doing and felt good about, even in a combat theater. He liked being part of an outfit that participated in events and made a positive difference. He also learned that even in war there are crimes, and the people who commit the crimes against others need to be identified and stopped. He came home changed from the rough young man who had left to go to war three years before. Still the muscle and grit, still the quiet anger, but some scars now, and a tempering, a seasoning. He came home believing he had to be part of the solution not the problems. He had two older brothers who became police officers, and Al saw something in them he wanted to be. He still looked for battle, but one with meaning. Al came home to be a cop on the streets of South Florida.

He stood now near the glass south wall of my office, staring out into my backyard filled with lush green foliage. I didn't know if his thoughts had taken him back to the jungles of Southeast Asia or to his first days as a rookie cop. Finally, without turning to look at me, he spoke.

"You know José Garcia. He's the Chief of FLPD now, but he was a captain when he gave me a chance to take on a rare job for a cop. By that time I had been with FLPD for years and had done all the stuff, road patrol, SWAT as a sniper, and some undercover narc deals. I was with Tactical Impact Felony Squad then, staking out and taking out the heavy stuff. We keyed on in-progress armed robberies, and man, that was not an assignment for the timid or slow. I liked it, liked kicking ass on those *hard* guys, and liked the people I worked with. It was a hot job, and a tight unit.

"I didn't know what the hell Garcia had planned for me. I had worked for him, and knew him to be all cop, so I guess my feelings were mixed when I followed him into the small Organized Crime office. At that time it was still located on the third floor of FLPD on Broward Boulevard. I wasn't impressed with the meager turf the O.C. guys had grabbed for themselves, but Garcia got my attention when he told me I was on loan to them from Tac so I could go out front on some deal of theirs. Said he was going to commission me as FLPD's first resident hitman. Yeah, *right.* Up until that time one of the things I had enjoyed most about undercover work was that I could be anything I wanted to *tell* people I was, and they seemed willing to believe me. But who was gonna believe *this?*"

Al was teamed up with a couple of younger but veteran Organized Crime, Tactical Intelligence detectives named Bill McBride and Don Stanley. He had shared some wild nights in Tactical Impact with both before they were transferred to O.C. McBride was a lean and quiet cop who had been raised in New York City. He was intense and hard, liked by women and serious about his job. Stanley was slightly taller, with black hair, a smooth friendly face, and a look of fun in him. He came from the streets of Chicago and could be tough when it hit the fan. Both were street-smart and dedicated.

"They gave me a cup of their bad O.C. coffee and told me about the Kenny C's Bar situation. Supposedly it would be a straight murder-for-hire deal, but there might be problems. Mc-Bride was wearing his famous tight grin, which meant he was pissed, when he told me that the deal might be tricky because there was some noise on the street that a couple of the local North Fork cops were somehow wired dirty into a couple of the lounges there. Hell, everybody in the county knew about the chief over there supposedly getting a new car 'donated' to him every year, but these were supposed to be street cops covering for the bar owners on small stuff and getting a little fun money for their trouble. McBride told me our guys would be the only ones I could count on in there, and not to look for local help if things went to pieces."

Two teams would go into the lounge first, Garcia and a female detective, then McBride and Stanley. Al would arrive in his new undercover T-Bird with the informant, Aries. Then he would cruise inside looking like a hired killer hoping to do the deed and meet with the owner for a close and personal discussion about contract murder.

"Before you could say crosseyed I was just that, staring into the business end of Cippaloni's forty-five. Like I told you, we came to a professional understanding, made the deal, and I left with Aries. The other teams waited a while, then they eased out of there too, and it looked like we played it just right." Al shook his head at the memory, and sighed. "Nothing can be easy though, and this case got the wind knocked out of it in a hurry. That same night a couple of bouncer-type assholes beat the shit out of Aries, putting him into the hospital with multiple fractures and contusions. We got the word that one of the dirty cops put the finger on him for Cippaloni after they recognized one of us, so we knew we had been blown. Aries told us the next day he was finished with the deal. He was *out,* and wanted nothing to do with us *or* being an informant. Who could blame him?

"We took what we had to the prosecutor, but he looked it over and shit-canned it. The laws were different then, and we needed more from the informant, who now wouldn't testify about a damned thing, and more than just my word against a suspect's. We only had enough to point the blue finger, and that wasn't good enough to take into a courtroom. So the case against Cippaloni died. I went into a slow burn. It wasn't bad enough getting a case chopped out from under me, there was also the bitter taste from the possibility that we had been blown by a cop on the take. We never got any more evidence about that part of the case, and maybe it was street bullshit, but just hearing the rumors was a kick in the balls. The cash from the deal went into evidence . . . probably still there. Aries would be limping for a while and looking over his shoulder, and I could have been killed if the timing had been slightly different. Cippaloni had put a gun in my face and offered me his crummy money. At least there was no murder. I mean, the old man is still collecting rent and wondering whatever happened to his nice young wife. We came close, but close only counts in horseshoes and hand grenades. But that sonofabitch Cippaloni walked away from that deal. And I felt hammered."

Al felt "hammered" after his first contract murder case fell apart, but he was learning.

ALLIGATOR

AL SMITH'S BACKGROUND IS similar to mine. We both grew up in South Florida working-class neighborhoods, stumbled through high school, joined the army, and served in Vietnam. In 1970 we were both rookie cops with the Fort Lauderdale Police Department. I knew him then as a rawboned, goal-oriented young patrolman, not afraid to get in and mix it up if the situation called for it. He was one of those guys you liked to see roll in as backup when the crap hit the fan on some hot Saturday night. We never shared time together as squad car partners but frequently worked in the same zones, answering calls together and covering each other.

When Al first left patrol and went to Tactical Impact, our career paths diverged and I didn't see much of him on a shift-to-shift basis. I knew he was out there, though. He's one of those cops who just seems to be where the action is. When the briefing room buzzed with some heavy felony rumble that had gone down the night before, Al's name was often one of those spoken. He impressed me as a cop, a man, and a person. Even though he was surely aware of his own reputation, he didn't do the macho hallway strut or act aloof around the poor unwashed troops in patrol. He was quiet and polite, and I always knew he was one of those cops I was glad was *out there.*

11

He left such an impression on me that I included a minor character based on him in my first novel, *The Patch.*

After I left the FLPD in 1980 Al stayed on, still doing the heavy stuff, still believing in the job. I kept my home in Fort Lauderdale, and many of my friends are former partners and fellow police officers. It is well known that the police community is a small one, so it was easy for me to keep up with Al's exploits, even though because of his sensitive undercover assignments most of his work was accomplished without the knowledge of the general public.

In 1990, ten years after I retired, ten years during which Al Smith still went out to do battle on those hard streets of Lauderdale, his name was mentioned to me by a mutual friend and former cop who had seen Al on a television talk show discussing contract murder. My friend was once a narc sergeant and former partner of Al's who had worked with him on some tough cases. At the peak of his career he got in the way of a sawed-off shotgun and took the full blast in the legs. I asked him idly who was doing the book Al was probably promoting on the show, but my friend couldn't recall a book being mentioned. I decided to contact Al and ask him.

Al was his usual quiet self when I called, downplaying his part on the talk show. Actually Al was on more than one show dealing with contract murder; he is, after all, an expert, one of a handful of undercover cops in this country who have hired on as hitmen time and again to make good cases. When I asked him about a book he said, "Yeah, Cherokee, I've been thinking I should write one, but I've tried and haven't been too successful. Some of the guys I work with told me I should get in touch with you, but ever since your first one was published I figured you get calls from guys like me all the time . . ." At that time my first nonfiction work, *Blue Truth,* was being released by Donald I. Fine and I had never collaborated on a book before. But I knew Al, and knew his story was one I wanted to help him tell.

The first couple of times Al and I sat down to begin discussions on the cases he did what all cops do when they are nervous and want to get the facts straight; they talk in courtroom-testimony style.

"I was contacted by a confidential informant who advised of the following criminal activities . . ."

"Made first meeting with suspect who stated he . . ."

"Set up stakeout based on CI's info. Then, based on probable cause, was able to secure a warrant for . . ."

This wasn't it, I knew, and after a couple of meetings I got Al to loosen up and look at it more like a bullshit session, to just *tell* me about the cases, as if we were all standing around the hood of a patrol car in a back alley on midnight shift, drinking bad coffee and eating stale donuts and swapping tales about dirtbags, crazy deals and bad arrests.

Al brought with him the police and public records of each case, the reports, statements from witnesses, transcripts of taped conversations, and even some of the cassette tapes made as Al wore the "wire." Cops are sensitive about the truth, and get defensive if the validity of a case is challenged. Al wanted me to work with him on his stories, but he wanted me to understand immediately this stuff was *real*, not some embellished cop nonsense that made lurid fantasy. Real people hired him with the absolute intention of causing other real people to be murdered . . . as in dead. He didn't have to convince *me*, of course, but the documentation made my job as collaborator that much easier and gave the stories a sense of real background even when they seemed unreal.

Most often we met at my home, which is located in northeast Fort Lauderdale near the Intracoastal Waterway and the ocean. It is a nice neighborhood with well-maintained homes occupied by working couples or retired types, close to good schools, restaurants and "old" Fort Lauderdale . . . the east side. My office is a small room at the back of the house, mostly glass. It looks out over a tropical yard with tall hedges, several types of palm trees, and lime, orange, grapefruit, and avocado trees. For over a year Al came to visit me with his tapes and reports, and his memories. I would listen and take notes and watch his face and eyes as he told me of treading that tightrope between being a cop and a contract murderer, Al Smith and Al Sanetti, undercover and exposed.

AL SMITH LEANED toward me, his expression one of mild distaste, and with a slight shake of his head began the story of the stockbroker who wanted to feed the alligators.

"I sat with this guy in Lum's, a small busy restaurant in the south end of town. He was an investment adviser, like a stockbroker. He was well-dressed, wore little jewelry, conservative clothes. He was almost my height but soft in the gut, about forty-two. He had a baby face, the same haircut he had when he was eleven, and cocky. He came across as intelligent, educated, businesslike, but there was a little spoiled rich kid in him, used to getting his way. He drove an old Austin Healey, restored. He told me he was a businessman trying to make it in this world where everyone was always out to beat him. Beat him? The last time this dude was beaten was when the doctor held him up by his heels and slapped him on the ass.

"He toyed with his breakfast, flirted with the waitress, and talked to me about murder. Said he'd pay me five thousand to kill his wife's new boyfriend, her too if she was there when it went down. 'Feed them to the alligators,' he told me. He didn't want to go to any funerals, and he wanted no bodies found."

Al stopped then, looked at me with a small grin, smoothed his beard with one big hand and went on. "Actually that was the second time I met with him. His name was Samuel Caruso, and the first time was at the Limelight Restaurant in Hallandale. I went there with the informant who had brought me in on the deal."

Hallandale is gently nestled on the east coast of Florida directly on the Dade-Broward County line. Al had attended junior high school there, and spent a lot of time at the beach during those years. Now Hallandale has become a community of senior citizens, most of them retired and living day to day on fixed incomes, housed in a multitude of condos that have spread over the beach like the man-o'-war that arrive with the tide from the east.

"Caruso had asked the informant for the meeting, and we first showed up at the fancy broker's office where he worked. The office was plush, quiet, and busy. Caruso fit into those surroundings, where he could nibble at the investment incomes of trusting elderly customers. They had those lighted panels on the walls that showed the ongoing trading, even in the entrance area, and we found Caruso in a big corner office after being ushered in by his secretary, a nice older woman. Caruso gave me a fish eye and ushered us right back out again. I didn't appreciate being treated like some kind of mold spore, but I knew I had to hang in there with this guy.

"We walked him to the Limelight, which is an open, friendly deli-type place. Caruso was cautious and very reluctant to talk about his 'problem' in front of me . . . didn't trust me. The informant, John LaSalle was his name, fed Caruso a line about me being a member of a local mob family for years, but Caruso stayed cold. Said he wanted a second meeting, like he wanted us to believe he could somehow check out my story. Sure. Then the second meeting was the one at Lum's, and it went okay until we were ready to split. It was one of those chance situations that bring the cold sweats to undercover cops. The whole deal almost went to hell."

Al was able to paint a picture of the intended targets in this case, Julie Caruso and Don Lombardi, with transcribed statements, reports, and memories of conversations he had with them during the course of the investigation.

Julie and Samuel Caruso were married in the early seventies. Samuel was a young and intense business magnate-to-be, and Julie was slim, blonde, attractive and sexually naïve. She believed Samuel was her man with all the answers, and she willingly let him take the reins of her life. During that time Samuel dabbled in various business enterprises and extramarital affairs, playing all the games he wanted and smiling as he lied to Julie.

After ten years the couple had some impressive shared financial holdings, bags full of bitter accusations and broken dreams, and a divorce.

Said Julie in a statement: "I was in my awakening stages then. I thought Samuel was out of my life, but less than two years later he was back, hounding me. He wanted to remarry, strictly for business reasons. He was having some kind of trouble with his new deals, and would be more financially secure if his holdings were jointly shared in a marriage." Julie was reluctant, but still making a transition to her own identity as a woman and person. "Samuel had always been the man in my life, the decision-maker, and even with all the problems between us I guess I still had an unreal attraction to him." Now he was back, persistent, pressuring and badgering her until finally she relented, told herself it could be good again and they remarried. It was an awkward time for her, a limbo time. "I learned almost immediately that he hadn't changed. Nothing had changed. I felt used and worthless. Samuel controlled me." He dominated their joint business actions and ignored her when it pleased him, which was most of the time.

"We didn't live together," said Julie, "I lived alone in the big house we bought as an 'investment,' and Samuel shared a condo with an ocean view with his new girlfriend." To Julie, the new girl seemed nubile and slightly bubble-headed, apparently impressed with Samuel's talk of money and power. Everything was going Samuel's way. In her statement Julie said, "I believe the only motivation Samuel has ever had has been money."

WHEN DON LOMBARDI entered the picture, things changed dramatically. Lombardi, tall and slim, dressed out of GQ, was one of those men whose hair always looks wet. He drove a white convertible Cadillac and owned a small flower shop where Julie, bored with sitting in the big empty house, took a job. They began seeing each other and the relationship grew. "Don has helped me to understand that I have a life *too*," Julie said. Samuel had lived with his girlfriend two years before Don came into Julie's life, and by that time Julie was a walking wound, starved for affection and positive reinforcement. Don gave it to her, and he also became a threat to the way Samuel had things structured.

In his interview Don stated, "As soon as Samuel found out we were seeing each other, that's when the problems started. So I would say it's been two years already that he's been making all kinds of accusations and troubles and so forth for everyone involved. As soon as Julie began sticking up for what's hers, he didn't like it . . . and he knew I was behind it."

Julie and Don became targets for constant harassment, hate mail, late night phone calls, threats. Samuel accused Don of retaliating by threatening *him* and sending thugs to stick a gun in Samuel's girlfriend's mouth. When the girl's car was stolen and stripped, Samuel blamed that on Lombardi too. Al told me that he felt Don Lombardi was more than capable of doing the things Samuel suspected him of, but it also appeared Julie had a calming effect on Don, which probably kept things from escalating. By April of 1983 the feud had degenerated to the point where Julie and Don were seeing an attorney about civil action against Samuel, in addition to Julie filing for her second divorce.

Al continued the story for me by talking about the informant. "John LaSalle had been in trouble in the past. He was a short guy, stocky, with unused muscle going to flab. He had thinning black hair, a pasty complexion and a wiseguy manner of speaking. He drove a new black Corvette and lived in a rat-hole apartment on South Federal Highway with a pretty wild and good-looking girl. He was an occasional singer and piano player and full-time opportunist. He had served hard jail time, and his name had been in the local news more than once. He rented a storefront in a small shopping center owned by our boy Samuel Caruso. Apparently Caruso saw LaSalle's name in the paper, and the word 'ex-con.' Caruso recognized LaSalle as one of his tenants and approached him about a 'problem' he guessed the ex-con could help him solve."

In his first statement to Al, LaSalle told him, "Caruso said he would like to have Don Lombardi killed. He asked me if I knew . . . you know, if I could have that taken care of. Caruso wanted Don killed, his body not found, and if Caruso's wife was there, also her body not found when they were both killed. The contract was for five thousand."

Next, LaSalle explained his motives for contacting the good guys. "I was trying to get my own life straightened out, you know? I didn't want anything that would bring me heat from the cops, and by chance I knew who this guy Don Lombardi was because we was neighbors in this apartment complex. I got hold of Lombardi, told him some of what was going on with this Caruso guy, and Lombardi made me go with him to see his lawyer. The lawyer heard only part of what I had to say, looked like he wanted to crap right there in his office, and called the cops."

Al said, "The call was eventually routed to me. By the time this case floated to the surface I had been permanently assigned to the Organized Crime Tactical Intelligence Unit. Captain Garcia presented me with my gold detective badge and suggested it might be a bad idea for me to carry it around in my wallet. I'd been assigned a geeky looking medium-sized Chevy rental and drove it to my first meeting with Don and Julie at their lawyer's office on East Oakland Park Boulevard."

The OPB Bridge was up when Al turned off U.S. 1 and he sat baking in the sun with all the beachbound traffic waiting for some hotshot on a booze cruise to sail on down the waterway. He walked into the lawyer's office hot and late. The lawyer's name was Jerry Stanton.

"Stanton was young, well-spoken, kind of . . . portly, and seemed sincere. I was glad to see he apparently only hired secretaries that were Vanna White clones. It took only a few minutes to learn he wasn't a boy scout, though. He stood to gain if any opponent of his client took a fall. It would make his job easier. He didn't seem comfortable talking to a cop, and that was fine with me.

"Don Lombardi seemed committed to the role of White Knight for Julie, nervous but determined. I saw Julie as a very good-looking lady in full bloom, like she was tasting some of life for the first time in a long time, excited and scared. There was something sexy about her, like you could tell she might be adventurous, just learning about the combination of her looks and sexuality. Seemed like she played with it, or maybe just played with me, watching the reaction caused by her heat."

Al grinned, shrugged and went on. "I forced myself to ignore the signals she was sending out and concentrate on the job. I wanted to get a feel for the case, gauging their words to see if the threat was real.

"Don told me about a recent conversation he'd had with Samuel Caruso, where Lombardi asked Caruso why he didn't get out of Julie's hair altogether by giving her what was rightly hers. Caruso's answer was he'd take his chances in court, and when Lombardi told him he'd lose in court, Caruso said, 'She wouldn't have twenty-four hours to enjoy it because I will kill her and turn myself right in.'

"I asked Julie about Caruso's motivation in all this and she talked about the deals, the money, the properties and a will that gave everything to Caruso if she died. With Lombardi out of the picture Caruso would have a better chance of keeping his financial status. When I told them I felt there was enough reason for me to take the case one step further, Julie and Don stared at me wide-eyed, and Stanton sat back in his plush chair behind his big desk and nodded, like he knew it all along."

Al left the lawyer's office feeling somehow depressed by the meeting with two people trying to be a couple and looking to him to keep them out of a matched set of body bags. He drove east over the bridge and found himself driving south near the ocean on North Ocean Boulevard. His head automatically turned when he passed *the* street, and he remembered the house, the night, his wife-to-be and the shooting . . .

"I'd been a cop for six years when I met Sylvia. A six-year cop, if he's into it, is a hard-case. I was working Tactical Impact then and we'd been shadowing a couple of nasty home invasion guys for weeks. These were the type of armed robbers who really cut off their victim's ring fingers to get at the jewelry, and pistol-whipped them whether they killed them or not. We knew they would hit again and even knew which area and a couple of houses they had already cased.

"We all wanted to be there when it went down, but life goes on, right? On that night I had finally managed to talk Sylvia into going out with me. I had been working the case hard with the other guys and needed a break. Sylvia and I went out to dinner, and I took my radio along, just to listen to any breaking developments. I could tell Sylvia wasn't thrilled with the radio bit . . . not sure if I was just trying to impress her or if I was already so hooked into the job anything else would just have to work around it.

"After dinner we drove toward the beach, and from the talk on the radio I could tell the two bad guys were getting ready to hit the home they had cased earlier. The old lady who lived alone there had been carefully joined by a couple of the Tac Squad people, including José Garcia, and there were more staked out and hiding around the edge of the property. When Sylvia and I got into the area the voices on the radio were a whisper. I put her behind the wheel of my car and told her to wait.

"I stood beside the car, listening to the night, and it had that feel, so I told her to just drive out of there when the shooting started and I'd meet her later. She asked me, 'How do you know there'll be shooting?' just as it all broke loose. She drove away as I ran toward the scene. She told me later she was scared, and said it was her 'baptism of fire.' The two badasses were blown away that night, no cops or citizens were hurt, and the guys who had been working the case for weeks were dancing in the streets."

Sylvia and Al have been married many years now and have two lovely daughters. Sylvia manages a doctor's office and has learned to cope with being a cop's wife. Al knows she has mixed feelings about some of the assignments he's had, like SWAT or the Bomb Squad. Now he works among the nocturnal creatures, and Sylvia has pretty much learned to put up with the late night calls at home. It's all very well to talk about not letting the job screw up your home life, but the reality can be a bitch.

One evening over dinner Sylvia told me one of the weirdest and most difficult things she had to do because of Al's job. It was nighttime at a local shopping center as she and the girls got out of her car and saw Al walking across the lot with a couple of strangers. Were they just cops from out of town? Were they players in some deal that was going down right there right then? She understood the danger Al could be in if a little girl ran up to him calling "Daddy, Daddy," so she kept them huddled beside the car with her until Al and company were out of sight. She told me she found it hard and unfair to be forced to brief her daughters to "know" their own daddy only when she said it was okay. I got her point. Al said nothing while she was telling the story. Less was better just then. Hell, it was best.

Al told me sometimes he wished he could be like one of those guys who work in a radioactive zone who peel off their special work suit and leave it lying on the floor of the shower when they're done for the day.

Now, on a crystal clear morning, with my small office brightened by the day, he went on with his story of contract murder.

"John LaSalle, the informant on the Caruso case, made the arrangements, and I wore the wire for that first meeting with Samuel Caruso at the Limelight on a Friday afternoon. LaSalle came along. A young detective, new to the unit, monitored the device from a car parked nearby. The reception was bad—in more ways than one.

"Caruso looked me over carefully, put his face in his drink and said something like, 'Uh, the problem is . . . my mother is having trouble with her car . . . won't run right, can't get any help from the dealer . . .' some such bullshit. LaSalle waited for Caruso to sputter to a stop, hooked a thumb at me and told him I had been with the family for five years and hits were my thing and he trusted me and so should Caruso.

"I remember asking myself how much I could trust LaSalle. I knew he thought Don and Julie would somehow take care of him for coming forward with this case. I hoped he wouldn't let his ambition get in the way of my investigation. Caruso listened, trying to be cool, and said he needed some time to check things out. He wanted to meet tomorrow and maybe he'd have five hundred dollars with him to get the ball rolling.

"As we watched Samuel walk off toward his office I wondered how serious he was. Talk is cheap, but contract murder takes time and a real desire to make the deal and see it all the way through. You really have to want to see the target *dead*. That kind of murder is not like a crime of passion, spur of the moment, when somebody's temper flares up and the wife makes a canoe out of the old man with a filet knife. Contract murder is something the killer really has to want, especially if they're trying to set it up with a professional like me. Hell, everybody knows there are guys running the alleys in Miami who'll kill you for a cheeseburger and fries. But a serious planner means to see it all the way through to a death—that's what they really *want* for an end result. At that point I wondered if this guy Caruso was made of the wrong enough stuff.

"Saturday morning was hot and sticky, you know how it gets, with a low buildup of cumulus clouds all around. Maybe there'd be rain, but for sure the heat anyway. LaSalle and I met and drove together to Lum's restaurant near Caruso's little shopping center and office. The place was popular and busy. There were even a couple of young cops, uniform guys, taking a break at a table near the front. We took a booth in the back, and Caruso came in from the rear entrance a few minutes later. He seemed more comfortable with me this time and wanted to get right into talking business.

"He began by breaking my heart with all of his business troubles with the small shopping center and his tenants, how the people were always ripping him off, how he had to struggle to

keep ahead of the market. He says stuff like, 'One of my properties is that small center across the street. The kind of people I
get in there! They take my eyeteeth while they sign a lease. One
wiseass, know what he got out of me? Free rent for a month, no
security deposit. I got so many fucking apartments and stuff, I
don't know, you know?' He was kind of cracking me up with
his tough talk, like he was trying so hard to sound like anything
but an investment counselor. He was really trying to make me
see *him* as the victim in this thing. What bullshit. He kept
eyeing the waitress and told us the tale about how Lombardi
once sent a couple of guys with a message for him, terrifying his
girlfriend, sticking a gun in her mouth, and so on. Then somebody shot a hole in his car windshield and it cost him big bucks
to get it fixed. Told us his girlfriend was so pissed off about the
whole thing she wanted him to get *her* a gun.

"At that point LaSalle laughed and said something like,
'Maybe she can do *this* job and save you five grand.' Caruso
made a face at that bit of levity and said, 'Are you shitting me?
She was *pissed*. That scared me, because, what the fuck . . . I
don't want to marry the girl.'

"This guy was a real sweetheart, no doubt about it, and we
made the deal. He would pay me two thousand dollars for the
hit on Lombardi, five hundred up front. Because LaSalle set it
up for us, he would get two years rent-free on his office in the
center. I walked out first, Caruso and LaSalle lagging behind
talking about the tip for the waitress. I was a few feet ahead of
them, passed the table with the two young patrol officers and
recognized one as a rookie I had recently instructed out at the
academy.

"I took my eyes away from his face, hoping like hell he
wouldn't recognize me. He did. 'Hi, Al,' he said with a big grin
on his face. I felt the ice cubes in my jockey shorts, made a face
at him with my back to Caruso and LaSalle, and walked right
on by as if I hadn't heard him. My mouth was dry as we walked
out of the place and I realized Caruso must have missed the

exchange, having turned away just then to say something to LaSalle."

I watched now as Al's eyes tightened and seemed to go out of focus for a moment. Then he looked at me and said quietly, "They say a common dream shared by undercover cops is the one where you find yourself walking buck-assed naked in a world where everyone else is dressed . . . you know?" I did know.

"Anyway," Al went on, "I guess Caruso maintained the small office in the center as some kind of tax write-off or something. When we climbed the stairs to the second floor I noticed that they seemed to be made of rust held together with mold. It looked like the whole building was in a similar condition. This office was dingy, barely furnished, and not anything like the one at his firm's building. Maybe he took off his tie, put on an old work shirt and mussed his hair when he talked about the rent with potential tenants. The office was barely big enough for the three of us, and we could smell each other's sweat.

"LaSalle and Caruso worked out the specifics of the free rent deal, and then Samuel Caruso handed me five one hundred dollar bills. He told me it's not how much you pay for something, but *how* you pay for it. I didn't know what he meant, until he went on to say he had used his MasterCharge to get the five bills. I thought making a down payment on a hit with a credit card was pretty weird. The three of us stood there looking out the window at his neat little car, then we wrapped it up, and those two rocket scientists started talking about the fine art of *tipping* in a cruel world. No kidding. Here, let me show you."

Al stopped for a moment, looked through the folder of reports and statements he had provided me and pulled out the typed transcript of the covert tapes that had been recorded at this meeting:

JOHN LASALLE: That fucking black girl never saw five dollars. Did you see that fucking smile on her?
SAMUEL CARUSO: Look, you left a *five dollar tip.*

LASALLE: Yeah. Well, yesterday, you know what happened? That fucking Greek guy, you left a three dollar tip . . . the tab was, let's say, five dollars. You leave eight, he puts the eight dollars in the cash register. He's the fucking manager, he's real shrewd.

CARUSO: Yeah.

Al shook his head, threw the transcript onto my desk. "Enlightened with this crap, we promised to keep in touch over the weekend, with another meeting set up for Monday in Caruso's office. As we left, LaSalle gave one more piece of advice to Caruso, a little tough talk about how Caruso was no longer fucking with him but with Al, the 'family' member and hitman. LaSalle wanted Caruso to understand that he had better pay for my services within sixty days after the job was done or he'd be answering to me. Caruso looked at me slightly goggle-eyed and nodded that he understood.

"John LaSalle dropped from sight after this case, but not for long. I heard later he got himself arrested for arson, trying to burn down a building for the owner on some insurance scam. Sometimes I think cops should be sprayed every day with some kind of disinfectant before going out and getting close to some of these tools of the trade."

Al shuffled through the tape transcriptions again, found the one he wanted and said, "On Monday morning I called Caruso at his investment office. I remember wondering while I was on 'hold' how he could be effective at his job, what with all the phone calls and restaurant meetings to discuss murder."

SAMUEL CARUSO: *(Bright and friendly)* Samuel Caruso.

AL SMITH: I've been following Don and Julie, trying to get a feel for their, um, pattern . . . you know? She had a rather active weekend.

CARUSO: *(Worried tone)* Let me ask you something, Al. What I don't understand, five hundred and the lease . . . what happens if it doesn't go down?

SMITH: Well, you've got my word it's going down, and John's word that it's going down. You know this isn't the first time I've done one of these.

CARUSO: Oh, yeah.

SMITH: I just want to make sure you've got something to do, you know . . . when it goes down.

CARUSO: I got a friend until midnight, uh, for dinner. Uh . . . also, I don't want to go to any funerals.

SMITH: Already taken care of, Samuel. Nobody will ever be found, I got a guy with an airboat.

CARUSO: All right . . .

Later that day Al met with Caruso in his dingy office. Caruso gave Al the finished lease agreement for LaSalle, and Al gave him a bogus surveillance report he had made up detailing the movements of the targets over the weekend.

"I told him I had it all planned for Tuesday night, around eleven. I told him Don and Julie were sharing an apartment now, and that got to him. His face got real tight as I went on with the plan, how I'd just take Don out of his car when he pulled into the parking area. I'd take him away from there, do the deed, then dump the body. Then Caruso tells me he bets when Lombardi figures out what's going on he'll offer me more money than the contract price not to kill him. He wanted to see my reaction to this, so I just acted impressed with his prediction.

"Then he threw another one at me. Wanted to talk about a little 'torch' job. He needed a place to 'burn down for business reasons.' He must have thought I was a jack-of-all-trades, the ignorant bastard. Arson guys are specialists. They have to be nowadays, with all the sophisticated technical equipment the fire investigators use. Torching a place and not getting caught isn't as easy as it used to be. I didn't say anything about that, though. I just told him I'd be interested after *this* deal was done.

"I felt like I could be employed by this guy all summer, but I wanted to keep things simple for the integrity of the case. He actually pouted. I don't think he liked being put off. Then he got back on the evidence thing again. He didn't want *any* found, and he again made it clear that if Julie was there when I grabbed Don, then she should go too. I shook his clammy hand and left.

"I had a real serious look on my face later when I told Don Lombardi I was going to kill him that night. I watched the color drain out of his face as he ran one hand through his wet hair. We were back in Stanton's office, the lawyer was there, and Julie too. I could see then that each of them understood at that point that if Caruso had been connected with any *other* hitman, and had hired him, the murder would actually take place. I told Lombardi he'd have to take a dive for a couple of days. He'd have to lay low, because it wouldn't do to have him pop up somewhere and have Caruso run into him when he was supposed to be rotting in the belly of some gator. He looked green around the gills at that one.

"Next I pointed at Julie and told her she'd have to telephone Caruso Thursday morning. We'd record the call. She'd ask him if he knew where Lombardi was. She'd be worried because she found Don's car in front of their apartment with the door open, and she'd suspect that Caruso had done something to him. Julie listened, and nodded real hard, determination all over her face. Stanton was nodding too, and for his benefit I told them Caruso's response to the call might strengthen our case."

Al spent the rest of that day getting his paperwork together and planning the next day with the other detectives who would assist him. On Wednesday he presented the case to a prosecutor for review before taking a warrant request before a judge. He had to show there was probable cause to believe Samuel Caruso had committed a crime in hiring him to kill Don Lombardi, that Caruso had conspired with him and had given partial payment to initiate the crime.

The prosecutor, always mindful of his conviction track record, wanted to see a case he could win. The judge wanted to see a case that not only clearly showed a crime had been committed but was also procedurally correct and didn't violate the defendant's civil rights. Al had to sit quietly while the reports and statements were examined, thinking of the patient alligators, who could care less about rights and procedures.

At the end of the long day he had his warrant. He drove home with a red orange sunset burning his eyes, feeling drained from pushing against the gelatinous mass that is our judicial system.

FROM THE THURSDAY tape transcripts:

JULIE CARUSO: *(Nervous, agitated)* Samuel? I know it's early, but listen, Don is missing. Can you help me? I can't find him. He left me last night and I don't know where he is. Do you know where he is?

SAMUEL CARUSO: *(Sharply)* Don?

JULIE: Yes.

CARUSO: How in the hell would I know where Don is?

JULIE: I don't know. I've called everywhere. I can't find him. Do you know anything about it?

CARUSO: I know nothing about him, Julie. I don't *want* to know nothing about him.

JULIE: But I just . . . if you do, please help me, can you help me?

CARUSO: I don't know anything about the man.

JULIE: *(Angry)* I'm very upset—

CARUSO: I can hear that but I don't know anything. I talked to him three weeks ago and told him to lay off, to give me a break, and he says, I'll lay off you if you'll lay off the IRS . . . and I says, you know . . .

JULIE: *(Hotly)* You don't know at *all!*

CARUSO: I haven't talked to him in three weeks.

JULIE: But do you know where he is?

CARUSO: *(After a pause)* How the hell would I know where he is?

JULIE: Okay, okay, I just thought—
    (Caruso hangs up)

"I told Julie she did good after she slowly hung up the phone and wiped the sweat off her hands. She sat almost rigid as Don hugged her, but after a few minutes she was able to relax again. Their taped conversation wasn't all that damning, unless a jury could hear the gloating tone in Caruso's voice.

"Not long after Julie's call I phoned Caruso at his office, the fancy one. I told him I wanted him to know everything had gone off without a hitch."

SAMUEL CARUSO: *(Cautiously excited)* Yeah, I understand that it did.

AL SMITH: You understand that it did?

CARUSO: Ah, somebody called me. Julie. Ah, looking for him . . .

SMITH: Yeah? Well, you were right about him offering me that money.

CARUSO: Yeah?

SMITH: Ten thousand.

CARUSO: *(Laughing)* I told you he would.

SMITH: He had another two thou on him, so I took that.

CARUSO: Good.

SMITH: How's business, Samuel?

CARUSO: Good, good, good. Today's my birthday, so I'm kind of celebrating. Lots of things to celebrate . . . you know.

SMITH: Happy birthday. I'll send you a box of cigars or something.

CARUSO: *(Laughing)* Kill me with cancer, you bum.

Al looked at me now with his big arms folded across his chest, his face set in a frown. "After I hung up the phone on his laughing I radioed the units waiting outside to move in with the arrest warrant."

Samuel Caruso was arrested quietly, but it still caused consternation in the prestigious financial office when he was led away in handcuffs by a small group of detectives. Caruso's secretary indignantly asked what it was all about, and one of the young detectives hesitated half a second before he said, "It seems your boss was doing some insider trading on contract murder." Many Adam's apples were bobbing up and down behind button-down collars, and customers and brokers alike couldn't help glancing first at the handcuffs, then up to the stock readouts on the wall. Caruso kept his head down, wouldn't look at Al, and later said to one of the detectives who drove him to jail only that the whole thing was about "money."

THE TRIAL QUICKLY grew into a local media event. The love triangle, financial wheeling and dealing and the undercover hitman all made juicy news. The judge on the case made it more interesting and newsworthy when he arranged to allow a class of law students to sit in on the trial. It would be good for them, he felt, and the attorneys for both sides agreed. Al had the feeling from the beginning that the judge was handling the case more like a showpiece teaching-aid than a real trial about real murder.

Caruso's attorney proceeded to attack Julie and Don, accusing them of manipulating Al for their own purposes, making Samuel out to be the real victim. The judge allowed his feelings of repugnance for the informant, John LaSalle, to show clearly. He didn't like LaSalle, and obviously felt that Caruso, the financial advisor, was a much more upstanding and believable citizen than LaSalle, the ex-con informant. (As an aside, Al said, "Actually, even though he *was* an ex-con and a dirtbag, I found it easier to relate to him as a street person than to Caruso. They would both lie to save their ass, but in this case I at least knew LaSalle was being truthful because *I worked it.*") It was hard to tell who was on trial during some exchanges. The prosecutor told the jury they would have to decide, considering all the other good evidence, who was lying, Caruso, the respected businessman, or Al, the undercover cop. The jury deliberated a short time, trudged back into the courtroom, and delivered a conviction against Caruso.

Al's feelings of accomplishment were short-lived, however, as the judge actually polled the young student audience to get their feelings on what the sentence should be! He studied the results and issued a sentence of less than two years in jail for Caruso, and prepared to release him on a ridiculously low appeal bond. Then he called for a meeting.

Al was up and pacing the floor of my office now as he remembered. "The judge, the prosecutor—who I thought had done a fine job with the case—the defense lawyer, and I all met in the judge's chambers. The judge began by telling me how he knew I felt this was an important case, but he was inclined to give Caruso a probationary sentence because he was a well-respected member of the business community, as compared to the main witness, LaSalle, who was a less than savory guy. Caruso also had a wife to think about, the judge said, and they had a child on the way. I just went kind of numb for a moment, speechless at what the judge was saying. But I saw the smile on Caruso's attorney's face out of the corner of my eye. My brain thawed and I told the judge his 'well-respected member of the community' had just been *convicted* of solicitation to commit *murder* by a jury of his peers. I reminded him that LaSalle hadn't paid me cash money to wax Lombardi—*Caruso* did.

"The judge went right on about how Caruso had a wife and a baby on the way, and how he thought Caruso could better serve the community by doing some type of counseling or some slap-on-the-wrist bullshit. I was just barely hanging onto my temper at that point and told the judge it didn't surprise me that Caruso had married and impregnated the girl he had been stringing along for years. The guy was looking at jail time and knew the image and sympathy factor might work on the jury. I told him I wouldn't be surprised if Caruso's attorney had advised him to do it, just like they tell their clients to get a haircut, wear a nice new suit with a tie and display a shiny crucifix on their chest.

"This pissed off Caruso's lawyer, naturally, and he got all red-faced and sputtery about my 'allegations,' and said this had nothing to do with the charges against his client. I just reminded him and the judge that Caruso had already been *con-victed.*

"We all just sat there a moment while the judge cleared his throat and we glared at each other. I went on, a little calmer, to argue that a murder would have actually taken place if I had not been the hitman Caruso made the deal with, that Caruso fully intended and planned to hear that Lombardi had been killed and fed to the alligators. Finally, dragging his feet to the end, the judge upped the appeal bond to fifty grand."

Al rolled his head on his shoulders, stretched his arms out in front of him with his fingers locked together, and shrugged. He sighed as he told me one of the constant problems he and other cops had to fight with these cases is the fact that the court has a difficult time accepting the intended result of these crimes. Everything about murder is set in motion, all the *intent* and premeditation is there, but the deed is not physically carried out in the end. We discussed the feasibility of borrowing a cadaver from the Medical Examiner's Office and setting it up in the front row of the courtroom. It could sit there stinking as it rotted for three days of high intellectual discussion on "human rights." It could be a mute representation to the court of what the intended victim would be if the accused's wishes and *intent* had been carried out. Said Al with an angry grin, "They want corpus delicti? I'll give them fucking corpus delicti."

SAMUEL CARUSO TOOK his appeal as far as it would go and lost. He finally went to jail for twenty-two months, but not before causing a little more grief. FLPD had seized his prized antique sports car under federal confiscation laws that allowed them to do so if the vehicle was used by the defendant while implementing the conspiracy. Along with the car came his briefcase. The young detective who had been assisting Al looked through the brief-case and entered it into evidence with a tag saying it contained "misc papers." Caruso later charged that there was five thousand dollars worth of jewelry in the briefcase and that the cops had stolen it. The young detective received a letter of reprimand in his file for "not properly itemizing each article of evidence," and Caruso's bogus claim was investigated and eventually blown off. But the smell of the allegation lingered. It usually does.

There was one more bizarre and ironic twist uncovered much later. Through another agency Al learned that his own name had come up when a suspect in some unrelated crime tried to get himself out of a jam by singing an interesting song to the cops who had nailed him. He was a black man, and told the cops he had been approached while in jail by a "soft white guy . . . business type." The white guy told the black inmate that he had been "put away" by a cop named Al Smith, who worked for FLPD. The guy offered to pay the inmate good cold cash if the inmate would kill Detective Smith when he got out of jail. The black man didn't agree or disagree, but just kept it to himself until he was later arrested for some misunderstanding. Then he came out with the tale to see if he and the authorities could be friends again. The other agency couldn't spend time working it, but passed it along for Al. He was busy on other cases by then, and knew, like all cops, that doing the job doesn't increase your popularity. No action was taken on that information.

As for Julie and Don, they went on with their lives, free of harassment for the first time in many years, but still haunted by the feeling that they should listen for footsteps in the night.

As we finished our discussion of the Caruso case, Al allowed a small grin and said quietly, "I doubt if anyone worried about the poor hungry alligators missing the meal Caruso had planned for them because I got in the way. Hell, this is South Florida. Alligators and people . . . not so different."

PERSONALS

FORT LAUDERDALE HAS VARIETY, intensity, and an eclectic mix of color, culture and crime. Al Smith and I have seen it grow from the sleepy vacation town it once was to the strident big city it has become. Fort Lauderdale was just too much of a good thing. The weather really *is* worth living here for, as long as you have air conditioning, and almost everyone has it now. Most of the bug problems have been wiped out, and you rarely hear about someone being eaten by an alligator, attacked by a mad Seminole Indian or swallowed by oozing quicksand. The place has become *too* livable. Of course, instead of being harassed by bugs we breathe pesticides, the Seminole Indians take our money at their bingo halls and try to kill us with their tax-free cigarettes, and all the quicksand or other spongy land has been artificially filled, sown with strange hardy grasses, or covered over with concrete.

When I was a teenager I used to laugh to hear the oldtimers say that someday Florida would be a solid slab of concrete from Daytona to Miami and from Fort Lauderdale to Naples. I don't laugh at that thought now, because it's almost true. The only things keeping us from interlocking parking lots with the malls in Naples and Fort Meyers are Lake Okeechobee, the big sugar company lands, the Indian Reservations and what's left of the "River of Grass," the Everglades.

Just as many coastal towns are centered on a river, Fort Lauderdale came to be because of the New River. It has been said the Indians gave it that name because one day it was just *there* as a result of some shift in the water through the heart of the Everglades. The river became the focal point for trade, and where the merchants dug in, early government soon followed.

For Fort Lauderdale, the river is just part of the water system. Port Everglades opens to the Atlantic, with Hillsborough Inlet and Boca Raton Inlet to the north, Miami's Haulover (a spot where the Indians hauled their canoes across a narrow spot between the ocean and the inland waterway) and Government Cut to the south, and the Intracoastal Waterway bordering the town on the east edge, running north-south like a huge flowing highway. There are over thirty miles of waterways within the city limits, and you can get to almost anywhere in the east and central parts of town by boat. We even have a water taxi service that does a brisk business in this Venice of America.

When South Florida grew and modernized to the point where people could begin enjoying themselves, they did just that. Hotels and motels popped up like fiddler crabs on an outgoing tide. Yacht clubs, country clubs, and retirement centers appeared anywhere a piling could be sunk without losing it, and behind these came the dreaded condominiums. Building booms have come and gone, and then come again just when you thought it was safe to spread your beach towel. The developers have been so successful and so determined that they have almost run out of virgin land on which to create a new "Red Squirrel Run" or "Nestling Pelican Point." It goes without saying that the last damn squirrel and pelican got the hell out of there when the first bulldozer showed up.

State and federal park lands, "environmentally sensitive" bits of mangrove, sea oats, sawgrass, beach, barrier islands, and tidal flats have not been "improved upon" . . . yet. There are many incredible and terrible stories of the lengths greedy developers and their backers will go in order to be granted permission to slap together another group of homes or condos. Acres of trees have been "accidentally" bulldozed, mangrove areas have been filled in while a "zoning feasibility study" is underway, and the state's aquifer, the pure subterranean water supply, has been poisoned while environmental charges against the big-money growers have languished in the court system.

Thousands of people move to Florida every day, and as is the nature of the beast, more people means more crime. Nowadays you would have to be from another planet not to know about Fort Lauderdale's great geographic location and why it has traditionally been a haven for a full assortment of illegal goings-on. The whole Caribbean Basin is just outside our front door, with South America, the Bahamas and Cuba enticingly close. Even before the rumrunners' day the ocean and waterways around here were busily traveled by opportunists engaged in bringing in salable goods, with fast profits to be made on the more illegal contraband. Pirates have always been around, swooping in like frigate birds to steal the fruits of someone else's labors, and we still see them today, lying in wait in their fast boats, guns ready. We've had Prohibition and the "Key Largo" days, more recently the narcotics smugglers and all the ticks and fleas that come with them, and always the roving packs of barracudas that follow the money.

Organized crime moved in early, and has stayed for the same reason as has the disorganized legitimate business sector: The money is here. Gambling is good business, whether it's Miami Beach, Nassau or Havana. Liquor licenses lead to action in lounges and restaurants, and hotels are great places for finding customers—often marks—seeking gratification. And as the customers congregate so do the sharks.

Fort Lauderdale has become a neon living-reef for all types of criminals to inhabit. It is nearly perfect for them, a place right out of the movies, a location that couldn't be better, and populated by herds of potential victims. We now cover the entire spectrum of crime, from the meanest little dope-related armed robbery to the most complex and sophisticated computer-assisted white collar ripoff. Newspapers play "can you top *this*"

with their stories and crime-fiction writers need only turn on
the five o'clock news to be inundated with impossible but true
stories, grist for the mill.

Most of the old money, and lots of the new, is located on Fort
Lauderdale's east side. The beach is jammed cheek-to-cheek
with hotels, from the sand edging the ocean to the concrete
seawall lining the Intracoastal less than a quarter-mile west.
South is the airport, with a now-continuous thundering stream
of heavy-metal birds impatiently packed with fresh vulnerable
skin and bulging wallets flaring out on final approach over I-95.
In the center, slightly inland from the ocean but straddling the
New River, is the old downtown area, modernized now with
lots of glass and a real skyline like Miami's or Atlanta's. Northeast residential sections are comfortably settled with nice
homes and manicured lawns, with many households on the water maintaining the almost obligatory yacht pulling on its lines
at the dock. Many of the finer clubs and restaurants are here
too, and along the beach, of course. U.S. 1 runs north-south
through town on the east side, and most of it is crowded with
new strip shopping-centers, fast-food places and service sta-
tions. Being on the cutting edge of the down-and-dirty enter-
tainment industry, Fort Lauderdale can also take credit for, at
one time or another, having (but not describing in tourist bro-
chures) at least one topless laundromat, topless carwash, topless
donut shop fighting to stay competitive with the usual topless
dance clubs.

Is traffic bad on the east side? There are only *nine* bridges
crossing the Intracoastal and the New River, one main north-
south artery, and maybe four east-west thoroughfares to negoti-
ate as you try to travel about. Add to the million or so who live
here the thousands in their rental cars, sunburned hands grip-
ping hot steering wheels while anxious eyeballs search in vain
for the sign that says "Jungle Queen," and it's a steel-and-con-
crete slice of heaven.

The northwest part of town (north of Broward Boulevard,
west of the railroad tracks) began as the "black section." Being a

part of the South, Fort Lauderdale cannot escape its own past. There were times when a black citizen would not be caught after the sun went down on the other side of Broward or the tracks. The heart of the lower-income area is still there, in the north-west, but it has expanded greatly since the early days, spreading north through once-cloistered residential communities, and south toward the traditional poor-white neighborhoods, there to clash and uncomfortably intermingle with the relatively new Hispanic enclaves.

Many bedroom communities have grown up to the west, forming small municipalities that cluster around Fort Lauderdale like barnacles on a slow-moving manatee. They in turn have been outgrown so fast that they had to keep pushing west. Naturalists were shaken when they learned that East Coast alligators got confused when they saw the Gulf of Mexico: they found themselves going south when they *knew* if the big water was on their right they should have been going north.

State Road 7, which for years marked the western terminus of growth, is now almost an east side road, swallowed up and passed over by the relentless march toward the setting sun and another half-acre to put a salable house on. Whole communites exist where hunters used to take deer and wild hog, movie theatres and burger places and gigantic malls squat where just a few years ago cattle stood gazing into a future no one would have believed possible. Many of those residing in the western parts of the Lauderdale area may as well live in any Southwestern city, where it is hot, flat and nouveau. They rarely see the beach, the ocean, or the waterways, the New River means nothing to them and commuting to and from work provides them with terrifying rides on superslab highways. I guess the theory is it still beats the snow and ice.

With all the growth, and the parallel growth in crime, Fort Lauderdale is now right up there with the big boys when it comes to murder statistics. And the perps aren't just drug dealers or trigger-happy robbers. Domestic-violence deaths, crimes of passion, have escalated too. Increased daily pressures bring increased chances for violent release. Since 1985 in Fort Lauderdale the murder numbers have steadily increased. Firearms are the weapons of choice.

Fort Lauderdale Police Department is approximately five-hundred strong, and virtually everyone, no matter what his other assignment, is in some way involved in murder investigations and prevention. There are homicide specialists, of course, and most of these officers have an aura of deliberate solemnity about them; even their humor is funereal. They look slightly tired, worn, but are unfazed by even the most bizarre crime scene. They have literally seen it all, heard it all, and done their best to keep chugging along, trying to "nail the bastard that did it."

Which brings us to Al Smith's specialty—murder-for-hire. In our world of customer service and retail value, where a person can buy anything he or she needs or wants, all kinds of people see paying someone for a contract hit as a logical way to handle a problem. But an effective murder can be a difficult thing to accomplish, especially if one wants to get away with it. Normally for some complex problem out of your everyday realm you would engage a specialist, an expert, and pay him to do the job right. So it is with many murderers these days—home-grown and, on the surface, just ordinary folk looking for a quick solution—a "hit"—to solve a nettling problem. And where there's a demand there's a supply. Many career criminals see contract killing as a rewarding and even satisfying occupation. With the organized crime elements and the narcotics groups often experiencing falling outs within their ranks, and hostile takeover attempts and so forth, contract hitmen find their services gladly paid for more often these days. But now that client-specialist attitude has moved from the streets and back rooms to the bedrooms and living rooms of the almost-average household.

No, murder-for-hire is no longer the sole domain of the professional criminal. Now there is the mother-in-law who will pay ten thousand dollars to have her daughter's husband taken out, **then** laugh about it when the hitman reports a successful job. **We see** a woman on the television news, her partner thoughtfully having taken a video of the act, calmly pulling out a gun **and** shooting four times a man tied to a tree as he cries for mercy—all part of a contract deal. We have seen a schoolteacher have **her** husband killed by her young lover, and a mom who tried **to hire** a hitman to kill the mother of her daughter's rival for a **slot** on the school *cheerleading* squad. A businessman will pay **a guy he** meets in a bar to throw a hand grenade at some cop who **arrested** his son, and a husband will pay a professional to run **over his** pregnant and heavily insured wife with a speedboat. **Competition** is fierce. A real blood sport.

As you've seen, Al Smith's job is to intercept as many of these **murders-for**-hire as possible, present himself as the professional **hitman, take** the money and arrest the employer-conspirator. He **tries to save** the life of the intended victim by interrupting the **chain of** planned events. People are killed for pay, and make no **mistake** . . . if Al Smith is not the hitman hired to do the job, **another,** a *real* one, will be.

> BUSINESSMAN—46, wants to take care of a
> pretty girl under twenty-five. Let's meet
> over lunch or dinner. Please write today.
> Dan, PO Box 12345, Fort Lauderdale.

A **voice** called out from the newsprinted page covered with ads **from** people trying to sell, to buy, to find, to make contact. This **voice** boldly stated what it needed, and hinted at favorable terms. **The** ad was placed in the hope that the right eyes would see **it, and** the right face and body and attitude would respond to it. **And another** voice *did* respond, an answering voice cried out "yes," **the** terms could be met. But like most things in this world, **nothing** can be that simple.

Dan **Rayburn,** the hopeful businessman looking for a lady of convenience through the above ad in the Personals section of the **Fort** Lauderdale *News-Sun Sentinel,* shared his post office box with an associate named Frederick Mack. Upon opening the box one morning, Frederick found a letter with the box address. Thinking it was for him, he opened and read it. Even before he finished the second page he wished he was proficient at resealing envelopes so no one could tell they had been opened. But he *had* opened it, and in doing so had learned more about the man he shared the box with than he wanted to know. To Frederick Mack, just the act of placing the ad in the Personals section had an exciting, illicit, tawdry feel about it, but the letter that came into his hands was something else. Still exciting, still with an undercurrent of potential sex, but now with the added ingredient of fear. Frederick Mack was the kind of man whose palms got sweaty at the thought of the kind of liaison the ad solicited and the kind of man who was frightened by the answering letter. He thought it over for most of the morning. Then he knew he had to call the police.

"Dear Dan," began the letter, "I am under twenty-five and could desperately use your help. When I was eighteen I married a man I thought I knew but I was wrong . . . he has turned into a man I barely know. I'm unhappy and afraid. There is no telling what he would do if I left, but I know the only thing that will help me is to become a widow. I am in a dangerous and desperate situation and would be grateful if you could help me. I have enclosed a picture of myself. If I don't look too happy, it's because that was taken on my wedding day. Please don't think I'm insane, because I'm not. I'm just trapped in a miserable life with a man who won't let me leave. I'll pay anything . . . but I don't have a lot of money. I could make weekly payments though. You're my last chance. Please help."

There was more, but Frederick Mack had seen enough.

When Mack finally made up his mind to call the police, he was routed from one office to another, through the detective division, and finally to an officer in Organized Crime. The detective examined what Mack had to say and show, recognized a potential contract murder in the making, and passed it on to Al Smith, the in-house hitman. The careful words on the paper hit Al with their poignant appeal, but this was darkly balanced by what the words were meant to accomplish.

Al told me that as he held the letter he thought he could almost make out the scent of inexpensive perfume, and he tried to form an image of the writer. This was not some witch, hardened by many years of failures, reaching out seductively with a poisoned apple, but a young girl trying to make a deal that might set her free. True, the apple she held out was herself, but the price of the gift was the same.

ON THE MORNING Al came to my house to discuss this case he seemed quieter than usual. He had some court proceeding scheduled for later that day and was dressed in a fine single-breasted suit and muted tie. This only enhanced his size, and made his appearance that much more imposing. He seemed reticent, almost reluctant to get into the case. While I sipped hot tea and prodded him, he sat glumly beside me, his big hands lying loose in his lap, his jacket open. After I had a chance to read through the reports and examine the photos and listen to the voices on tape I understood part of what bothered Al, and why he had trouble generating enthusiasm about successfully nailing the culprit. A monstrous act was planned and put into action with careful deliberation and absolute intent, but the planner was anything but a monster.

Al started slowly, then picked up speed with the momentum of the case, "I arranged a meeting with Frederick Mack through the other detective he had contacted. There was an hour or so to kill before he came into the station, so I hooked a recorder to the phone and dialed the number given at the end of the letter. The writer said the number was at her workplace, and had signed it, "Sally."

VOICE: Can I help you?
AL SMITH: May I speak with Sally, please?
VOICE: This is Sally . . .

SMITH: Sally, my name is Al Sanetti. I'm a friend of Dan's, uh, from the ad? He talked to me and asked me to call you to see if I could help you with your problem.

SALLY: *(After a very brief hesitation)* Oh . . . okay, Al. Then I'm pleased to hear from you.

SMITH: Listen, I don't like talking on the phone, you know? I might have to call you back from a pay phone, and then we can try to meet soon.

SALLY: I understand, Al, and that sounds good to me.

SMITH: Okay, Sally, bye.

"I hung up, slightly disoriented and caught off guard by her bright and cheerful voice on the phone. I had the impression she would have talked the whole deal out right there on the phone without even thinking of me being a cop or some other kind of setup. Kind of pissed me off. I mean, we weren't trying to set up a frigging kitchenware party, we were talking about murder, and I began to wonder if she was serious."

Using Al's memory of conversations he had with Sally, and the reports, transcripts and other written materials, I was able to determine some of Sally's history and feelings about her situation.

Sally married Bobby when she was eighteen. Even while it was happening she wasn't sure why she did it, other than to break the monotony of her life and to get out of a restrictive and depressing family situation. In her young mind it seemed she and Bobby could break away from the things that were dragging her down. They could set up their own little home, make their own decisions, live their days the way they wanted, and get on with a life that had some promise, things most young couples want. She saw it as a doorway to an expanding life, but it quickly became a cave entrance to a darkening and diminishing world. Less than two years after the marriage began, Sally wanted out.

Bobby was a lean, hard young man, jealous and possessive and dominating. He would fly into a rage over trivial things, accuse her of flirting if she even looked at another man in a friendly way, and slowly insulated her from any friends. She stated later, "He won't even let me go out in a bathing suit. He wants my life to be centered on *him*, and if I even start to have some outside interest he shuts it right down. If I get a job I like, or I mention that there are nice people working there, he makes me quit or stay home 'til I'm fired."

Bobby worked at manual labor, sweating in the heat, doing what he saw as the manly thing, and he resented Sally's forays into the world of potential. His temper would flare when they argued, he would come close to striking her, then direct the blow against some inanimate object in their apartment, smashing it. Sally recognized with frustration that sex with her husband was not the lovemaking they showed in the movies or wrote about in romance novels. Where she longed for patience he was aggressive, where she desired gentleness he was rough. She found that the most pleasureable time for her was after he was spent, and they lay huddled together until he fell asleep.

In her statement Sally went on, "He's made my world smaller and smaller, to where now I just feel trapped." Her life became strictly controlled by Bobby. She was alone in a dull and emotionally stressful world, she wanted an escape. "I know he'll never let me leave him," she said, "Like, get a separation or divorce. He keeps track of where I am all the time, like he always has to know where I am or where I'll be in a few minutes." Bobby, it seemed, couldn't make a prisoner of her mind, her imagination . . . and he couldn't stop her from reading the ads in the newspaper Personals.

Al was speaking more freely now that we were into the workings of the case:

"Frederick Mack came into the station on Broward Boulevard later that day. He was small and trim and neat. Looked like a professor, you know? You could tell by looking at him his desk at work was orderly and organized, his personal checkbook probably balanced to the friggin' penny. He wore a crisp white shirt and a paisley tie. Even the gold-wire rims of his glasses were polished.

"I told him what I wanted him to do, and he thought it over and nodded. He seemed nervous but excited about playing a role in a real police drama. Before we got started he needed a little reassurance. He wanted to know if there was some possibility he had misread the meaning of the 'young lady's' letter. He looked at me wide-eyed through his polished glasses and wanted to know if I thought he might have overreacted by contacting us.

"I told him we have this woman crying out in apparent desperation. Maybe *I* got caught up in playing a role in a real police drama, because I asked him if she cried out to the angels in prayer in her desperation. I put my face real close to Mack's and told him, *no*. She had worded the message so it could only be answered from the dark side. I reminded him that one of the things it said in the letter was that it would be impossible for them to meet for lunch 'until he was gone.' She was looking for someone to *murder* her husband, I told Mack, and she just might find him. He nodded slowly, wiped his compressed lips with a nice monogrammed handkerchief, and picked up the phone, which was attached to a tape recorder."

SALLY: *(Brightly)* This is Sally, can I help you?

FREDERICK MACK: Um, yes, this is, um . . . Dan. Did my friend contact you about the, um, *problem?*

SALLY: Yes he did, Dan.

MACK: He, um, understandably doesn't want to talk business on the telephone, so it would be better if the two of you could meet somewhere. Do you think that would be possible?

SALLY: *(After short pause)* I can take a break around ten. I could meet Al in the Howard Johnson's parking lot, you know the one off Commercial Boulevard?

MACK: Um, yes, that would be fine.

SALLY: Okay, Dan, what kind of car does Al drive? I'll sit there
and look for him.

MACK: (After pausing while Al passes him a scribbled note) It's
a Z-28, a Camaro, black. It's a black Z-28.

SALLY: *(Very pleasantly)* Great. Thanks for your help on this,
Dan. And, Dan . . . when do *you* and I meet? I'd like to
meet you, you seem so nice, helping out and all. Do you
think we could get together soon?

MACK: (After a moment of panic during which he stares at Al,
pearls of sweat on his brow) Uh . . . yes . . . um, later,
after . . .

SALLY: *(Sweetly)* Yes, Dan. You're absolutely right. It will have
to be after . . .

"After they hung up, Mack looked at me and wiped his face
with the now soaked handkerchief. I could tell he was taken
with Sally's matter-of-fact attitude and nice voice. I thanked
him, told him he'd done the right thing as a citizen helping out
the cops and all that, and tried to send him back to his world.
He wouldn't leave, though. Got all sheepish-looking and
wanted to know if I thought Sally really wanted to meet him,
like could they get together after this deal was done. He seemed
both sad and excited, and I had the feeling he didn't want to step
aside now, he wanted to stay with the game.

"Maybe he thought he could somehow get next to Sally, this
brave and desperate and sexually adventurous 'young woman'
who needed a man to help her out of a jam. Frederick Mack
could be Walter Mitty as some tough private eye in a
trenchcoat, doing a sticky job for the cops, helping the little
lady land on her feet and in his arms, or some such bullshit. I
finally got him to leave by walking him to the elevator, shaking
his hand and making sure he was aboard for the short trip down
to the lobby.

"I walked back to my office thinking about the guy who had
placed the ad, Dan Rayburn. I wondered how bad it had to be
before he finally did it, and if he was a geek, somehow so

screwed-up that it was hard or impossible for him to meet people. Being a cynical cop I couldn't help figuring he might just be
a guy with the bucks and the time to work out an 'arrangement'
with some lonely or opportunistic woman. Maybe he already
had a wife and kids and the whole deal, and this was a way for
him to have an easy piece of strange on the side whenever he
wanted it. Bottom line, this guy was pissing me off, and I'd
never even met him. I put my soap-opera brain back onto the
operational stuff, made arrangements for another detective to be
my eyeball and monitor the recorder, and went out to meet a
would-be future widow."

We took a break for a moment so Al could make a couple of
phone calls in response to the pager he wore at his waist. One
was to his office about the court appointment later that day.
The other was to his wife, Sylvia, who was just checking in. I
could tell by what I heard as I waited that one of Al's daughter's
had stayed home from school because she was sick, but after Al
came back and sat at my desk he told me she was okay, just a
cold. He talked for a moment about the never-ending battle of
raising children, shrugged, and went back to the story about
Sally and the Personals case:

"It was already hot out when I pulled into the hotel-restau-
rant parking lot in the Z-28. I was glad I'd placed my bugging
device in the console of the Camaro and not on me where I
usually wore it. I had begun to sweat, and it always made me
nervous to have those damn electronic devices so close to my
balls."

Al Smith is always a cop, and while he sat there waiting for
Sally he knew he had to make the pieces fall together for a tight
case. At the same time he was Al Sanetti, killer for hire, and he
had to will himself to think like Sanetti, to come across like
Sanetti. His tight short-sleeved pullover showed his arm, chest
and shoulder muscles to good effect. He had worn it to the
meeting with that in mind, and with his beard and dark scowl
and heavy gold jewelry, he hoped Sally would see what she
wanted to see. It turned out Sally was already in the parking lot,

sitting in an old beat-up car, looking at Al. She hesitated, then jumped out of her car and hurried over. She got into the passenger side of the Z-28, she and Al introduced themselves, then Al leaned back in his seat and asked Sally how he could help her.

"She told me flat out then that she wanted to get rid of her husband. It was the first thing she said after our names, and it just came out easy as hell. She said it, then looked at me, then down at her feet. She was petite, almost tiny, not quite twenty. She was an attractive young woman with a pretty face and long blonde hair. Her eyes looked slightly puffy and strained, and when she wasn't talking she kept her lips pressed tightly together. Her clothes were inexpensive but clean and looked like she chose what to wear carefully, like it was important to her. She seemed nervous, but like she had her mind made up. I asked her if she actually realized that for me to 'get rid' of her husband I'd have to kill him, and she looked right at me and said she knew that, and that was what she wanted.

"I started asking her questions about her husband and their relationship, trying to get a look at her motivation behind this deal. She told me about the marriage. She saw this meeting with me, and the action planned, as a means of escape, like she had no way out of her situation and she had to take this drastic step. Tell you the truth, she made me uneasy, she seemed so sweet, but her plans were murder. I wondered if I wasn't making a deal with a girl who had mixed reality with some soap-opera drama. I still wanted a confirmation that she really understood what we were talking about here, and really wanted it to happen. She got rid of any doubts I had when we got down to the nuts and bolts:

"She said she thought the best way to do it was for me to break into their apartment while they were at work. Bobby got a ride home from some guy he worked with, and he always made it a point to get home before she did so he could time how long it took her to get home from the job. She was nibbling on her lip as she told me I could be a burglar in the house when Bobby came home. It would be like he surprised a burglar in the act. Then I was supposed to kill him.

"I sat there a moment, like I was thinking it over. Then I nodded and told her that could work but that I'd probably take him out of there after I killed him and dispose of the body. I always like to get rid of the body, I told her, because that way there would be less for the cops to work on. I didn't know how she'd react to that, but she just stared out the windshield and nodded. I told her I usually charged five-thousand dollars, and she turned and looked at me and said she figured it would be that much, still very matter-of-fact. She told me she had about five hundred in her checking account, and could make some kind of payments to me.

"I still pretended to be thinking it over. I knew she couldn't afford the price and I was worried that she might try to shop around and stumble onto some scroatbag who would actually *do* the hit for less. I told her I'd be willing to let her give me one hundred dollars up-front. I needed the hundred to buy a gun, because I always dumped the gun when I was through with it, it was stupid to walk around with a gun you had used to kill somebody. She just sat there taking it all in. I told her I knew she didn't have a lot of money but I was sure we could work it out somehow.

"She looked right at me with her big eyes, and held my gaze so I would really hear her, and quietly told me how important it was that I really *do it.* She had an important meeting at work on Saturday that she wanted to go to, and besides that, if Bobby saw the money missing from the account, he'd get really mad at her. She moved a little closer to me then, ran her little pink tongue around her lips, and in an even quieter voice, came on to me big-time. She told me she knew that *I* knew she and Dan were setting something up where they might 'get together' once in a while. She told me it didn't *have* to be with Dan, she felt 'comfortable' around me. I seemed 'nice.' Can you beat it?

"I stared back at her with my eyes wide, smiling as if it sounded like a good deal to me. Then I told her to make the check out to Al Sanetti and spelled it for her. She hesitated, her head cocked to the side, so I told her she'd be single by Saturday. She wanted to hear it again, so I told he she'd be single by Saturday. She said, 'Okay.' She took out her checkbook and sat there and wrote out a check for a hundred dollars to Al Sanetti, nice as you please. Then she tore it out of the book and handed it to me right along with a smile.

"It hit me right then that if I really *was* one of the street animals she thought I was, she would not stand a chance. I could take advantage of her in so many different ways, none of them good. I almost got angry at her then, and wanted to grab her by those shoulders and shake her until she paid attention while I reamed her butt about the big bad fucking world and all the absolutely badass barracudas out there who would have her and her stupid little husband for lunch. But hell, she was paying me to kill her husband, not lecture her.

"She gave my hand a quick squeeze as she left. And then the only one I wanted to lecture was myself."

WE TOOK A break then while I made a cup of tea and Al made a couple more phone calls. I opened a soft drink for him and we sat at the dining room table shooting the breeze. He told me that after he left that first meeting with Sally he had the radio on in his car and the station was playing oldies. He said he didn't know if it was the old songs or the bizarre time he was spending with this young, pretty, and very reckless young woman who had designs on her hitman, but something about the whole thing triggered memories in him. He told me his mind was filled with thoughts of his earlier years as he drove back to the police station, how he had enjoyed them. "It's got nothing to do with these stories I'm telling you," he said, "Just some of my early experiences with the opposite sex." Hell, we *were* taking a break, and they *were* a part of the Al Smith I was writing about, so I told him to share some with me, and we kicked back and had at it.

It turned out that horses were Al's first real love, but then horses and girls were mixed and tied together in his adolescent memories. Jan was the first name he remembered, from the fourth grade, and she hurried to a barn near the school every day after class and went riding off on a large chestnut quarter-horse which dwarfed her. Al, standing duty as a school-crossing guard, thought she was the most perfect thing he had ever seen at Lake Forest Elementary School. He watched her and longed to be her friend, and through her he knew his first conflict over a girl.

One day during recess Al and some of the other kids were playing on the basketball court. Jan was there, and some kid whose name Al couldn't remember was trying to get her attention. When other forms of communication failed, the other kid picked up a basketball and threw it at Jan, causing Al to flip out and jump the kid. They wrestled around until a teacher broke it up. Jan just walked away, ignoring both combatants, and Al was embarrassed and heartbroken. "Neither me *or* ol' what's-his-name made out on that deal," he said.

Then there was Joann. She was the daughter of a wealthy rancher who had about ten acres and a fine home with a large barn not too far from Al's home. The pasture where her horses grazed bordered the elementary school, and on weekends Al would take them apples or carrots just to get near them. By that time he was an older guy, enrolled at Hallandale Junior High. Al's best friend, a boy named Lee, lived nearby, and he and Al rode around on a horse that belonged to Al's uncle. When Lee finally got his own horse, he and Al became the talk of the school. "There wasn't a girl at that school who didn't want to spread her legs across the back of 'Joker' or 'Flair,'" he told me.

Al and Lee got a job at a place called Grass Hill Farm, where they tended to the horses and grounds while rich kids took riding lessons. One of the perks the owner gave them was permission to attend all the camp barbecues and hayrides and dances. As Al described it, "We jumped at the offer like two young Brahmas cinched in the nuts and spurred sideways out of the gate."

On the first day of camp Joann showed up on a perfect Arabian, pure white, wearing brown English leather riding boots, jodhpurs and a white blouse, which to Al's eyes seemed to be straining to hold in her chest. Al tried to talk to her about the horse but she told him to take care of the animal and just walked away. He felt then she was stuck-up, but still found himself doing everything he could for her when she was around. He said he couldn't help noticing Lee was sniffing around a lot too, so he got in his face and his friend admitted he was after the same thing Al was—some of her time, and whatever came with it. They agreed to both ask her to an upcoming hayride, and whichever one she chose, the other one would back off. To Al's surprise, Joann picked him.

Al had a faraway look on his face as he told me about that hayride, explaining that hayrides are wonderful, magical places to learn about kissing. He swore he could still remember the sound of the wagon wheels on the dirt road, the feel of her blouse, the scent of her hair in the hay and the spine-chilling, toe-numbing thrill of that moment when you get so close to an actual living girl that your lips touch.

That summer flew by, another school year began, and into Al's life came Judy. He told me he still doesn't know why he had such a hard time in his early years getting past girls whose names began with J. Judy had the wildest strawberry hair Al had ever seen. According to Al's memory the word around the school at that time (innocently accepted in naive and hopeful ignorance of substantiated fact) was that if Judy liked you "she would screw your eyelids off," *plus* she had her own horse. This seemed to be a prerequisite in Al's budding love life. Judy's best friend was a girl named Terry, and she and Al's friend Lee hit it off, so things were shaping up. They would ride Joker and a new horse named Blackjack to where the girls waited, pull them up on the wide backs of the horses, and take off. Al loved to ride bareback with a girl behind him. The movement of the horse would shortly bring the girl flush against his back, and every once in a while he'd give Joker a little bit of the heel of his boot to make sure she hung on tight.

Al remembered it was weeks before he got up the nerve to even kiss Judy. They went for a night ride, November, clear air in the low sixties. They set off for some wooded trails around the Dade-Broward County line in a place called Hidden Lakes. After about an hour they decided to "rest the horses" for a bit. Al dismounted Joker and reached up to help Judy, and when she slid down into his arms he lost all inhibition and kissed her. He was sure at that moment he knew what love was all about. But as soon as Al began to feel comfortable in the male role Judy dropped a challenging bombshell on him by asking him if he'd ever French kissed. Joker waited patiently while they practiced.

Al went with Judy through that school year, and most of his buddies were convinced he was quite the successful stud. He would neither confirm nor deny their speculations, but did take on an all-knowing air when the subject came around to the opposite sex. In reality his experimentation and experiences with Judy were innocently tame, but it was pleasing to them both.

As Al grew, so did his experiences. He had a kind of young *American Graffiti* life, with horses often replacing the cars. He went from one relationship to another until he came out of the army and joined the FLPD. He found it odd then to be working the beach, on the infamous "strip," where he had sown his wild oats. Being a cop had an unexpected effect on him. He still maintained a healthy and aggressive interest in women, and shared time with different ones when he could, but he found himself really getting into the job, doing for others instead of doing for himself.

His love for horses, he says, will never fade away. He told me his other constant now is his wife Sylvia and his daughters. Like many young cops, Al played the field with enthusiasm when he was single, but "ran into something solid and real" when he met Sylvia. He feels his relationship with her as compared with others he's known is something like the difference between working as a standby Pony Express rider and standing deep in a hundred acres of Kentucky bluegrass, gently holding the reins of a glistening thoroughbred.

All in all, an incongruous background for an undercover hitman. Al only smiles when this seeming contradiction is put to him. "It's what I do," he says, and lets it go at that. . . .

IT TURNED OUT Al had to leave after that break to meet with the prosecutor on the court case he had later that day, but he was back in the morning dressed in a pullover and jeans, ready to get back into the "Personals" story:

"I went about my business of being hired by Sally to kill her husband and finally got home in the early evening. I was just closing the front door when I was surprised by my "safe," or undercover pager kicking in. The number that showed on the digital display was Sally's home number. I'd forgotten I'd given her the pager number earlier so she could contact me if any problems came up. She'd given me her number then, apparently trusting me not to call at the wrong time. I dialed and she answered on the first ring. She sounded nervous as she told me she had only a minute because Bobby had gone next door to visit a neighbor.

"I told her it was okay because I wanted to tell her that I'd found a gun and it looked like the deal was shaping up. Apparently she'd had time to think about the deal and was beginning to get nervous—not about murder but about getting ripped off. Hey, I could almost see her staring at the front door of her apartment as she told me she was afraid I wasn't going to go through with it and Bobby would find the check missing and wonder what she'd spent it on and get seriously mad at her. I told her I still intended to do the job for her, and needed a description of Bobby. She asked me if I'd like a photo of him, in a faint voice, and I said sure. We agreed to meet during her lunch hour in the Winn Dixie Supermarket parking lot on North Federal Highway. I reassured her again and hung up.

"As I cradled the phone I saw that my wife Sylvia was watching me, and I wondered what she must think. I had called all types of low-lifes—hookers, druggies, mob guys. Now I was talking to a young attractive female about killing her husband. Sylvia kept her thoughts to herself, but it sounded like the plates hit the dinner table harder than usual when she reheated my dinner and put it out for me.

"First thing in the morning I got my reports typed up and transcribed my tapes and high-tailed it over to the State Attorney's Office for the bullshit obligatory nod from our overseers. The young prosecutor listened to my facts so far on Sally's case and agreed I had enough to make a Probable Cause arrest if she showed up with the pictures. She had conspired with me, given me money, and now would positively identify the intended victim. I had the green light.

"It was Friday, clear and hot. I had promised Sally she would be a widow by the next day. I guessed she had gone through another long night. Was she going to chicken out? I made arrangements with a patrol sergeant whose squad covered the north end. He would have a couple of officers, one a female, ready to move in and make the arrest on my signal. I had the wire in the car again, and set it up for another detective to eyeball the Z-28 from the back. When I wanted them to move in I'd hit the brakes a few times and they'd see the lights.

"Heavy lunchtime traffic slowed me down but I was in position a little after noon. I sat there watching the people bustling in and out of the supermarket, trying not to think too much about what was going down . . . if it was going down. It was. Sally pulled into the lot in her old clunker a few minutes later. She climbed into my car, face flushed, ran her fingers through her hair and gave me two photographs of Bobby. She pointed at one and told me Bobby didn't have the beard anymore.

"I took the photos from her and as I did I noticed the perfume scent on Sally that wasn't there when I first met her, new stuff. She looked fresh and clean and young, and I felt her eyes on me and forced myself to glance at the photos instead of returning her look. It was quiet for a moment, there was a tension she didn't seem to want to break. Finally she took a deep breath, leaned closer to me and started asking questions in her soft voice."

From the taped transcript:

SALLY: Will anything actually be taken in the burglary? I mean, when I get home I'll know because the apartment will be trashed, right? I'll know something has happened then because everything will be thrown around and Bobby won't be there? I'll call his friend that drops him off after work . . . then should I call the police?

AL SMITH: *(Tersely)* Yeah. You'll report the burglary, and your husband missing.

SALLY: Won't the police be suspicious if nothing is taken from the apartment?

SMITH: No. It will look like your husband came home while I was breaking in, we struggled, he got the bad end of the deal and I took him outta there.

SALLY: He'll be gone? He won't be there when I get home?

SMITH: No. I have a friend with an air transport business. We'll put the body in the airplane and throw it out over the Everglades so it won't be found. Ever.

(The poor Everglades have become a traditional dumping ground for bodies after some foul deed or another. Corpses are found almost daily along Alligator Alley, Highway 27, and all the miles of saw grass in between. Hunters and fishermen stumble across them, or firefighters sent to battle a blaze started by the torching of a car find a couple of dead ones baking in the trunk. What the gators and turkey buzzards don't get just rots away. Some bodies are never found, and others are found but never identified. At least they're biodegradable.)

SALLY: Oh. *(Pause)* And when the police arrive I should be upset and all, right?

"By then I was tired of this little girl. I was convinced that she was fully aware of what we were talking about, and she absolutely expected me to carry it out. I nodded at her, and pumped the brakes.

"She was startled a few seconds later when the uniformed officers opened her door, leaned in and told her to get out. She sat frozen for a moment, stunned, and stared at me. She pulled away from the officers, looked at me once more, then slowly climbed out. She was put in the rear seat of a patrol unit and told she was under arrest for Solicitation to Commit Armed Burglary and Murder, First Degree.

"I sat alone in my car for a few minutes after they took her out, still holding the pictures of her husband. I remembered the check she'd given me with both her and her husband's name on it. If I'd actually killed him he would have helped pay for his own murder. Weird thought. I was really into it. I looked at the pictures closely. Bobby was smiling for the camera, never knowing that one day his little wife would pass along the pictures so a hitman would recognize him when he came home to die."

Sally was held without bail, but Bobby, no kidding, showed up to try and get her out anyway. He had been shocked when Al had called him, identified himself and told him he had arrested his wife for conspiring to kill him. Bobby, his voice cracking, *told Al he wanted her back.* He *knew* she loved him, he told Al, and later he said Sally had told him she hadn't *really* wanted to kill him, and she was sorry for all the trouble she'd caused. A real beauty, our little Sally.

Bobby was finally made to understand that Sally's alleged change of heart did *not* change the facts and he reluctantly, very reluctantly, agreed that the police couldn't just say, "Okay, you're sorry, you can go home now." Bobby left the station that afternoon saying he'd do everything he could for his wife, and Al went home feeling like he'd been a player in some kind of macabre, surrealistic cartoon. When he told me about it, I said it sounded to me like the couple deserved each other.

In court Sally's attorney would berate Al, accuse him of "grandstanding." Al should have gone straight to Sally's family, he said, when he first learned about the case instead of turning it into a big criminal deal. Al stood his ground, explaining to the judge (for the record, of course, since the judge already knew it) that though there were legal avenues a police officer could take to help someone with "emotional problems" they were, after all, limited. He *had* to let the case go forward to learn Sally's true intentions, and during his investigation the intangible line between unbalanced flailing about and calculated, criminal machination had been crossed. Sally saw Al Sanetti as a real hitman who would in fact kill her husband for pay, Al argued, and with Al Sanetti she made *real* plans that she expected to be carried out.

Possibly because of Al's determination and the carefully prepared case (Sally's attorney would argue it was to "save his client from the trauma of a trial"), Sally pled guilty to the Solicitation for Murder charge. And who spoke to the judge in her behalf, urging leniency because Sally needed professional help? Bobby, of course. Al figured they both needed help.

The judge, examining all the strange stuff that had taken place, and all that was now compiled on Sally's background, went along and sentenced Sally to two years in Community Control, which would allow her to live at home on probation while she underwent psychiatric counseling. Bobby said that was fair and took Sally's arm as he led her out of the courtroom. Sally was smiling as they left. No wonder. Al remembers hoping that smile wouldn't come back to haunt Bobby, *or* him.

As it turned out, that day of sentencing was a late one for Al. After he left the courthouse he went back to the Organized Crime office to complete the record of Sally's case and handle some other paperwork that was overdue. It was early evening by the time he headed home, but he wasn't through with that day yet.

"What happened was, just after I left the station a northwest patrol unit got into a chase with a stolen car occupied by two dudes wanted in a string of armed robberies. It was funny, because I was thinking of Sylvia and how patient she was with my goofy job and its stretched-out hours and stuff, and the next thing I knew I was roaring down this dead-end street where the bad guys had crashed the stolen car. One patrol cop was continuing the chase on foot, and when I pulled up to the scene the other one asked if I'd stay with the hot car while he went to help his partner.

"So I found myself standing there in a quiet neighborhood just off ol' Sistrunk Boulevard, the main drag through the northwest, the so-called black section of Lauderdale. My mind began to wander back to my first year as a patrolman in that area with Bill McBride as my partner. I knew I was near a little market called Ray's Store, and thought of a man many people in the northwest knew as the poor man's friend . . .

"McBride and I were dispatched to an armed robbery in progress with a report of shots fired, one man down. We ran Code-Three to the scene, and as we jumped out we saw a black male lying on the sidewalk just outside the front door of the business. There was an angry crowd of almost one hundred people around the store, yelling and shouting. We checked the guy on the sidewalk, saw he had been shot and was bleeding and called for an ambulance.

"Just then a young white guy came running out of the store and yelled, 'Quick! I think my father is having a heart attack!' So I ran inside the place and found Ray Efird inside his small office in the corner of the market, gasping and clutching his chest. I notified the dispatcher we'd need more help and another ambulance, then asked the young guy what the hell had happened.

"He told me his father had been working the register in the front of the store. The guy out on the sidewalk had come in, lingered around, then picked up some steaks and carried them to the front. When he got to the register he pulled a sawed-off shotgun from under his coat and pointed it at Ray Efird. He took all the money, then smiled as he walked out the door.

"I guess the smile was too much for Ray Efird. He grabbed his own gun, jumped over the counter and headed out the door after the robber. Outside, he shot the guy, then turned, came back inside and collapsed. The son told me his father was over sixty and had a bad heart. The med units arrived and things were getting sorted out. I checked with McBride to see how the crowd was behaving. He told me it was kind of strange, the crowd was definitely angry and threatening, which was usual. But what was unusual was that they were angry at the black robber for trying to hold up the white store owner. Seems Ray Efird had dealt with the people in the area for years and was known to carry a lot of them on credit when they needed the groceries but couldn't pay the bill. He was really liked and respected, and the people didn't like anyone hitting on him.

"We got the wounded robber out of there before the people did a job on him, and Ray Efird went to the hospital, too. He was released the next day, ready to go back to work. Ray and his family and I would become very close about six years later, after I met his daughter Sylvia and married her."

AL HAD ONE more thing to tell me before he left for the day. I watched his face and eyes as he talked, and saw in them that it's not the car chases and punch-outs and shootings that leave the deepest scars on a working cop.

Al stood at my front door, his car keys in hand, and said: "You know, some of the, well, saddest moments of my young life were when I waited for *my* father to come home from work to do things with us, his kids. We lived at the end of a small street, and as soon as his car came around the far corner I could tell it was him just by the sound. His car didn't make any specific noise or anything, it's just that I'd sat so many times waiting and listening that I knew that car as soon as I heard it. I'd always promised myself it would be different with my kids, but here I was, working late while they waited for me. I wondered if they knew the sound of my car yet.

"That night after everyone else had gone to bed I sat in the kitchen and scanned the Personals in the classified section of the paper. There were some ads for colon massage and hair weaving, a couple for private nude sunbathing, escort services and couples-referrals numbers, messages from men and women 'seeking companionship' or 'someone to take care of.' I wondered how many people who answered those ads would do anything to get what they thought they wanted. I went to bed, very damn glad to be there."

AMATEURS

KILLING. It can be easy, or hard. One little hole in the belly of a three-hundred-pound man, made by the unplanned entrance of a tiny .22 short caliber bullet, leaving a tiny spot of bright red blood, and he's gone after two or three deep, shuddering breaths. There was a good-looking guy dancing with a beautiful woman in a nightclub owned by an ex-football player and a couple of other business types. An older, chubby man in a shiny suit laid the barrel of a small-caliber automatic pistol against the base of his skull and popped it once. The good-looking guy died in his beauty's arms. The music kept on but the dance was over, and the chubby older man just walked away.

Then again, we've had cases locally where an intended victim is beaten, shot two or three times, tied up and dumped way out in those convenient Everglades, only to bob to the surface of the swamp, wriggle out of the rope, stagger through the darkness to a roadway and flag down a passing car. These guarded-by-angels types have lived to testify in court and send their bumbling attackers to prison.

What I'm getting at is that bringing violent death to someone is an inexact science, with variables and unknowns. Which is one of the reasons it's so scary. Professional killers who train, study weaponry, plan their job with finesse and accuracy, these are rare birds. The pseudo-professional killers, those who have seen more than two violent movies, who can easily obtain a real gun anywhere and then slide out to attempt to murder someone, these defectives make every ordinary and routine moment of life potentially dangerous for everyone.

From transcribed taped conversation:

INFORMANT: I was frighten . . .

AL SMITH: Frighten?

INFORMANT: I was frighten my balls off.

SMITH: Frighten your balls off?

INFORMANT: When I heard Clarence say they were gonna do the *real deal* to this guy, I didn't understand, that's not my mentality. I figured that they're gonna go and talk to these guys, you know, have a powwow . . . you know, we've had powwows in the business before. I figured there might be a fight, at best. I saw the blood on their faces, and I said forget about that. I don't walk in that circle. I'm sitting there, I can't believe this, I think I'm in the wrong car. Really, I was so frighten. This guy is like some, you know, wild and crazy Al Capone guy.

SMITH: Yeah?

INFORMANT: This guy tried to blow somebody away . . . just over the deep end.

SMITH: Tell me more.

INFORMANT: Okay . . . but not here . . .

Al Smith and I had met for a drink. We picked one of the nicer clubs on the east side of town. He had work to do in the area involving an ongoing investigation into parking-valet turf-wars and I saw it as a chance to spend some time with him out and about. He wore one of his tight-fitting polo shirts, but slacks this time, not jeans. Still the look of latent power on him. He drank club soda and let the noise and smoke and music and people swirl around him as if he was comfortable. The nighttime atmosphere of the Fort Lauderdale club scene was where many of his "jobs" began.

We talked for a few minutes about his work for that night, and then I asked him about the Amateurs case. The first meeting with the main informant on the case was to take place at a bar called Montego Bay. He explained that the action in the case, meeting places and the like, all took place on the east side of Lauderdale, so apparently the informant felt more comfortable in a bar on the west side of town. Al got that far, and then a big grin crossed his face.

"I had gone in there, Montego Bay, with one of my partners, crazy Don Stanley. We went early, which is the practice on a meet with an informant you don't know. We wanted to get the feel of the place, see if there were any faces we knew, that stuff. So we're there and everything seems cool and we're waiting. The place was really jumping, loud music, people coming on to each other, all that. Lots of fine-looking women, which Stanley was quick to observe and point out.

"He keyed on this one lady at the end of the bar. She had dark red hair, early thirties maybe, nice. She wore a black blouse stretched over what appeared to be a serious pair of breasts. They looked so good they looked *too* good, and we got into a discussion about the chances of them being real. She seemed to be with a couple of other girls, but they were out on the dance floor, so the lady was standing there alone. She knew we were looking at her and talking about her, and even gave us a sort of wary smile.

"My man Stanley says he can't stand it, he's friggin' got to know. She was about ten or fifteen feet away from us, sort of in a corner. Stanley goes over to her—she probably figured he was going to ask her to dance or something—but he says to her that he and his friend, that's me, had a bet going about her. She's smiling, so he goes on with it. Tells her he's bet me fifty bucks that her magnificent and wonderful-looking breasts . . . I don't know, he probably said all kinds of nice things about them . . . were real. He asks her if there was some way she could help him win the bet.

"She kind of cocked her head to one side and looked him over real good. Then she took a long look at me. Then she told him to go back and stand next to me. Stanley came back, shrugged, but when we looked at her she had turned her back on us and the rest of the room. Seemed like she waited for a minute, maybe for the bartender to move to the other end of the bar. Then she turned real slow and just opened that black blouse all the way out nice as yóu please. She had her head back a little and a small smile on her face and, man, she had every right to be proud of those beauties. You know that expression about the room seeming to stand still? Well, that's what it was like. There was nothin' going on around us, just me and crazy Don Stanley staring at that beautiful woman.

"She finally closed up her blouse, buttoned it, then turned her back on us while she tucked it into her slacks. When she turned back we both bowed to her, and I made a show of handing Don a fifty dollar bill. We had the bartender take her a drink, and a few minutes later I was sitting at a back table with the informant on the case, Stanley watching my back. Never did see that woman again, but she surely left an impression. One of the unexpected pleasures that go with the territory."

RentReferrals was one of those shady businesses that grow like a fungus in any rapidly expanding metropolis. Supposedly it kept an up-to-date and comprehensive listing of all available apartments for rent in the northeast section of Fort Lauderdale. A customer paid a fee and the people at RentReferrals rooted through their files. Apartment managers and building owners paid to be in their listings, and potential tenants paid for the locations. Problem was, the people at RentReferrals could really give a "Florida Native" bumper sticker if the renter found a place or not, as long as the fee was paid. If anything, most often the customer paid and then was handed a book of addresses and phone numbers, out of date and inaccurate, and told to "look through this and see if you can find anything." Consumer complaints piled up but little action was taken against the borderline scam.

Again, like fungus, these places seemed to huddle together in certain parts of town, clustered for support and protection. Scam or not, it is profitable. Many people moving to South Florida are either desperately seeking employment or have jobs lined up and need to get to them. They need to get settled in a place, *any* place, quickly and without hassle, and they'll often put some of their hard-earned money into a referral place to make it happen. Because of the profits, some of the turf wars that erupt for dominance of an area can get real hairy.

In this case, some amateurs with a Roaring Twenties mentality, a bellyful of booze and a gun decided to eliminate a competitor who wouldn't cooperate. No doubt wanting to experience the satisfaction of a job well done by their own hands, they had a go at it themselves. After the dust and gunpowder cleared and their target was still walking, talking and doing business, they decided to seek out some professional help. That's how Al came into the picture.

"We used the signs of the zodiac to identify our CI's," he said, meaning confidential informants. "These work names were picked at random and had nothing to do with the month the CI was recruited or personality traits or any of that. Libra, who put me on to George Chianti and RentReferrals, was a little guy with hair that looked like he'd been in a wind tunnel, dirty clothes, a runny nose, and expensive-type shoes. You figure the shoes. He was a squirmy little junkhead, scared of his own shadow, dog-paddling behind the barracudas. People like Libra put even people like George Chianti higher on the evolutionary scale. Libra was on hand when the RentReferrals gang went into action, and when it was over he went home, changed his underwear and began making his way through the pimps, hustlers and liars that would bring him to me.

"After that first meeting with Libra we set it up again for the next afternoon. I bought him coffee and we sat in my car behind an elementary school on the north side of town. I had the feeling Libra was intimidated by my size, my job, and that here I was sitting next to him expecting to hear a straight story. I was intimidated by the smell of him, and kept my cup of coffee tucked up under my nose.

"He wanted to tell me what had happened, but he also wanted to make sure he came out all innocent and smelling like a rose. A *rose* . . . According to Libra he advised this guy Chianti he was crazy to do any shooting, and that he, Libra, didn't know there was gonna be shooting until it happened. Told me he was an 'innocent bystander' in the thing, he could see himself in jail because of it, because of these 'assholes,' he said.

"I was tired, to tell the truth, and didn't feel like playing the game with this guy. You know, you've got to act like you're really interested in the informant as a person, not just what he's got to say, and I was having a hard time at that, playing the part of a father confessor. It had already been a long month that week, and I felt like I was going to spend the rest of my life talking make-believe to junkie liars. The shrinks talk about cop burnout, and I knew it could happen from too much exposure to people like Libra and situations where your life's on the line.

"I've had hookers inform on their pimps who mistreated them, drug dealers sing about other dealers to keep from going to jail, porn sellers put the finger on child molesters to take the heat off their own slimy backs. And this paragon of virtue, shit, he'd been impressed that I bought his coffee. He kept sipping it while he told me about the rent-war guys who thought they were tough, guys with guns who would use them. I knew about tough too, and guns and shooting people, and about how sometimes it's tougher *not* to shoot."

Al looked at me, hesitating. "C'mon," he said as he stood, "let's go for a ride." He wanted to talk about shooting and not shooting but was afraid to wander away from the story we were working on. I told him to say what he wanted to say. This was his story, after all. We cruised the night streets of Fort Lauderdale's east side and beach side as we talked . . .

*   *   *

A<small>L HAD BEEN</small> a member of the Tactical Impact Unit on the night he wanted to tell me about. Their specialty was armed robberies in progress. There had been a bunch of holdups at convenience stores all through the southwest section of town. This was before silent alarms were installed in most stores, so the most common method of prevention was the stakeout. Al's unit would be sent to the south end of the city with orders to sit on a store right through the night. On this particular night Al was watching a small market located across the street from the baseball fields at Croissant Park near the railroad tracks. He had his radio, a flashlight and a .12 gauge pump shotgun, and got permission from a homeowner to sit in his backyard. He lounged in a lawn chair, deep in the shadows, and could see clearly into the side windows of the store, where the clerk stood behind the counter. Less than a mile east of him nighttime Lauderdale Beach did its thing with loud music and hot cars and sleek women and dusty noses and money, money, money. From where Al was, in his small dark place, all of that could have been the sewer system of Uranus.

"There was also the usual cop stuff going on over the radio, not too busy, when one of our other units broadcast a BOLO for a yellow Volkswagen with three occupants. The vehicle had been observed driving slowly around several stores, apparently casing them. Minutes after I heard that, the car came slowly down the street in front of me. All three people inside, two black males and a black female, were concentrating on the store as they went past. I tightened up, felt my heart begin to pound, and then they were gone. I listened to the radio for any other word, but no one else spotted the yellow VW after it left my area. I sat back on the lounger, still keyed up, and thought about armed robbery while I waited."

A possibility for any cop on stakeout is that he might be sitting a few feet away, watching, while someone gets blown away. If you see activity that makes you think a felony is about to go down you still have to wait until it actually begins. Our laws back way off when it gets to "maybe," or "it appeared about to." Until an armed robber does his thing he's just another suspect with a gun or knife, and the court, buried under real cases, will often let the "suspect" walk, if that's all he or she is.

It's frightening to be sitting there in the darkness, hoping you'll time it just right. Do we really need more studies to explain why some punk will shoot an unarmed, unresisting, elderly female convenience-store clerk in the face with his stolen .357 magnum *after* he gets the lousy thirty-four dollars out of the register? It's a power thing, we're told. Compensation. Poor little oppressed punk who's had to live his young life under the crushing weight of an apathetic society, experiences his first taste of having real power over another human being, and "makes a statement" reflecting his sorry life. What horseshit. The clerk most often is some poor soul working two jobs, raising a family, makes minimum wage for putting up with all kinds of abuse and probably believes in and *voted* for most of the legislation enacted to give the designated oppressed a chance in the first place. The last thing she sees before her brain explodes is the face of someone she probably would help if given the opportunity and time. Spare me the sociology . . .

"One half hour later they were back," Al said, picking up his story. "They cruised slowly by again, then disappeared from sight. One of the other officers on my team located down the street whispered into the radio that the VW had pulled off the road, one occupant had exited and was walking back toward the store. The rest of my team would keep the eyeball on the vehicle and I'd take the one headed my way. Sure enough, in a moment a young black guy wearing dark clothes came out of the shadows. He waited for a minute in front of the store, looking all around. Then he went inside. Through the window I saw him standing in an aisle until a customer finished paying the clerk and walked out. Then the guy walked up to the counter and pulled out a gun. I whispered into my radio that it was going down, a forty-one in progress!

"I watched as the clerk handed a paper bag full of money from the cash register to the guy. The clerk did not appear to be resisting, but for some reason the robber leaned over the counter and pistol-whipped the clerk until she fell down behind the register. Then he turned for the door, and I was up with the shotgun in my hands, running across the yard toward the street. As I ran I was thinking, 'Okay badass, let's see what you're made of.' The guy came out the front door, stuck the gun in his waist and began to turn to his right. I stopped in the middle of the street about twenty feet from him, racked a shell into the .12 gauge—can any cop tell me of a better sound when it's face-to-face time with an armed suspect?—and yelled 'police' and for him to freeze.

"The guy looked startled but turned toward me and took a step. I yelled for him to put his hands up, and he stopped and raised his arms. I saw the paper bag fall from his left hand, then saw his hands jerk downward toward the gun at his waist. I could see his wide eyes staring into the darkness at me, trying to gauge the distance, and maybe to see if I was real. I gripped the shotgun tighter and pointed the barrel at the center of his body as his hands neared that gun, then lifted away, then back down to the weapon. 'Do it, asshole, do it,' I yelled. I admit it sounds like Clint Eastwood now, but remember, he got it from us. He makes movies, make-believe. We're in the real thing."

In those wonderfully terrible microseconds all of the cop in Al Smith knew that this one was his, a righteous shoot-to-kill situation if ever there was one. He could waste the sonofabitch right then, right there, and not a grand jury in the land would censor him for it, even if the suspect was a black man and Al was a white cop. (Despite what the media would have us believe, grand juries as a rule are not swayed by skin color one way or another. They are usually made up of people intelligent enough to look hard at the evidence and to understand that not all robbers are black, not all cops white. And no skin color has a monopoly on good or bad.) The warm weight of that beautiful pump shotgun rested in his police officer's hands (hands that had been *ordered* to make our streets safe), and the barrel was aimed at the center of one of those Al was trained to hunt down and stop by whatever means necessary. This suspect was not a black guy or a white guy, he was an armed and dangerous asshole who had just pistolwhipped a defenseless victim right in front of Al's eyes, and now his dirty criminal fingers were inches from that oh-so-bad Saturday Night Special riding near his crotch, and his wide eyes were staring in anger and confusion and fear. Al felt his finger increasing the pressure on the trigger. He leaned slightly forward to absorb the recoil . . . and the robber froze. The man in Al recognized what would happen next and groaned in frustration. But the cop in him obeyed the man.

"He froze. The fucker *froze* right there, absolutely fucking *still*. So I didn't pull that shotgun's trigger, and another robber lived that night. I let him surrender, I stayed right on the edge of the fucking rules, and let him fall to his knees on that street instead of cutting him in half with a load of hot buckshot like I could have.

"His buddies in the VW, when they saw what was going down, hauled ass without him. They were chased by my team and finally crashed and bailed out on foot. There was a brief search, a K-9 chewed on one and they were both captured. Score one for the good guys. I disarmed and handcuffed the one I had lying in the street. The reason I'm telling you this as one example of what I've seen out there is because I think about it when somebody like Libra tells me about some asshole trying to be a badass with a gun, like shooting at someone makes a person tough. I stood there in the street waiting for a transport for that supposedly bad little robber, and an ambulance for the clerk. Crap . . . I knew about tough."

That night and others since then have helped Al understand clearly the difference between twisted predatory tough and honest tough, evil kicks and protective reality, anarchy and the badge. I thought it was one example of the subtle but deep and real differences between murderous opportunists, freelance or hired killers, and cops.

*   *   *

AL AND I talked as we drove around town for another half hour or so, then he took me back to the club so I could get my car and we parted. He was at my house the next morning, ready to get back into the "Amateurs" story. Again we got things started with his narrative memories backed by the police reports . . .

George Chianti liked to think of himself, Al said, as a flashy guy, a with-it guy, a successful man who took what was there to take and put up with no crap. He ghosted out of Boston with his pockets stuffed with other people's money, left a trail of scams and broken promises and legal actions already under way. He settled in South Florida after deciding a buck could be made there. Trusting people were walking the streets with their hands full of money waiting to give it to him. He set up Rent-Referrals after recognizing its ambiguous borderline-legal possibilities. He enjoyed the power other people's money gave him. He liked the way the dancers at the nude clubs looked at him when he pulled a banded wad from his pocket. It had a near-hypnotic effect he used to get what he wanted. He never considered for an instant the pain and suffering he created by taking money from people who couldn't afford to lose it.

Chianti was a lot like his jewelry—glittery, heavy, showy, cheap, fake. *He* saw himself as a leader, a thinker, a doer, an action guy and didn't like the wishy-washy types who got in his way. Right across the street from his RentReferrals office was another fee-rental business that somehow compiled fewer complaints from consumers (possibly actually delivering the services they advertised). It bugged George to see the customers hurrying in and out of that business all day. The name of the outfit was RentSearch, which to Chianti had a "poofter," yuppie sound to it anyway. The guy that owned the place looked sort of like a biker, with muscled arms and long hair. He had a girl's name, Gayle Girard, and seemed stubbornly reluctant to go along with Chianti's great business idea. George thought it would be better if Gayle let George bring RentSearch under the wing of RentReferrals, sort of merge them, with George, of course, in charge. Or maybe Gayle could just take his business and move it to another part of town. 'Simple,' was the way Libra described it to Al, 'but Gayle just couldn't get hold of the idea.'

Al picked up the story with the first long meeting he had with the informant while they sipped coffee:

"According to Libra, Chianti thought the location for his business was perfect—one of the best things about it was that they were right across the street from the nude bar Goldbody's. The place opened before noon, served strong drinks and had 'fabulously delicious honeys dancing naked, right there, live.' Chianti liked to have what he called his business meetings there. Libra reminded me there was no cover charge or minimum, that the booze oiled the folks, and George told him that the girls not only appreciated the bucks he slipped into their garters but likewise his sharp business mind when he told them about the great deals he had going. Chianti met there with owners of similar businesses and always took his two employees, Clarence and Mike, for the important talks. I wanted to know more about Clarence and Mike.

"Libra hesitated when I first asked about the two sidekicks but finally he told me Clarence O'Neal was a skinny guy with an 'unkempt' look about him (this from Libra, the grubby little scuzball). O'Neal seemed to stay drunk all the time, and he was a *mean* drunk. His partner, Mike Warner, was a fat hairy guy, kind of dumb and easygoing. He seemed content to be a gopher for Chianti.

"Libra started playing with his empty coffee cup, seemed to relax some and told me that one afternoon the week before our meeting the three of them, George, Clarence and Mike were sitting around the office talking tough in front of the secretary, Rita. Libra grinned at me then with his half-size-too-big stained dentures and described Rita: 'Wears a lot of makeup and smokes too many cigarettes, and Clarence and Mike are all the time arguing about her incredible breasts, and I mean olympic class, big-nippled kachungas.' The boys in the office had a running bet about those 'kachungas,' whether they were real or implanted, and Chianti would wink and shrug to let the others think he really knew for himself.

"Like I said, I was tired of sitting with this guy and wished he would stop shooting all over the place and just tell it like a police report. But I was dreaming, and I knew if I pushed him he might dry up, or hurt his little CI's pride or something. He sat in a daze for a few minutes, apparently dreaming of making a close examination of Rita's kachungas, then he shook himself and got on with it.

"The tough talk got around to the RentSearch problem. That guy Gayle Girard had to be made to see the light. Chianti handed Clarence the phone, and Clarence called Gayle and told him to meet Chianti at Goldbody's for a drink. When Gayle turned him down Clarence told him they were going to go over to RentSearch and smash the place up. He hung up and glanced at Rita to see how she reacted to his macho number. At about that point in this story I was massaging my forehead wondering if they needed cops in Fiji or the Seychelles or Resume-Speed, Kansas. No, I had to sit there with Libra and listen as he told me that Chianti and his two boys were all pissed off after Girard told them to go pound salt up their ass. They decided to go get a drink at Goldbody's anyway. It was Chianti's philosophy, according to Libra, that watching the girls move on that stage was good for a man's thought processes, among other things.

"An hour or so later they were all back in the RentReferrals office, full of juice and a plan. Here Libra admitted being there, and doing a little macho strutting in front of Rita just like the others. They were all talking dirty and saying how they were gonna take care of business, and do the 'real deal' on that guy. But Libra began to get nervous when Mike Warner pulled a small silver .38 and some bullets from Chianti's desk drawer. He said he began making noises to Chianti about how it was time for him to take off, but George slapped him on the back and told him he didn't want to miss the action. Libra said Chianti was actually talking out of the side of his mouth, like a movie gangster, Edward G. Robinson, and said all they needed at that point were some running boards on Chianti's Chevy Nova.

"Hot-headed Clarence O'Neal called Gayle Girard again and told him they were on the way to 'destroy' the place. They all piled into Chianti's car, Libra in the back seat trying to stay low, drove across the street and into the alley behind a row of small businesses where RentSearch was located. I knew the area. There is a popular chili restaurant there that has customers coming and going day and night. Along the same block are a lot of nice businesses, including a baby-supply store that's baby-boom busy with young mothers and new grandmothers rushing in and out." I said what Libra was describing to Al sounded like superimposing a scene from *A Clockwork Orange* over the background from *Bambi.* Al said he guessed so and went on.

"Chianti let Mike and Clarence out so they could get the plan started. They were supposed to charge into the front of Rent-Search, start a fight with Gayle Girard and force him out the back door into the alley, where Chianti would be waiting. Libra insisted he didn't know the plan, he just watched it all happen, helpless and innocent. I stayed noncommittal, not cutting him any slack until I had a good picture of what the hell had taken place there.

"I knew the incident had gone down in the middle of a workday afternoon. Real people, with real lives, doing *normal* things, you know? And here came George Chianti with an attitude and a gun.

"Apparently Gayle Girard may have had what sounds like a girl's name but according to Libra he didn't fight like a girl. Once they got into it he beat the piss out of Clarence and Mike, knocking them both down a couple of times, and gave Clarence an 'almost perfect' shiner on one eye. He may have thought they came in the front to draw him from the back, but suddenly he turned and ran through the store to the rear, maybe to lock it up. And that's when Chianti opened fire.

"I had already seen the reports, of course," Al said. "The witness accounts varied, par for the course, but the info was that Chianti fired at least twice, probably more. This was confirmed later by the discovery of two bullet holes in the wall *inside* the doorway, inches from where Gayle Girard's head had been. You know that most common business-space construction these days has all the interior walls made of aluminum framing and drywall, right? Those two .38 caliber slugs could've punched through that drywall easy if they had hit just right. Once through, where would they go? Into the back of a young mother? A baby? A salesgirl?"

Al was up and pacing again. I made some notes and looked over what we had done so far that morning while he took a moment to ease up. He kind of grinned, shrugged, took his seat, and charged on:

"After the shots were fired O'Neal and Warner came stumbling back to the car and got in. They hauled ass then, and all the way down Middle River Drive, according to Libra, Chianti chewed out the other two bozos because they hadn't flushed Girard all the way into the alley. All the yelling didn't really matter, though, because pretty soon the three of them were acting like the whole thing was a big victory. O'Neal and Warner talked like they were proud of their cuts and bruises, making it sound like they had thumped Girard pretty good, and Chianti was all puffed up about drilling a couple of holes in the wall beside Girard's 'goggle-eyed' head. They drove down to the park beside the river, parked the car and began talking about going back to finish the job. Libra suggested they 'back off awhile so things could cool off,' so they finally gave it up and went back to the RentReferrals office. Libra, still insisting he was there by accident, left then and went home, worried sick about the heat that was sure to follow.

THE POLICE REPORTS stated that the police had been called by several people through 911. Many witnesses heard the shots, and a couple had seen the fight and the getaway vehicle. One young businesswoman not only saw and heard most of the incident, she told the reporting officers she was willing to give statements and testify in court. Amazing. Reports were done with all available information, and the case was kicked to the Detective Division as an Attempted Homicide, possible Extortion. Al Smith was familiar with the incident reports because copies had gone to his unit in the event that there were Organized Crime tie-ins. Within a week Libra's shaky little voice was calling out from the shady side of the street, searching for Al Smith/Al Sanetti.

Libra was now supposed to find a contract hitman for Chianti, and, scared to death, he was looking for a cop to save his butt.

Al looked at Libra squirming in front of him and his mind's eye was filled with clear pictures of those stupid bullets from Chianti's gun, spinning out of the barrel in a blast of powder and fire, rocketing through the normal day. Al remembered we had a recent incident where an angry drug buyer who had been ripped off opened fire with a shotgun at the street corner where the dealer usually hung out. Part of that blast hit a little girl in the head. She had every right to be there, living her normal life. She didn't die but she was blinded forever in one eye.

Al drove Libra back to where he had met him and dropped him off, then stopped at a car wash on the way back to the station and made sure they did a good job on the interior. Later that afternoon he raised a sweat mucking the stalls at the police Mounted Patrol Unit stables. Seeing my reaction to this, he explained that after his talk and visit with Libra he felt depressed and unclean. He needed to recharge himself before he went home, and not surprisingly, he did it by going back to the horses.

"Hey, I was one of the officers that started the FLPD Mounted Patrol Unit," he told me. "If we had to choose between people or horses . . . well . . . I stayed with the unit until it was established, then to the high impact work that led me to my current undercover assignment. But I still like to drive out to the stables near the trails at Sunshine Ranches and help with the grooming and cleaning and repairing the tack. Being around the horses helps me get my perspective back, get my head on straight after it gets twisted around by all the bullshit. The honesty of horses makes me feel good. Even on that day I'm talking about, while I shoveled the soiled straw from the stalls, I knew I could work there for an hour and somehow wash away all the crap I had been wading through on the job."

GEORGE CHIANTI DIDN'T waste time grumbling about a temporary defeat. Girard and his pain-in-the-ass RentSearch apparently wasn't going to go away, and it was obvious that O'Neal and Warner, good guys, just couldn't really *handle* it. He doubted he should do the hit himself, though he toyed with the idea, even liked it. But no, maybe it was time to call in the pros.

After Chianti put out the word that he wanted to issue a contract on Gayle Girard, one of the first nibbles he got was from a group of dirty-neck bikers in Pompano Beach. Through an intermediary they set up a meet. It took place under the Fourteenth Street Causeway Bridge next to the Intracoastal Waterway in Pompano. All the participants carefully covered the license plates on their trucks and cars, wore dark sunglasses, bandannas and, in Chianti's case, a ball cap with the Goldbody's logo on the crown. The conversation was exchanged in low voices.

Perfect assholes don't have pimples, and some of these clowns had them, so maybe they weren't perfect—which was the way Al described the group to me. To Chianti the bikers seemed serious enough but they were such a *visible* bunch. If they got into trouble with the cops on one of their many other criminal enterprises they might give away Chianti's little hit to save themselves. Chianti left the meet with vague promises of recontact, and put the word out for a *real* professional. Through the efforts of his pal Libra, who was acting to save his own sweaty skin, Chianti finally made contact with Al "Sanetti." They began their relationship on the phone:

GEORGE CHIANTI: So, Al, you see my problem here, why I might need someone who can guarantee a sure thing?

AL SMITH: Sure, George. That's a hell of a story. Sounds like you almost did the deal yourself.

CHIANTI: Yeah, but close isn't good enough, and I want this guy *done.* I already talked to some other people, some guys out of Pompano, but they didn't impress me, ya know?

SMITH: There are a lot of amateurs out there, George.

CHIANTI: That's no shit, Al. Listen, maybe we can work somethin' out on this guy . . . but not on the phone, understand?

SMITH: Maybe we can, George.

The case was already snapping and popping by the time Chianti and Al began their dance. O'Neal and Warner were getting antsy, Gayle Girard was cooperating with the police, witnesses to the shooting were coming forward all over the place. It didn't look like Al would have time to consummate a deal with Chianti before other action took over. The detectives in Al's unit, pulled into the case, were close to moving toward arrests. Then Chianti, again through Libra, finally asked for a face-to-face with Al Sanetti. All proceedings went into suspended animation while all the players waited to see if Chianti would dig himself an even deeper hole.

"We had gone through a day of waiting for reviews from the prosecutor's office, you know, to see if we had enough to get warrants for solicitation or if we should just go out and bag Chianti and the other two for the attempted murder of Gayle Girard. I got a number on my pager from Libra, called him, and he told me George Chianti wanted to see me that night at Goldbody's. Libra said Chianti wanted him there too, but he was scared and was going to try and back out. He'd call me back in a half hour to let me know his situation.

"He never did call back, and I didn't think too much of it because he'd already told me the time Chianti would expect me at the club, around nine. That gave me time to go home and have dinner with Sylvia and my girls. The girls were pumped up about a school thing scheduled for the next night, and Sylvia didn't act too concerned about me spending the evening at a nude dance club since I had actually been *home for dinner*. I tried to reassure her with that old one about why go out for tired hamburger when you've got USDA Prime waitin' at home, but she gave it back to me with, 'Even cheap stuff tastes good if you add enough sauce.' She was laughing as she said it, though, so I left the house that evening feeling like things were still cool at home.

"Goldbody's, one of your premier nude dance clubs in town, located right on a major artery on the east side, was doing a hot business by the time I got there. My instructions were to look for an older heavy-set guy sitting on the upper level near the back bar. He would be wearing a gray vest over a pink shirt, and a little American flag pin would be on the vest. I knew him from photos, of course, but paid for a beer at the first bar near the door and wandered around for a few minutes before I walked up and stood beside him.

"Libra was nowhere in sight. I didn't see Warner or O'Neal either and figured Chianti was making his deal with Sanetti and keeping it to himself. He might have had someone watching his back, I don't know. I do know the music was loud, the drinks were flowing, the girls were dancing, and Chianti wanted to show me how careful and tricky he was right from the git-go. He looked me over after I leaned close and said hello, then cocked his head for me to follow. He got up and walked quickly back toward the bathrooms. Real original, I remember thinking, the goddamned bathrooms, but he went into the hallway to the rear fire door, pushed it open and just kept going. I followed him across the dark parking lot to the rear of the club, figuring we were headed for a car. Nope, he just stopped, turned, looked around for a moment, then grinned and waved me on again. We walked across the lot, along the driveway and back to the front doors. We hesitated again as he looked around, then went back into the crowd, past the dancers on the stage doing the 'table-tops,' and finally stopped at the rear bar where we'd started.

"I guess he thought if I had someone watching my back they would panic and try to follow us out the back door into the lot, or rush around to the front doors and then along the driveway looking for us. He didn't see any of that, so he relaxed. He didn't see Bill McBride, either, who had entered the club before me by attaching himself to a carload of guys from some bachelor party as they charged in yelling for drinks and naked women. When McBride saw me heading out the back he didn't panic, he just began moving slowly toward the front door, knowing Don Stanley, who Chianti missed too, would pick us up from where he sat in the darkest corner of the parking lot with a view of the rear door and main entrance.

"Chianti was right about two things, though. One was that most people there were either too busy working the customers or too busy staring at the dancing girls to notice or remember us. The other was that the place was so damned noisy there was no way Stanley, out in the car, could get anything worth a damn off the wire I wore. I can give you the conversation I had with Chianti, but it will have to be from memory. It went like this:

GEORGE CHIANTI: This place is great, huh, Al? Tits and ass all
   night long.
AL SMITH: Yeah, there's no denyin' that. Funny place for a busi-
   ness meet, but this is your turf, so maybe it's okay.
CHIANTI: Believe me, it's okay.
SMITH: Where's our little friend, the one who called me for
   you? I thought he was supposed to be here. It makes me
   nervous when things don't look like I was told they would.
CHIANTI: What? You think this is some kind of setup? *I'm* the
   one who should be nervous. You could be a cop.
SMITH: And so could you.
CHIANTI: And so could that fucking broad up there with no

pubes, okay? Shit, I don't know where that little idiot is, I thought he'd be here too.

SMITH: *(Laughing)* Maybe *he's* a cop!

CHIANTI: *(Laughing too)* Holy shit, then we're all in trouble. All right, let's talk about a job. I want you to know I very quietly asked a guy here and there about you, your name, Al. Seems you've been heard of, that you've done jobs like these around here before.

SMITH: It's what I do, George.

CHIANTI: Yeah. So I need a guy done. I need somebody to do the *real deal* on this bastard. A clean job, a sure job, know what I mean?

SMITH: Yeah, but even when you told me the story on the phone you didn't tell me the guy's name, just that he was a competitor of yours.

CHIANTI: *(Finishes his drink, and orders another before talking again)* No names right now, I mean tonight. I'm still thinking about doing this thing myself and I don't want too much info out—

SMITH: Doing it yourself isn't always the best move.

CHIANTI: Don't you think I know that? I'm still not absolutely sure, that's all. I definitely want this guy whacked, though.

SMITH: I hear you. It would just make my planning easier if I knew who the target was.

CHIANTI: Later. Tell me how much.

SMITH: Five thou, half up front, half after he's down.

CHIANTI: I can handle that . . .

SMITH: Let's make a deal then. I don't want to sit on this too long.

CHIANTI: It won't be too long.

SMITH: All you have to do is say yes, give me the half up front and a name and I'm on the way.

CHIANTI: Good. But not tonight. I got some more thinkin' to do on this, then I'll get back to you.

SMITH: All I can say is, don't think too long, yeah?

"I got back to my office, McBride and Stanley right behind me, and had the gut feeling that Chianti was still giving serious thought to doing a *real deal* himself."

THE NEXT DAY Don Stanley and Bill McBride showed Al what they had compiled on the case against George Chianti. They felt it was ready to go to a judge for warrants on the Attempted Murder and Extortion charges, and after looking it all over, taking everything into account, Al agreed. He reminded himself they were trying to save Gayle Girard's life, and if they could get good warrants on Chianti for that first messy attempt it would pull him off the streets that much faster. Al still had the nagging worry that while negotiations for the hit were in progress Chianti would come charging out of Goldbody's with his stupid little gun and somehow manage to kill Girard—and anyone else who might get nailed by one of his shots. They got the warrants for Chianti and O'Neal and Warner, and made ready to scoop them up that evening.

"That was the evening my oldest daughter got ready for her part in a school play. She was excited and happy because it was her first time in something like that, and both her parents would be sitting in the audience, her dad had promised her he would be there no matter what. I was almost hoping the damned lawyers at the State Attorney's Office would give us some grief about the case and delay the warrants—which is what usually happened, but not this time of course. But it all came together, the warrants were hot in our hands, and the word on the street was that the three hairbags at RentReferrals might take off for good at any moment. We had to go.

"Sylvia hesitated on the phone when I called home late that afternoon to tell her I wasn't going to make it, and for a scary second I thought she was going to put my daughter on the line so I could try to explain it to *her*. She did her best to keep the anger and disappointment out of her voice as she told me to 'be careful.' I hung up the phone feeling like a total schmuck, a cardboard cutout of a father.

"Well, that evening Stanley, McBride and I eased into the RentReferrals office to bag 'em. I hoped they were there and not across the street at Goldbody's staring up between some dancer's thighs. Clarence O'Neal and Mike Warner were in the office and didn't put up any fight when we flashed our tin. We cuffed 'em and stuffed 'em. George Chianti was *not* there, and I wondered if our meeting had somehow spooked him, or if he was blessed with a ratlike sense of trouble, or if the still-missing Libra had flipped back to the bad guys under pressure. Rita the secretary was surprisingly loyal to him, shrugging and pouting and telling us nothing as she sucked nervously on one of those extra-long cigarettes. Chianti was out of town, on the lam, gone."

So GEORGE CHIANTI became a Federal Fugitive, wanted in Florida and Massachusetts. He stayed on the run for over a year, but he couldn't change his con-man ways, and his flash and bluster finally led the FBI to his new scammer's office in upstate New York. He was extradited back to Fort Lauderdale on the Extortion and Attempted Murder charges and made a lot of noise through his attorney about how he would fight the case, trumped up and bogus as it was, all the way through a trial that would "vindicate" him. His lying mouth runneth over, and at first it looked like he might actually slide.

Al was up and pacing in my small office again, punching one fist into the other palm. Frustration, even in memory, still burns hotly.

"We began having problems with the trial part of the case soon after we got Chianti behind bars here in Lauderdale. Libra surfaced, but no longer living in Florida. He was still 'frighten his balls off' he told me. He'd talk to me on the phone but didn't want anything to do with coming back for the trial. I knew we could force the issue, but wasn't sure at that point how important the loss of his testimony would be.

"Even though I had talked to Chianti on the phone and then had met him face to face at the skin joint, and even though we both *for sure* knew we were discussing him paying me to kill Gayle Girard, we hadn't taken it far enough for me to bring charges for Solicitation against him. He had never clearly identified his intended victim, and although the initial price was agreed on, no money ever changed hands. It was just going to have to be one of those very real truths that never gets looked at in the courtroom.

"Then there was the original prosecutor assigned to the case. He was one of those who looks only for some type of conviction, even if it means reduced charges, ready to play 'let's make a deal' with the defendant even before he's done his homework enough to know what the case is all about. I felt we had worked hard and had put together a solid case, the charges were serious, we had citizens who had witnessed the action and were willing to put themselves on the line in the courtroom. No way Chianti should get an easy deal. The prosecutor tried to intimidate me, but I made him understand that I wasn't going to go quietly. He backed off, and the case was then assigned to a female State's Attorney who turned out to be a real fireball. She began from scratch and read every report and studied every aspect of the case, committing it all to memory. She wasn't a hundred pounds soaking wet, but she had a heart for the fight fifty times her size. She didn't scare easy either, and as it turned out, that was a good thing.

"On the day of Chianti's bond-hearing I met the prosecutor out in the hallway near the courtroom. She seemed tired, and when I asked her what was up she told me she'd been getting hang-up phone calls all through the week, and last night someone had tried to break into her apartment. I didn't say anything to her then, but I was getting the late night hang-up calls too, and was already arranging for the phone company to put a lock on my line. Alarm bells were going off in my thick skull as I talked with the lawyer. We were both likely targets for this type of bullshit harassment, me even more than her, but there was only one case she and I were working or had ever worked together. Chianti. And I also knew it was his M.O. to use the phone to make his threats, the slimy no-balled bastard. When we went into the courtroom I was steaming.

"Why we were even *having* a bond hearing for this recent Federal Fugitive was beyond me, and then I had to sit there and watch while the judge allowed him to bond out of jail before he went to trial because the other two defendants in the case, O'Neal and Warner, had been granted bonds in exchange for their cooperation. Chianti stayed close to his attorney after the proceedings, looking smug but apparently sensing that to get too close to me might not be good for his health. At least this time he didn't skip town, probably was confident he could win the case by getting to O'Neal and Warner. We got ready for trial.

"We never could prove it was George Chianti behind the phone calls, or if he paid some dirtball to try to break into the prosecutor's apartment, but I wasn't through. The prosecutor called me early one morning just before the trial. She told me she'd been run off the road the night before by a man in what appeared to be a medium-sized rental with Dade County tags. She wasn't hurt, just shaken up, but she told me it frightened her some because she was sure the man in the rental had *purposely* forced her to swerve away to avoid him. Then he stopped a short distance from where her car came to rest and stared at her for a moment before speeding off. I had heard enough."

Al stopped for a moment, got up and went into my kitchen and came back with a soft drink. He took a long pull from the bottle, then gave me a grin.

"I don't have to tell you there's no documentation on this next part of the story, right? I'll give it to you from memory, or rather *Sanetti's* memory." It seems later that same day Chianti had a meeting with his lawyer. When the meeting was over the lawyer went back to his business and Chianti headed for the parking lot, where his car sat angled across two spaces in the shade of an old oak tree. He got the key in the lock when Al Sanetti leaned against the door, smiled into his surprised face and began to talk real quiet.

AL SMITH: You are fucking up *big* time, George.

GEORGE CHIANTI: What the hell? You can't . . . I'll tell my lawyer you're—

SMITH: You'll tell nobody. This is between you and me, George, and I want you to pay close attention so you'll understand what I'm tellin' you here.

CHIANTI: I don't have to listen. I already told my lawyer you're the cop who tried to pass yourself off on me, tried to *entrap* me, made things up about me. I don't have to listen—

(Sanetti takes the car keys out of Chianti's hand. There is just a "but" of resistance, then Chianti's hand flies open and gives up the keys, which are tossed onto the ground under the car.)

SMITH: You weren't leaving just yet anyway. Now *listen*. The phone calls are spineless bullshit. The attempted break-in is more serious. Now we've had a near-accident that looks like a deliberate attempt to intimidate an officer of the court.

(Chianti stays quiet, sweat forming on his upper lip. He tries to step aside to give himself more room but Sanetti gets even closer and puts his face in front of Chianti's and brings his voice even lower.)

SMITH: *(Continues)* I don't care if they waste a lot of time and taxpayers' money trying to bring charges against you for hiring some asshole to pull these stunts, George, but *I* am gonna take a more personal interest in you from now on. Up 'til now you've just been another case, nothin' personal about it . . . whatever happens happens. But now, George, you've gone and changed the rules here. Now I am looking at you in a new light. *You*, asshole, are going to have to think about how you want to play this game. Go cryin' to your lawyer if you want, tell the court about how nasty ol'

Al Sanetti threatened you, and see if it does any good, scumbag. You do whatever you want in court, but if there are *any* more bullshit games goin' on outside the courtroom you'll be looking at somethin' you do *not* want to see late some night. Understand?

(Chianti stares at Sanetti.)

SMITH: *(Continues) Understand?*

(Chianti nods rapidly, sucking in his breath. Sanetti pats him on the cheek, three times, hard, then walks away.)

SMITH: *(Continues)* That's good, George.

(Chianti watches Sanetti walk away, then slowly goes to his knees and tries to reach for his car keys.)

"After that no more phone calls. No more attempted break-ins. No more prosecutors getting run off the road by mysterious assholes in rental cars," said Al Smith with satisfaction.

THE CIVILIAN WITNESSES hung tough, and Al felt good knowing how strong the police can be when the public they serve backs them up. The witnesses weren't swayed at all by the defense attorney's badgering, and their testimony was clear, concise and damning to Chianti. Al was proud of them.

O'Neal and Warner managed to stay on track too. They had made their deals with the State, knew they would be going to jail for short sentences, but they also knew Chianti was looking at a long fall and they were smart enough to separate themselves from him. There is no doubt he tried to get them to change their testimony—we can only imagine the methods—to weaken the case, but Clarence and Mike had seen enough of Chianti's doings and decided to save themselves. Maybe they figured they could be back in their favorite seats at Goldbody's if they stuck with their deals. In addition to the witnesses and Clarence and Mike rolling over, the case was also helped by Chianti himself. He failed to come clean to his own attorney, and it badly undermined his credibility in the courtroom:

DEFENSE ATTORNEY: Tell me, Detective Smith. While you were investigating my client and his business interests did you have occasion to run a criminal history on him?

AL SMITH: Yes, I did. It's standard procedure in a case of this nature.

ATTORNEY: And would you tell the court what, if anything, your inquiry found?

SMITH: (Looking over at the prosecutor and hesitating. He knew in most circumstances that information would not be admissable unless introduced by the defense.) Yes, sir, I did.

ATTORNEY: And what, if anything, did you learn?

SMITH: I learned that your client, the defendant, has been arrested three times for DUI, and twice for assault. He was listed as a fugitive by the FBI for charges stemming from this jurisdiction and others, and he has two outstanding warrants for his arrest currently on file.

(Defense Attorney, his face pale, looks quickly through his notes. In a final effort to free the hook from his client's mouth he asks if Al has his personal notes relating to that criminal history or a copy of it. Al does not, so the attorney asks the judge to strike that portion of Al's testimony because it's hearsay and could not be verified.

The prosecutor asks to approach the bench. She hands the judge a copy of the criminal history on Chianti and states this is the same copy Detective Smith refers to.)

JUDGE: Detective Smith, is this a copy of the same criminal history you had reviewed, and does it accurately reflect your testimony?

SMITH: Yes, your honor.

JUDGE: It is admissable. Are you ready to continue?

ATTORNEY: Your honor, we'd like to take a moment from the proceedings for a short discussion.

The judge ordered a recess during which Chianti and his attorney had an intense whispered exchange. When the trial resumed the attorney notified the court his client wanted to change his plea. Chianti pled guilty to the charges in the stated hope that the court would look favorably on his decision.

"The judge," Al said, "was one of those who kept himself informed about all aspects of the case, inside and outside of the court, and did a thorough background check on the convicted defendant before sentencing. He handed George Chianti a fifteen year sentence (total for all counts), and George went bye-bye to the Graybar Hotel, where if he wasn't careful, maybe someday *he'd* be a dancing girl."

FUNNY MONEY

IT WAS LATE AT NIGHT, my house and the neighborhood were quiet, and I was alone with Al's notes, reports, and papers. He and I were scheduled to meet for breakfast in the morning to begin work on the next story, so I thought I'd get a head start by looking over the copies of the police reports of the incident that sparked the whole investigation, and led to Al's once again playing the role of hired killer.

OFFENSE REPORT (FLPD)

OFFENSE: ROBBERY (Armed) Date/Time: 8/25/88
0853 OR#88-123456
LOCATION: Pearl's Gateway Jewels, North Federal Highway
VICTIM: Thomas Pearl (WM, dob 2/15/40, Res: 500 Gull Drive, Ft. Laud.)
SUSPECTS: Three Latin males (see supplement for description), automatic weapons
VEHICLE: Unknown

Victim advised he opened the above store at 0815 hrs and went to the rear to make coffee. While there he looked to the front door and saw suspect #1 standing at the door, well-dressed, carrying briefcase. Victim buzzed door to unlock it and admit suspect, thinking it was a customer. Suspect then pulled out long-barreled handgun and told victim to go to rear of store. Suspect ordered

91

victim to open rear entrance door which opens to alley behind shops. At that time two suspects wearing shorts entered, both with automatic weapons, one with a tan shopping bag. Suspects ordered victim to open safe, then ransacked it.

Before leaving business one suspect used black electrical tape (shiny finish) to tie victim's wrists and ankles together. Victim was left on couch, and was later observed through the front windows by a passing construction worker, and the police were notified.

Suspects fled through rear door of business into alley, leaving behind one brown paper bag which contained a weapon. Bomb Squad was called out to scene since the contents of the bag were unknown to officers on scene at that time.

Loss:
Victim advised this officer that four hundred thousand dollars ($400,000.00) in jewelry and stones was taken.

Supplement to Armed Robbery Report #88-123456
This patrol sergeant arrived on scene shortly after the first unit. Found victim on couch, sitting up, with both wrists and ankles taped. He complained of some discomfort, but could stand up and move around. I cut the tape *between* the wrists and ankles, but did not *remove* tape around same. Officers on scene then discussed brown paper bag left on floor near rear door. I advised them to leave it alone by stating, "You never know, it might hold a bomb." At that time the victim quickly stated that there was no bomb, just a gun in the bag. Loss reported at $400,000.00. See further supplements.

Supplement to Armed Robbery Report #88-123456
This bomb squad captain and one bomb squad detective arrived on scene and found brown paper bag (grocery) on floor in back room. Careful examination showed an Uzi-style weapon w/ magazine full of live rounds. Silencer device also found. Magazines, silencer, and weapon each wrapped separately, then in one brown bag, then this bag inside the exterior grocery bag. No explosives found other than live bullets in magazines. All items turned over to lab for processing and evidence.
For Further, see supplements by Detective Division.

The next morning, which turned out to be clear, hot and beautiful, Al and I were joined by our friend Randy, the retired (because of shotgun wounds) FLPD sergeant who had first told me he had seen Al on a TV talk show. He and Al Smith had been partners in Organized Crime for several months, and were comfortable with each other. We went to a breakfast restaurant on U.S. 1 near my house and took a quiet booth near the front windows. The waitresses knew us and didn't mind if we sat there for a couple of hours drinking coffee and shooting the bull. This restaurant specializes in huge and exotic pancakes from all over the world, so while I took notes Al told me the story as he and Randy threw themselves with frightening intensity into a *serious* breakfast:

"Even in plastic, glittery, money-hungry Fort Lauderdale a four-hundred-grand jewelry robbery is a pretty impressive hit, and this one came in the form of an armed robbery with automatic weapons, which always makes us sit up and take notice. I was sitting around with Bill McBride and Don Stanley in the OC office waiting for that first cup of coffee bean battery acid to jump-start my heart, and copies of the robbery report were being passed around. I didn't connect the name at first, but finally a few of my neurons sparked and it hit me. Thomas Pearl, the innocent 'victim' listed as owner of Pearl's Gateway Jewels, was actually a shithead bad boy. I didn't know it then, but in this Funny Money case, Pearl was playing the dual role of victim *and* scammer. I tuned out all the bullshit around me and remembered my first meeting with the real Tommy Pearl, representative of the Giancana family out of Chicago, local carwash and bar owner, shady deal player, extortionist and a genuine motherfucker."

As Al remembered it, spring had crept in quietly that year, after the traditional New Year's Eve bash and riot that occurred annually on the strip on the beach in Fort Lauderdale. Usually the approach of Spring Break made the FLPD cancel all vacations, and the overtime budget would swell like the ocean that sweeps the city's edge on the east. Bad publicity and aggressive wooing tactics by other Florida towns caused the once flowing stream of college students to dwindle down to a trickle of what it had once been.

Where thousands of boisterous beer-drinking student bodies swarmed the beach streets trying to party their brains out and take some memories home with them, now there were a few hundred, mostly quiet, polite, well-dressed and well . . . *touristy*. Hotel rooms that traditionally held twenty or thirty kids in various stages of intoxication now slept one or two who *might* have finished most of a half-carafe of house wine at the Pizza Shack. I mean, *these* Spring Breakers lined up with the last of the winter season Canadians to get tickets for the Jungle Queen cruise!

"For me it was kind of depressing to see the tradition of row-diness die off," Al said. "From the time I was fourteen I spent many nights on the strip learning the things kids are only supposed to wonder about. It seemed ironic to me that I'd spend the first three spring seasons of my police career arresting college breakers on the beach for doing the same types of stupid things I used to do as a teenager. When the seasons did change I was no longer a rookie cop on the strip but an undercover OC cop, swimming with the barracuda marinara."

Al got a call from a Henry Burns, the manager of the Pirate Hotel on the beach. Al knew him from different cases he had handled there and remembered him to be a pleasant undemanding man, very overweight and bald. When Al got to the hotel and went into the manager's office he could see Burns was pretty nervous. The man's voice cracked when he said hello and his hands were shaking. Burns closed the door, looked out the window and asked Al if he had ever heard of a guy named Tommy Pearl, who claimed to be part of the Chicago Mafia.

Al said he had never heard of Pearl, and added that in Fort Lauderdale every guy who wanted to talk tough and have a touch of mystery about him says he's in the Mafia, and they don't even have to be of Italian descent. Burns lightened up, blew a little puff of air out of his chubby cheeks and told Al this guy calling himself Tommy Pearl had called the hotel. He said he had a nephew who had stayed there for several days and that the nephew claimed a man named Henry, the manager, had made homosexual advances toward him.

"I shook my head when I heard that and told him I knew he was a good family man. I even tried to joke with him about it, saying he had never made a move on *me*, but he just looked at me funny, so I told him to go on with his story."

Burns then told Al that Tommy Pearl said to him on the phone that he was going to come to the hotel and *take care* of the manager, in person. Burns, sounding desperate, told Al he was not gay, didn't do what he was accused of and was sure there was some mistake. He said he didn't want to press the issue but he didn't want to wake up with a horse's head in bed with him either. Al told him he had seen too many movies. He would try to check this Pearl guy out, and Burns was to call him if there was any more contact.

"Things were kind of quiet around town then, as I said, so when I got back to the office I ran a background check on one Tommy Pearl. Well, according to the files the guy really *was* connected. Both his carwash and bar had been fingered as places where illicit activities went down, and Mr. Pearl himself had a pretty impressive dossier of arrests and criminal associates. I wondered how it was I'd never heard of him and figured it had something to do with that old policeman's lament—so many scumbags . . . so little time. Anyway, as I read up on Pearl I felt the old anger. It was so typical of these types to take advantage of people least able to defend themselves. Burns was a family man, a businessman, a nice guy. Just the kind of mark predators like Pearl feed on. I also felt that Pearl's threats to Burns were somehow business related . . . he was applying pressure to the manager of a prominent beach hotel and it for sure wasn't just because his nephew had been insulted. One way or another, once he had Burns neutralized, Pearl would either grab a piece of the action or slide one of his own operations into the place . . . the lounge maybe, or the parking valet service. Typical muscle bullshit."

Don Stanley was out of town for a few days so Al got hold of Bill McBride, who was off duty but due in soon. Al told Bill he wanted to make an unofficial visit to an asshole in reference to an attitude adjustment. McBride responded that he just loved unofficial visits, and was in the office ten minutes later. He and Al then headed for the bar Pearl owned up in the north end of town:

"The bar was one of those small places in a strip shopping center, very dark with a big-screen TV. It had lots of colorful sports team pennants scattered around, a bored bartender and fast action in the back if you knew who to ask. McBride and I walked in easy to look the place over, and the first person we saw was a guy named Jack Carp. Carp I knew about, he was a sidekick of Pearl's from the files but I didn't know he had an interest in the bar. Carp was about fifty, slightly overweight. At one time he was in charge of all the gambling for the Chicago Mafia. He had come south for a weather change, and to get away from the heat of a probing Federal Strike Force."

Jack Carp looked up when he saw McBride moving toward him, looked over at Al, and grunted unhappily. Maybe he had that veteran's intuition about cops. And at that moment Tommy Pearl stepped out from the back room. Pearl was a slim well-groomed man in his mid-fifties with hair as black as pitch and as shiny as the bumper on a cherry '55 Chevy. He wore lots of oddly delicate jewelry and a neatly pressed shirt tucked into casual pants. His light-gauge leather loafers looked comfortable and expensive. He saw Al coming and gave an uncertain smile. He held it as Al told him, with a grin, that they just might be cops. Al moved to stand very close to Pearl, his shoulder touching Carp's back. The bartender didn't like what he saw and began to move closer from behind the bar, but McBride leaned over and whispered something to him and the guy backed away, wiping his hands on a small towel. McBride then put his own back to the wall in a good position to watch the bartender and the rest of the room. Al kept his voice quiet as he said again that they might be cops, or they might just be friends with a man who runs a hotel out on the beach. He held up a cassette tape, and watched as Pearl looked at it and then back at him. He told Pearl the tape might be of a conversation he'd had with the guy in the hotel, a conversation in which Pearl threatened and promised to go to the hotel and "take care" of the guy. Al told Pearl if he *was* a cop he'd be thinking that tape was pretty good evidence reference threats or extortion charges, because obviously there was more to it than the "nephew" thing.

Jack Carp kept silent, probably wishing he was back in Chi-town where cops acted civilized. Tommy Pearl tried to play tough. He told Al to go ahead and arrest him if Al had a signed complaint, if not, to get out of his business. Now Al leaned even closer and laid the edge of the cassette tape against Pearl's nose. He told Pearl if he was a cop he had Pearl's ass right there in his hand. The local State's Attorney's office would love to hear the tape, and the Feds, just imagine. Pearl's eyes widened a little and Carp's round head seemed to try to disappear down his jacket collar. Al put the tape in his pocket and took a slow step backward for leverage if he needed it. He shrugged and told Pearl they might just be friends with the guy at the hotel. Either way, Pearl should never bother the guy again, and hope the guy didn't have any accidents:

"I could always tell when I was about to lose control. Some guys bounce on their toes or poke a finger into a suspect's chest as they made ready to jump, but not me. My upper lip would begin to twitch, sort of like Elvis with the hiccups. I looked at Pearl and let myself get angry. I really hate that kind of shit he was trying to pull, trying to do his sleazy business by threatening a guy with something almost anybody dealing with the public would be vulnerable to. My anger showed in my eyes and my voice, and my upper lip too, I guess. I told him if the guy at the beach hotel heard from him again I'd come back to that little bookie joint of his and feed it to him in small pieces. Then I'd turn him upside down and use him for a urinal. McBride and I waited on the balls of our feet. Pearl turned gray, and the skin around his eyes tightened. For a second I thought he might actually jump, but that passed and he showed how much of a badass he really was. He put his hands out slowly, palms up, and said that he didn't deserve this trouble from the cops or anybody else. We were threatening him over something that somebody else did, not him. The tape meant nothing to him, he said, and he had never heard of the hotel guy. He had absolutely no reason to call him again so he wouldn't. I forced myself to come down when I heard him squirmin'. I let my muscles relax and took a slow deep breath. I really had wanted him to make a move and knew McBride had been ready too. That would have been a pleasure. We left, and Henry Burns never heard from Tommy Pearl again. You win some . . . This time we won.

SHORTLY AFTER THAT little social call Bill McBride's partner, Don Stanley, came back from vacation and the team went back to work. Stanley, originally from the Chicago area, was in the office talking about some guy named Tommy. Stanley had managed to get undercover with Tommy in a sports betting ring run by none other than Jack Carp. Tommy turned out to be Pearl, of course, and Don Stanley had been surprised to learn Pearl and Carp were still hooked in with the Chicago wiseguys. McBride was working with Stanley on the case, and teased his partner about being the ten percent that never got the word, since he and Al had already rousted the "asshole." Apparently street-sharp and experienced Tommy Pearl had not recognized McBride from their tête-à-tête, maybe because Al's face was so much in his. McBride had been telling Stanley all along that Carp and Pearl worked under a crime boss in Miami named Sam Gold. Gold was *the* South Florida rep for the Chicago groups:

"During this time I'd developed an informant we called Leo who was deep in the Carp-Pearl organization. He'd been pleased to learn I knew of Pearl, because it would mean more money for him as an informant if we took down a big fish through his information. Leo told me he had heard Tommy Pearl was not in good standing with his boss Sam Gold in Miami. Word was that Pearl was running the gambling for Gold but skimming the proceeds. At that point it made interesting Mafia gossip for us, and we could hope that Pearl would wind up in a fifty-five-gallon drum floating in Biscayne Bay, but there was nothing we could really work at that time. I didn't know it then, but Pearl's path and mine would soon cross again in a weird way."

Al and his ex-partner Randy finally managed to eat all of the food in the breakfast restaurant and we took off.

Supplement to Armed Robbery (Pearl's Gateway Jewels) #88-123456:

This detective interviewed the "victim" Thomas Pearl at the scene after the patrol units secured it. I spoke with the bomb squad captain about the bag with the weapon, and with the patrol sergeant about what she saw and heard. I made the following observations:

Although the victim could move around in spite of being taped, no attempt was made to activate the alarm. There are several panic-button locations in the store. Victim waited until he was observed by a passerby. Then, when the civilian help arrived and tried to cut the tape off his wrists the victim stated, "Don't cut that off, I want the police to see it."

Victim told the patrol sergeant there was only a gun in the bag, no bomb, but the bomb squad captain stated there was no way to see the weapon, which was wrapped and double-bagged.

This detective examined the rear room area by looking in from outside through the rear door. The carpet is short pile weave. I was unable to observe any footprints on the carpet. The building complex is still under construction, the rear door area outside the victim's business is very sandy. I examined the sand by the rear door where the victim claims two of the suspects entered and all three exited. The area was void of any shoe prints of any kind. I found this to be inconsistent with what the victim claimed had occurred.

When other detectives arrived I watched them enter the rear door from the alley. I noted that they left shoe impressions in the sand and heavy sand impressions on the carpet. Had the culprits entered the rear door they too should have left such impressions.

Negative fingerprints on the grocery bag or weapon. Negative prints on any of the tape used to bind the victim. Lab later examined and test-fired the weapon. It is a .380 caliber fully automatic with silencer. It is the type in which the parts are made from different sources and assembled later. No numbers or markings.

No witnesses saw anyone (vehicle or foot) enter or leave store.

When asked why the safe alarm wasn't activated the victim stated it has a sensor that can be accidentally activated when six inches from the safe. Victim stated he wanted to make coffee so he turned it off. This detective noted that the coffeepot unit is more than *three feet* from the safe, and a person standing there would not activate the sensor alarm.

Victim stated all three suspects wore gloves, but also stated that when one suspect hit him in the face he saw a tattoo on the suspect's hand. It was also observed that although the suspects took the jewelry and stones from the safe, they left all identifying documents, descriptions, photos behind . . . without which the victim would have difficulty making an accurate report of the loss to the police, and an insurance claim.

Note: Because of these inconsistencies the victim has been asked to take a polygraph test reference this robbery report. He stated he would come in for the test, but as of this date he has not done so.

Summary: It appears at this time that this robbery report is unfounded, and probably fabricated.

He might have added: not all "victims" are victims.

* * *

THE DAY AFTER our breakfast meeting Al settled in at my desk in my office and we went back to the "Funny Money" case. He said he had not heard from Leo the informant for some time, then suddenly the guy was calling for him all over the place:

"Leo was a heavy-set guy in his early forties with light brown hair cut like a monk, a bowl around the ears and bald on the crown. He always dressed like he was on his way to play golf— pastel shirts . . . those shiny kind . . . and checked pants and white loafers. He had babylike skin, as if he'd spent hours in the bathroom after a shower dusting himself with all kinds of powders and stuff. He was a scammer, of course, always on the fringes of some deal, out to make an easy buck. He was usually friendly and easygoing, had a quick sense of humor and a knack for picking up pieces of info on the street that somehow mostly seemed to pan out.

"I first met Leo about four years earlier. He called the office one day saying he had been arrested by Plantation PD on fraud-related charges. He had done a short jail term and was placed on a very strict probation. He knew that the Plantation police wanted to hammer his ass again, so he was going to walk the straight path. He had a gun at home, which was contrary to his probation so he decided to get rid of it. He took it to one of the local pawn shops and turned it over for some quick cash, not thinking any more about it. Soon after that he was arrested for violating his probation. The Plantation cops had a pawn-shop detail that found the pawn ticket with Leo's name on it for the weapon and zinged it to his probation officer. Leo was waiting for a hearing in front of a judge he felt already disliked him, so he wanted to better his chances of staying out of the slammer.

"Which was where I came in. Leo said he wanted to trade some info with me. I took it before the judge and his probation officer, and after getting the necessary seals of approval I called Leo and set up a meet. I told him the judge would allow him to work with me, and anything he did that panned out would help the judge make a decision on his case. Leo gave me a shit-eating grin and reached into his pants pocket and pulled out two one-hundred dollar bills. He asked me to look at them carefully, and when I did I saw they were fine quality, but counterfeit. I asked Leo if he could get his busy little hands on any more of the stuff, and he told me he could put me onto the printer and two and a half to three million more. We worked the case with the Secret Service/Treasury people, and everything turned out just like Leo said it would. The judge reinstated Leo's probation, and he was able to stay out of trouble—*and* the morgue, amazingly—long enough to complete it. He was grateful, and stayed in contact with me off and on ever since."

Al now got back to Leo's sudden attempts to call him and how they set up a quick meeting because he wouldn't say anything on the phone. They met in the downtown parking garage, third level. McBride and Stanley had the eyeball, parked in the shadows four or five spaces away. As Al backed into a space Leo climbed out of his leased Lincoln, looked around and got into Al's car looking tense but determined:

"He began to tell me he had some hot information, then stopped when an old Ford Falcon driven by a tiny elderly woman who could barely see over the wheel passed slowly by and went down the exit ramp. Then he got started again, said he had info that a person, one Tommy Pearl, was going to be eliminated. I asked him how he meant that, 'eliminated.' Then he says 'terminated,' so I said, 'terminated, like killed?' and he says, 'yeah, killed.' I was thinking I already knew what was coming when I asked him how he had heard about this, and he told me it was through his 'association' with a guy named Nunzio Spinelli. At the time Leo had some kind of telephone-marketing consulting service.

"I nodded at Leo while I ran the Spinelli name through my mind. I knew that all kinds of telephone scams are run through so-called service consultants. Leo gave me Spinelli's home address, which was out in Plantation, the small town west of Lauderdale, and said that's where their offices were too. Leo proceeded to chew on his little finger for a long ten count, then scrunched down in his seat, turned toward me and told me this

Spinelli had told him to get all the info he could on Tommy Pearl, where his house was, the phone number, tags on his cars, all that stuff. Then he said Spinelli had asked him to find somebody to come in and 'do the execution.'

"I thought, Well kiss my ass if Spinelli isn't looking for a hitman to fill a contract on *Tommy Pearl*, and that hitman might be *me*. Of all the targets I had ever been hired to take out, none would have given me more pleasure than to waste *that* scuzball. I remember wondering for like a split second if there was some way I could *actually* carry out the hit as a contribution to society, then arrest Spinelli and donate my fee to the Police Athletic League. Nah. Well, can't hang a man for his thoughts. I asked Leo what stupid Tommy Pearl had done to Spinelli that was bad enough to die for?

"Leo fidgeted around some more, then says Pearl apparently turned around and reneged on a drug deal by trying to give approximately four hundred thousand dollars in counterfeit money in payment for maybe fifteen kilos of good cocaine. So now I had to ask Leo how he knew about *that*, and he tells me it was Spinelli again, because Spinelli was the middleman who had set up the deal between Tommy Pearl and these three Colombians who had the coke. Leo, Spinelli and his wife would get forty thousand for being the go-betweens. Nice. Nunzio Spinelli would get ten percent just for setting it up. I asked Leo for names on the three Colombians, he says he never met them but knows they're called Paco, Rosie and Chico." (I had to smile at that last one—Chico. A Marx brother's name was just right for a funny-money caper.) "So," Al went on, "Tommy Pearl greased them with a load of funny money. I settled in and told Leo to sing me the whole song . . ."

As Al remembered the meeting, at this point Leo the informant brought out a container of small green breath mints, shook about a dozen into his palm and pushed them into his mouth. He offered some to Al, who declined. Al opened his side window slightly to let in some fresh air and let out some of Leo's fragrances. Leo told Al that Nunzio Spinelli's wife Alicia had the Latin connections from Miami and farther south, and Nunzio had ties to the Buffalino family up in New York. So Alicia could get the coke, and Pearl came to Spinelli and asked him if he could help him put a deal together. Leo told Al he didn't know if Pearl and Spinelli had something going before, or how Pearl knew to contact Spinelli. All he knew was that Tommy Pearl told Nunzio Spinelli that he'd like to get into the coke business, and fourteen or fifteen keys seemed like a good amount to start with, and as it turned out four hundred thou wouldn't go any further than that anyway:

"Just then a new Cadillac with dark-smoked windows cruised into the parking area in front of us," Al said. "You know, war wagons. The car seemed to slow in front of us, then went on its way. I knew Stanley and McBride would snag the tag and keep an eye on it if it came back, but old Leo got nervous, suddenly decided this was a hell of a place for a meeting, what with all those cars driving by and everything. I told him to ease up, that people parked there to go to the friggin' downtown public library, and how many spitballs did he know that went to the library for Christ sake. He looked at me and shrugged, then slid even further down into his seat and went on with his story."

According to Leo, Tommy Pearl asked Nunzio Spinelli for the coke, and Nunzio's wife Alicia in turn contacted the suppliers, the three Colombians, to get the stuff. Spinelli met with Pearl at Pearl's jewelry store and the exchange was made. Tommy kept the coke and Spinelli walked out with a briefcase of money, forty grand of it for him. Then Spinelli took the cash to Chico, Paco and Rosie. It required about two seconds for them to see the money was bogus. They were not pleased.

"Nunzio Spinelli has been around long enough to know not to panic in front of the Colombians, he just puts the fake cash back into the briefcase and tells the suppliers he'll clear the problem right up. Spinelli goes back to Pearl, who gives him a song and dance about somehow giving him the wrong suitcase. (Al: "Don't you *love* that?"). Pearl asks for a couple of days to make it right. He'll be able to come up with the real money because he's going to stage a fake robbery at his own jewelry store and then he'll fence the 'hot stuff' and have the cash in hand. So now Spinelli goes back to Chico, Paco and Rosie and tells them things are going to be covered, and everybody waits."

When Leo paused for a moment, Al remembered the robbery report that had been passed around, and made a note to contact the robbery-squad detectives to let them in on the info about the phony heist—and who and what their "victim" was all about. He found out later they had already seen through the scam and had noted it in their supplements. They had also alerted the insurance company to take a close look before paying off on Pearl's claim. The insurance company eventually refused to pay, and charges were pending against Tommy Pearl for filing a false police report. Al reflected that robbery-squad detectives tended to dress a bit more conservatively than the guys he worked with, but it was apparent they didn't need any help from him in seeing through a bullshit story. Then he told Leo to carry on with the events that followed:

"Leo seemed to be finally relaxing a bit, cracking his knuckles and sitting up straighter. He told me the deadline passed and Pearl didn't get back to Spinelli. The Colombians tell Spinelli they're gonna kill Pearl, and Spinelli goes crazy trying to find the guy. Finally he gets Pearl on the phone, and Tommy tells him something like, 'Tough shit, I've got the coke and the funny money (which Spinelli had returned to Pearl for his own reasons, probably because he didn't want to be caught with it) and you can go fuck off.' The next time Spinelli meets with the Colombians they tell him *he's* responsible for the whole pile of shit. They want Spinelli to recover the money *and* kill Tommy Pearl for being such an asshole.

"So Nunzio Spinelli gets back to Leo and tells him Tommy Pearl has got to be taken care of. Leo didn't know if Spinelli was serious at first, but when he found out he was, he figured he better come up with something to help out. Spinelli was really hot, and Leo wanted him to chill out, so he made up a story he knew about a guy who filled contracts out of West Palm Beach.

Spinelli knew Leo had been in and out of jail and had plenty of contacts, so he accepted it when Leo told him he had a guy who might do the job. He meant *me.*"

After that meeting Al didn't hear from Leo for a couple of days. Then Leo called, very agitated, and told Al there had been a change in the scenario. The Colombians had informed Nunzio Spinelli *they* were going to kill Tommy Pearl, *that night.* They were coming up from Miami, first to Spinelli's place to get all the info on Pearl, then out to find Pearl and do him:

"It was just after noon, and I was standing in my kitchen in an old pair of jeans and a T-shirt," Al said. "Sylvia had left a list of things that needed fixing around the house and I was doing my best to change light bulbs and nail down loose floor trim and all that stuff. My pager had gone off and the number turned out to be a phone booth occupied by one worried Leo the informant. He told me what was going on and I asked him if there was a time-frame. He said he only knew they were coming up that evening, with the intentions of doing the hit that night. As I hung up I realized it was Friday, and that Friday evening I was supposed to drive Sylvia and the girls up to Deland, where my in-laws have their property and keep two horses for the girls, who dearly love to visit there. Sylvia likes it too, a chance to visit with her parents and get out of Lauderdale for the weekend. She had told me earlier in the week that *this* time she did *not* want to drive up there by herself and spend the weekend telling our girls that daddy would show up any minute. *This* time we were all going up together, no buts about it."

Al grimaced now, and rubbed his face hard with his two big hands, then shrugged. "*But.* But now Chico and Paco and Rosie were coming up from Miami to do one of my all-time favorite scumbags, and it looked like I was going to have to prevent it. I made all the arrangements with the guys in my unit, and when Sylvia got home from work early to get ready for the trip I told her what was shaping up. If it went down tonight, I told her, I could be on my way early and be up there in time to have breakfast with her and the girls. It was lame, and we both knew it.

She just looked at me, then quietly told me I knew the girls wanted to ride this weekend and they were counting on me being there. Amanda wanted to ride Happy, a goofy Shetland pony that could be a handful. If Carolyn was going to ride Bourbon, then they would need me there to go with her while Sylvia watched Amanda. She turned her back on me then and asked if I planned to spend the rest of my life protecting every damn person in the city, including the bad guys. I left her standing in the bedroom while I went to make my promises to the girls."

Al paused a moment again, staring out the windows of my office. I tried to think of something appropriate to say, stuff about duty and responsibility, but I knew there are many levels of duty and responsibility, and I was still struggling with it when Al summed it up by simply saying *"shit."* He stood and stretched, then sat down again, looked through some of the notes and transcripts and went on with the story:

"I was sitting in a rental car half a block west of Nunzio Spinelli's house by five-thirty that afternoon. McBride and Stanley would watch Tommy Pearl's house, which was located on the east side of Lauderdale on Gull Drive, one of the isles off Las Olas Boulevard near the beach. I settled back in the car seat, not exactly thrilled about the situation. By nine that night I was even less happy.

"I called those guys on the radio again and asked if anything was shaking. They said it was quiet, the same as what I was seeing . . . *nada.* They said an occasional car came down the street, for sure no tan Bronco—the Colombians would be driving a tan Bronco, according to Leo. I had already checked with him twice by phone, and he'd heard nothing more from Spinelli. He wanted to call Spinelli again but I told him not to, I didn't want him to seem *too* interested. Captain Garcia buzzed me too, checked on the progress of things, then told me I should cover our asses by handling this thing 'by the numbers.' He made a suggestion that left a bad taste in my mouth, but what the hell, orders is orders. I went to a phone booth to do as advised."

AL SMITH: Tommy Pearl?

TOMMY PEARL: Maybe. Who's this?

SMITH: This is your old friend Al, who might be a cop.

PEARL: I got no friends buddy, *especially* cops. But I remember you, tough guy. What the hell do you want, calling me here at my home?

SMITH: I've been ordered by my boss to call you and advise you there will be plainclothes officers watching your house during the night. We have information that a hit is planned on you, and the word is it will happen some time tonight.

PEARL: Yeah? A hit on me? By who? For what?

SMITH: I can't get into the details with you right now, Tommy, all I'm doing is telling you we'll be out there, and it might be a good idea to stay away from open windows and maybe stay home tonight, you know?

PEARL: Yeah, yeah. You cops are protecting *me?* That's a laugh.

(Al hangs up.)

He wasn't laughing as he left the Spinelli stakeout and joined McBride and Stanley on the east side of town. It made the night a little easier with two undercover cars—they could take turns going for coffee or checking the adjoining isles off Las Olas or just going for a ride to ease the boredom. The long night also gave Al plenty of time to think. He didn't particularly like himself or the position he was in then. His family had to make the trip without him, which was bad enough, and the reason was this total slimeball in his fancy house on Gull Drive where no cop could afford to live. It was an unsaid truth that the Colombians would be doing Fort Lauderdale a favor if they did a job on Tommy Pearl, but here was Al, with good partners, sitting through the wet night to try to stop them if they tried. To serve and protect . . . who?

By the time the first probing orange fingers of the sun came up over the tops of the coconut palms lining the isle Al felt like he was wearing clothes taken off an old corpse, and the inside of his mouth had the consistency of a wet saddle blanket. "Fucking terrific," was how he put it. He and McBride and Stanley went to the Floridian Restaurant for an early breakfast, then decided to pull the plug. They would have to be on standby for that night, depending on what info Leo came up with. Al still had hopes of making it to his in-laws', but they were fading. As they left the restaurant Don Stanley took a toothpick out of his mouth, and with a grin said they should ask Captain Garcia to write them up a letter of commendation because "Tommy Pearl made it through the night, didn't he?" Bill McBride looked at his partner, shook his head and summed up: "Oh, bullshit."

"Later that morning," Al said, "I called Sylvia at her parents' home. She was great on the phone, said the kids were having a good time and everyone missed me but that they were okay. She didn't lay any guilt on me, and I hung up feeling relieved. Sylvia, as you've probably gathered by now, is a good one."

THE NUNZIO SPINELLI-Tommy Pearl deal was apparently still up in the air. Leo called Al in the afternoon and said he was going down to Miami with Spinelli to meet with someone and he'd call when he got back. Three hours later Al's pager went off and they set up a meeting in a lot behind a country-and-western bar alongside State Road 7. For this meeting, because he felt the info learned might be detailed, Al experimented with a small directional mike near the window on the driver's side of his car. He knew Leo liked car-to-car meetings and decided that even if Leo came and sat in his car beside him the mike would still get it all. On the tape Leo's voice is faint but distinct, and Al's is almost too loud, but he lets Leo do most of the talking. Background noise was very muted, as the meeting took place in a back lot surrounded by trees and shrubs. Al remembers that Leo was nervous and excited:

CONFIDENTIAL INFORMANT *(Leo):* The Colombian named Chico was there when I got to Spinelli's. He was driving the tan

Bronco and only stayed a few minutes while I was there. He was pissed off, man, and Spinelli was trying to calm him down.

AL SMITH: Describe him for me.

LEO: He's a big guy for a Latino, six foot, maybe six-two. Two hundred thirty pounds, real stocky. Maybe forty-years-old, like brownish grayish hair. Chubby face. He wore the typical shiny black pants and white Cubanstyle shirt. He had some kind of big automatic under the shirt.

SMITH: So what happened?

(Al adds here that Leo's head was barely visible over the top of the window ledge on the driver's side of his leased Lincoln. Al had the urge to reach out and grab him by the hair and pull him up to where he could be seen, but he *was* Al's informant, and Al had to put up with his on-again, off-again bravado. Leo kept looking nervously across the lot while he talked.)

LEO: They were talking in and out of Spanish, you know? I mean, the wife is Latin. So I didn't get it all. Spinelli gave the guy the info on Tommy Pearl, his cars, his home address, all that crap. *(Pause)* I'm really sorry about last night, Al. Goddamn Spinelli *told* me they were comin' up to do it . . . he acted like it was a sure thing . . . or I woulda never passed it on to you.

SMITH: No problem, you did right. So what's the plan now?

LEO: They'll probably go over to Pearl's house and uh, wherever, and probably either kidnap him or kill him, one of the two.

SMITH: Spinelli or the Colombians?

LEO: Well, that's the thing. I'm not sure who's gonna do it, but it's gonna get done. (Al cuts in to say that at this point Leo sat up slightly and his nose came over the window ledge, across the chrome strip, and that he looked like Kilroy when his fingers came over too.) That's why I wanted to tell you about me riding down to Miami with Spinelli, Al.

On the way down he told me Tommy Pearl works for Sam Gold, and as you know, hell, *everybody* knows, Sam Gold is the boss down here. I was nervous as shit just going there, you know? I told you before that Tommy was skimming from the top of some of the mob's money, so I guess Spinelli figured Gold was already pissed. I got the idea that Spinelli needed Sam Gold's approval before anything could happen to Tommy, like it had to be a sanctioned hit or something. Spinelli is connected, but none of these hotshots down here do something as serious as this Pearl hit without old Sam's nod.

SMITH: Describe the meeting, Leo.

LEO: On the way down I thought, you know, we'd be going to one of those Miami Vice houses with all the pussy in the pool, and the old man on a lounger with a drink in one hand and a big cigar in the other. Nope. We get down to like One Sixty-third, off Biscayne, and pull into a small lot beside this ratty little pawnshop.

SMITH: A pawn shop?

LEO: Can you believe it? All-Miami Pawn, or something like that, was the name over the door, and we went inside and it looked just like it was supposed to, with all the junk guitars and old military rings and crap. There was some nice stereo stuff in there too. Anyway, these two young hard guys are there, and they ran those metal detector things over us while we stand there smiling. Those things don't make you sterile or anything, do they? So they told us to wait, and a minute later here comes the old man, looking like some geezer out of a retirement home. Needed a shave, wore bedroom slippers and an old pair of pants with a moth-eaten sweater. What a piece of work.

SMITH: But he's still got the power, yeah?

LEO: Oh, yeah. As soon as he spoke, man, you *knew* it. Those hard guys hung on his words, and Spinelli looked like he was trying to shit a basketball. I tried to look respectful. Spinelli introduced me, which I thought was nice . . . and they went into the back room for about three minutes. I stand there looking at the stereo stuff, Spinelli comes out, and we go.

SMITH: And it went well, the meeting?

LEO: I guess it did. Spinelli's takin' it in the ass either way on this deal, because he comes out looking like a jerk for giving Pearl the toot before checking out the loot, dig it? So he's pissed, but he seemed pleased as we drove back to Lauderdale. I asked him what happened, and all he'd say was, 'It's all right, that's it.' To *me* it was like old Sam said like, 'You got my blessings on the Tommy Pearl thing,' or some such baloney.

SMITH: So the hit is still on, but we don't know if the Colombians are going to do it, or if Spinelli is going to need help.

LEO: Tell you what, Al. I think the Colombians are smart enough to know about Sam Gold and the way things work and all that. I think they'll lay the whole thing on Spinelli, like, 'get us our money and kill that goddamned Tommy Pearl for fucking with us.' That's what I think.

SMITH: When are you supposed to go back to Spinelli's?

LEO: Tonight, Al.

SMITH: We'll wire you before you go in.

LEO: Now, Al, that's a scary thing, Al, that wire. I mean, shit, I'll be sitting there with him, talking about this stuff. If he thinks I'm hooked into you guys I'm history in a very messy way.

SMITH: Leo . . . Leo, my *man*. Look how hard you've already worked on this case. You want somethin' out of it when it's all over, right? Not to mention good protection in the future because you've been so helpful and cooperative and all that stuff the state's attorney likes to see. Hell, at this point the silly prosecutors might even see you as a *co-conspirator* in all this, *capish?* Leo, wear the wire, we'll be listening, and we'll cover your ass when the shit hits the fan, right?

LEO: *(Obviously unconvinced)* Right, Al.

"After Leo and I went our separate ways," Al said, "I decided to go into the OC office to make a couple of calls. It was going on Saturday evening, Sylvia and the kids were probably getting ready for dinner at her parents' and I didn't want to go home to an empty house. It was obvious now that I wouldn't make De-land for even a part of the weekend. The first call I made was to Sylvia. I spoke with her, my daughters and both of my in-laws. They said they were sorry I couldn't be there but that they understood. My daughters said they *didn't* understand, and Syl-via told me they would leave there in the morning and maybe we could get together at our house for lunch. She recited our home address slowly, and in her messing-with-me voice said: 'Be there,' before she hung up."

Stanley and McBride came into the office a few minutes later with a DEA agent in tow. They all knew him because he used to be a local cop before signing on with the feds. He took the usual ribbing about being an agent with an outfit most police agencies called "brand X," and gave some back about how the local yo-kels got all sweaty and excited every time they saw a one-ounce baggie of coke. On that note of mutual admiration they decided to go to dinner, and at the restaurant one of those crazy little off-the-wall deals came up that makes cops just shake their heads at how people will react to what they think they see.

To RUB ELBOWS with the players you have to look like a player. Al's DEA agent friend wore a subdued but expensive Italian suit and shoes, and his Rolex had the almost obligatory diamond bezel around the face. Al, as I've mentioned, wears lots of heavy gold, and both McBride and Stanley pride themselves on look-ing sharp as only big city boys can. They have the gold too, and the walk and the persona that says power, adventure. They de-cided on a nice little restaurant, a steak house on Federal High-way and took a table in a corner of the main room. The place was only half-full, it being still too early for the Saturday night crowd. They had a good meal, garnished with energetic and interesting conversation including professional and personal matters. Lots of information is exchanged when cops from different agencies get together, and the informal times can be the best. Al and the others were there for just over an hour, and during that time Al noticed the young maitre d', who kept moving around them, hovering. He was a sharp looking guy in his twenties, tanned and fit, and his tux looked like he belonged in it. His nails were manicured, his teeth were white and perfect and he had a hungry energy about him.

But he was sort of bugging Al the way he kept coming to the table to ask if anything was needed, or to stand by as a waiter removed a plate or whatever. It seemed he was trying to pick up on the dinner conversation. Al wasn't worried about being made as a cop because the conversations between a group of undercover Organized Crime cops and a group of Organized Crime members would sound very similar to an outsider—deals and names and jobs and connections and money.

As the group got up to leave Al did a spur-of-the-moment thing. He carries business cards he had made up that have SANETTI'S SPECIAL SERVICES, Al Sanetti and his undercover pager number printed on them. Al wrapped a ten-dollar bill around one of the cards, and as they walked out of the dining area he tagged the maitre d'. "Here, my friend," Al said to the guy with a big smile as he slid the bill and card into his palm, "take this for being so attentive. But listen, the next time my friends and I come here for dinner we'd like a little more breathing room so we can discuss business, got it? And call me if there's ever a project I can help you with." The young guy nodded, thanked Al and pocketed the bill.

About two weeks later Al got a number on his pager he didn't recognize. He dialed, and found the young maitre d' from the steak place on the other end. The young man asked if Al could meet with him to discuss a profitable situation and Al agreed. They met in a parking lot, car-to-car, and the guy told Al he knew Al was a player when he saw him with the other hard guys in the restaurant. He represented some people who had four kilos of really fine coke, and they needed a buyer. Was Al interested, or did he know anyone who was?

Al thought it over for about ten seconds, then told the guy he specialized in another line of activity but knew a standup guy who moved a lot of nose candy and could always shop a little more. Al told the maitre d' he'd take his cut from his man if they made the deal, and the maitre d' would have to work out *his* slice from his own people. The young guy thought that was perfect, gave Al his home and business phone numbers and said he'd be waiting. As he drove off, Al snagged his tag number. It was worse than shooting fish in a barrel.

Al hooked the maitre d' up with his friend from the DEA because the feds were working several fast-moving cocaine groups in town. As it turned out, the maitre d's friends were a splinter group of something DEA already knew about, so it tied in nicely. The feds made a simple buy-bust with the maitre d', hammered him, turned him inside out, and put him back on the street as a scared informant ratting on his buddies and never knowing when the DEA was going to yank his chain and send him up for hard time anyway.

"Stupid bastard thought he could just walk right out onto the battlefield with a nice smile and a reference from a real 'player' he had scoped out in his restaurant. Cannon fodder in a tux," was how Al put it.

"As LUCK WOULD have it," Al said, "the Sunday after that Saturday night dinner at the steak place with the DEA agent turned out to be a very nice day with my family. But Saturday night, workwise, fell apart after that dinner. Leo got hold of me and said the whole thing with Nunzio Spinelli and the Colombians was on hold until Monday, because everyone thought things should calm down and it was moving too fast. Leo's Saturday night meeting with Nunzio was off, so we all cleared out and got a decent night's sleep. My gang arrived back home just before lunch and let me cook them one of my forest-fire specials. I spent the afternoon with my daughters, sharing some pretty close time, and that night after the girls went to bed, Sylvia and I became reacquainted. She acted like she wanted no part of me at first, but after I moped around with my patented woe-is-me look on my sorry face . . .

"The next day, Monday, it was back to the wars."

The morning was just getting a good start when Leo contacted Al and told him Nunzio Spinelli had already called and wanted him to come to his place later that day to "discuss the situation." Leo wanted to know if Al still wanted him to wear a wire, or could he go in clean and give a statement later. The wire, he was told.

"I sat in my car down the street from the Spinelli residence," Al said. "I was backed into the driveway of a house that looked like it was closed up for the summer. McBride and Stanley were in their car a couple of blocks away. I had observed Leo get out of his Lincoln in front of Spinelli's house, wait a moment at the front door after he rang the bell and then go inside. I could hear the static sounds the cloth of his shirt made as it brushed against the small microphone taped to his breastbone. He was told to go sit at the kitchen table, and then they got right to it."

MALE VOICE: . . . yeah, so Chico told me to take care of it, they weren't going to mess with it. They want me to get the money owed to them, and do that goddamned Tommy Pearl.

CONFIDENTIAL INFORMANT *(Leo):* Sure, Nunzio.

MALE VOICE: *(Identified as Nunzio Spinelli)* This whole thing is a pisser, it really is. Chico said to follow him as he drives away from his house, run him off the road, take him outta the car and drive him someplace where we can make him give up the money. Then kill the bastard.

LEO: What if he doesn't have the money, or won't give it up?

SPINELLI: He's dead either way.

(Unclear conversation, possibly Spinelli turning to say something to female identified as his wife, Alicia.)

SPINELLI: So what about this guy you know about, this guy in Palm Beach?

LEO: I spoke with him already, Nunzio . . . no names or nuthin' . . . just that there might be the need for a hit. He said he gets twenty-five hundred up front as good faith money, a total of five thou for the job.

SPINELLI: Good faith money? He wants money up front before he does the hit? C'mon, what is this guy?

LEO: No, no . . . that's the way—

SPINELLI: Shit. I give him the twenty-five hundred and then I wonder if I ever see him again.

LEO: Nunzio, you could give him some of that money Tommy gave to you.

(Leo laughs. Spinelli doesn't. Leo stops laughing.)

LEO: Listen, Nunzio. This guy Al is for real, you know? I mean, he *does* this. I heard he's done work here for people, you might know some of them, or heard their names before. As far as I know he'd have to be . . . uh . . . approved . . . sort of like, sanctioned by somebody to work here, know what I mean? He says he gets half up front, five for the job.

(Note: Al had coached Leo on Al Sanetti's history.)

SPINELLI: Okay, say I give him the half. Here's what I want. He takes Tommy outta the car, like Chico said. Or, what the fuck, take him any way he wants. He takes Tommy somewhere to talk, and presses the asshole until he gets that fucking four hundred big ones, *real* ones.

LEO: Yeah, all right.

SPINELLI: If he can't do that, grab Tommy and get the money, within twenty-four hours . . . *then* I'll give him the twenty-five up front and he can make it a simple hit on his own schedule.

LEO: And if he *can* hold Tommy somewhere and get the money outta him?

SPINELLI: Then he kills Tommy anyway. I got the go-ahead on it, and I'm tired of fucking around with that asshole. Now

you get out of here and get back to me when you hear
something . . .

(Pause, sound of movement, unclear voices.)

SPINELLI: One more thing. I want to *see* this guy Al before we
go much further.

"Back at the office we debriefed Leo, wrote up our reports to
that date and talked the case over with Captain Garcia. We met
with one of the state's attorney prosecutors, sketched out the
case for him, told him our plans. He told us we should call the
intended victim again to warn him once more (I liked that
about as much as riding bareback and bareassed on a sandpaper
horse), and that it looked like preparing warrants for Spinelli
and his wife would be no problem. He felt it would really
strengthen the case if Spinelli actually met 'Al Sanetti' face-to-
face and talked murder, so we wouldn't have to rely on the
testimony of an informant, and that we try somehow to make
contact with the Colombians so we could charge them on the
conspiracy too. He said his office would of course work on it
with us. Of course. We went back to our own office and I made
the call to Tommy Pearl.":

TOMMY PEARL: How'd you get . . . my car phone number . . . ?

AL SMITH: Just good solid police work, Tommy.

PEARL: Fuck you.

SMITH: Probably be the best piece of ass you ever had, Tommy.
Listen, can you meet with me? I need to talk with you
about something important.

PEARL: Meet with you? Get out of here.

SMITH: I'm dead serious Tommy, it's important.

PEARL: When?

SMITH: Right now.

PEARL: No way, buddy. You want to meet with me, you meet
with me in my lawyer's office. You know Paul Albert?

SMITH: Sure, I know Paul. Let's meet there right now.

PEARL: Nuh-uh . . . no way . . . I'm . . . on the other side of town. What's the big deal?

SMITH: I'm calling because there's a contract on your life . . . I've just been hired to kill you.
  (Pause. Muted traffic sounds, a horn, bells, like a bridge or railroad-crossing guard.)

PEARL: *You've* been hired to kill me?

SMITH: That's right . . . and we want some cooperation from you.

PEARL: Fuck you again. You want . . . cooperation from me . . . for what?

SMITH: *(Strained sincerity)* So you don't get killed.

PEARL: Listen. If they're gonna kill me, they're gonna kill me. Let 'em kill me.

SMITH: Tommy, you don't want to talk with me about this?

PEARL: No. I don't want to talk with nobody about nuthin'. If there's a contract on my life, let 'em come and kill me.

SMITH: Okay.

PEARL: *Okay?*

"Fifteen minutes later I got a call from Paul Albert, Pearl's attorney. I explained the situation, and told him we only needed Tommy to lay low for a day or two so we could work the case without him getting blown up in the middle of it. Albert seemed somewhat amused that we were protecting his client, but told me he would speak with Pearl about cooperating. He called later and left a message that he had discussed the situation with his client, and that Tommy Pearl had agreed to stay invisible for a couple of days."

In the early afternoon of the next day, Leo called the Spinelli house on a tapped phone, with Al listening in. Alicia Spinelli answered:

ALICIA SPINELLI: Hello . . . ?

LEO: Alicia, this is Nunzio's friend. Do you recognize my voice?

ALICIA: Yes. What is it? Nunzio's not here.

LEO: It's about this Tommy Pearl thing . . .

ALICIA: Oh, um . . . don't say that name on this phone . . . um . . .

LEO: But . . .

ALICIA: *Don't.* Don't say any more unless you can come here . . . to the house . . .

(Disconnect)

"We hit a snag that evening. Leo made contact with Nunzio Spinelli and was told to go to the Spinelli house that night. Leo tried to set it up so Al "Sanetti" could go along, but Spinelli wouldn't go for it. He told Leo he never wanted to meet Al, they would have a business deal, that's all. Leo reminded him of what he had said in their earlier meeting about wanting to see Al, and Spinelli said, 'Yeah, *see* him, not meet him.' Spinelli laid it out that he wanted Leo to take this Al to breakfast at a nearby deli place. Spinelli would be there. He'd put the eyeball on me, uh, Sanetti, and he'd watch to see who, if anyone, came with me. He told Leo something about being able to 'spot a shill,' and would not go any further with any hit deal until he got a look at me.

"I told Garcia about it and added that I wanted to make the setup alone, no backup. Garcia didn't like that, and for sure neither did McBride and Stanley, who felt they could at least take positions in the parking lot to keep an eyeball on things. They came around to my way of thinking when I told them that Spinelli was being very careful. I didn't think he was totally convinced of Leo's story about Al Sanetti, and he was already touchy about being burned by Tommy Pearl. Three of our faces there increased the chances that he might somehow recognize a cop in the crowd, and even if he didn't know our faces he might have been around long enough to sniff out one or two guys watching my back. I thought he was too spooky to risk it, and felt we had come too far with the case to blow it now. It was agreed I would go to the meeting alone.

"It was at one of those plain little deli places that have all the kosher breakfast foods, ten million kinds of bagels, plastic plates and utensils, loud waitresses and a line of people out the door and onto the sidewalk. It was on the east side of University Drive, across from one of the big malls there. I got there a few minutes early, didn't see anything and was joined by Leo. He seemed in a good mood, and hungry.

"We were on our second cup of coffee when I made Nunzio Spinelli outside on the sidewalk. I could see him through the front windows of the place, standing near the newspaper machines. He was alone, and seemed pretty cool, kind of gave the impression that maybe years ago he had been some kind of street player, maybe in his early days with the wiseguys, or whatever. A few minutes later he's a couple of tables away from us, looking his newspaper over and giving me a quick glance now and then. I ignored him, and saw that Leo was doing his damndest not to see him too.

"When we were all done, Leo threw a tip on the table while I stood in line at the cashier. Spinelli came up behind me, close, and I had the feeling he was undressing me with his eyes, as they say. I walked out, stood and talked to Leo for a couple of minutes in the parking lot, got in my car and drove away. I'm not sure if Spinelli followed me as I left the area or not, but just for Al *Sanetti's* sake I drove down to I-595, hooked it east to the turnpike, grabbed a ticket and took a ride north toward Palm Beach. I got off in Boca Raton, did some curlycues, U-turns and other fancy stuff to check my rear and headed back to the office. My partners were glad to see me, and we settled down to see what Spinelli's reaction was after his inspection of Al Sanetti, man of the hour."

It was only a couple of hours later that Leo called Al with the word. He had been contacted by Spinelli and told to give Al Sanetti all of the info on Tommy Pearl. It was a go, and Spinelli didn't want to hear anything from Leo again until Sanetti had done his thing.

"We gave him the rest of that day, and all that night, and the whole time we were praying stupid Tommy Pearl wouldn't get himself on national TV, or decide to contact Sam Gold or Spinelli or somethin' himself. We hoped he would stay *gone*, and hoped the long silence would make Spinelli more ready to hear the good news. We gave it to him late the next afternoon with a call from Leo, who insisted on a meeting right away. Spinelli told him to come right over. Leo was wondering if the wire was going to become some kind of electronic growth on his skin by this time, but he grudgingly suited up and we followed him out to the Spinelli place for one more meeting."

MALE VOICE: So what's the word?

CONFIDENTIAL INFORMANT *(Leo):* Al's all done . . .

MALE VOICE *(Nunzio Spinelli):* All done? What about the money?

LEO: Al told me it took some persuading, but Tommy finally came up with the cash. I don't know how it happened, and I sure as hell wasn't going to ask Al for details, you know?

SPINELLI: Yeah. Well, he *is* a big sonofabitch, ain't he? My impression of him at the deli was that he looked like he'd been around. Had a cold look to him, like he didn't give a shit, I don't know. I got up close to him once, and I'd bet he was carrying a piece, even at that fuckin' deli . . . I bet he tore Tommy a new asshole . . .

LEO: Like I said, Nunzio, I didn't ask. All I know now is Al told me he's got your money, and he already did Tommy.

SPINELLI: Pearl's dead now?

LEO: Yeah.

   (Pause)

SPINELLI: Okay.

   (Pause. Female voice indistinct in background, possibly Alicia Spinelli)

SPINELLI: Here's the twenty-five hundred. I'll pay the rest when I get the money.

LEO: Okay, Nunzio, but this is the thing. Al told me he wants to deliver the money to the Colombians for you, minus your cut, of course.

SPINELLI: *(In angry voice)* . . . how's he know about them? I told you not to . . .

(Alicia Spinelli's voice in background, angry but indistinct)

LEO: . . . the fuck? Hell do I know how? The guy's a pro, ain't he? Nunzio, this guy just spent *how* many hours fuckin' with Tommy's mind and breakin' his goddamned legs. Fucking Tommy probably told him his life history *and* the whole story on this deal before Al waxed him.

(Pause. Silence. Tinkle of ice against a glass)

SPINELLI: Okay. Whatever. So now Al has the cash. First of all, *no way* I want him delivering it to the Colombians. I don't want him to meet them. My wife's . . . good name, and my . . . honor are at stake here. *I'm* gonna hand over that money, get my cut, and be done with this crazy deal once and for all.

LEO: Sure, Nunzio. He told me he wants to deliver it to the Colombians because he's a businessman. He wants to meet people with . . . connections, you know.

SPINELLI: He's got my four hundred grand! How the fuck do I know he'll even deliver it *or* bring it to me? Goddamn it! He's gonna hand over that chunk of change and take five grand for doing the job?

(Note: Leo had been carefully coached by Al about this question.)

LEO: *(Sighing)* Nunzio, I told ya . . . the guy's a *pro*. These guys got their own thing, you know? He doesn't want to run with the money and spend it looking over his shoulder for you or the Colombians! He hired out to do the job, and if nobody fucks with him or plays games with him he'll deliver what he said. He'll take the five from you, and he'll be in damn good standing with guys like Sam and . . . others . . . right?

(Pause. Muted conversation between Nunzio and Alicia Spinelli)

SPINELLI: This better go down like you're saying, my friend . . . or it will most definitely be *your ass!*

(Pause. Silence.)

SPINELLI: *(Continues)* Okay. Here's the twenty-five hundred for Al now. He gets the rest when I get the large cash, the *real* shit. You tell him there's *no way* he meets the Colombians and there's *no way* he meets me. *You* take this half-payment for him. You get my money, come *right* back here and hand it over. You know we'll stroke you with a chunk for your help in all this and you also know that at this point I'm in no mood to be fucked with *any more* . . . yeah? Al took Tommy *out*, now get me my money and that's the end of this mess. Understand?

LEO: Perfectly.

They met Leo a few blocks away. Captain Garcia was there with warrants for Alicia and Nunzio Spinelli. McBride and Stanley were there too, and they all had to spend a few minutes assuring a shaken Leo he'd be protected after the arrests. Then they sent him on his way and listened to the last tape. They heard Spinelli's responses, read over previous transcripts, checked the warrants, and decided there was enough to move on it.

Captain Garcia pointed out that the case was still hot. There was no way of knowing if the Colombians would hit Tommy Pearl anyway, or when, or if Spinelli might have something else worked out with Sam Gold to take care of it through another hit team. Scooping up the Spinellis now might, they figured, freeze all the players, give Tommy Pearl another lease on life, and give them a chance to cover Leo's tracks before all or some of these players began looking for him. They notified the Plantation PD patrol units in the area to stand by in the event they needed backups (they had already coordinated with a supervisor from that jurisdiction and he was on scene), and headed toward the Spinelli house.

The arrests went smoothly, so quietly that most of the residents in the area didn't know about it until they read the papers the next day. Nunzio did, after all, meet face-to-face with Al, the hitman, and when he came to grips with the news that Al was one of the cops crowded into his comfortable living room his shoulders sagged and he let out a deep sigh. His wife was in a nightdress, fighting mad and indignant. When she figured out who Al really was she unleashed a fiery torrent of Spanish and English at the cops, and even used Leo's real name in her frustration before she was shushed by her husband. She calmed down when they let her change into something more appropriate for booking while a female officer stood by. Nunzio got dressed quietly and asked only that he be allowed to take his prescription medicine (heart) with him. These were collected from the nightstand.

The Spinellis were handcuffed and taken out to the waiting cars for the ride downtown. They were both made aware of the Miranda warnings, and booked for Conspiracy to Commit Armed Kidnapping and Conspiracy to Commit Homicide, First Degree. Al's partners tried to get a statement from Nunzio and asked him some questions, but he just shook his head and kept silent.

The state had a good solid case against Nunzio and Alicia Spinelli, and a few months later they both pled guilty to the charges. Their well-known defense attorney made a statement to the effect that of course his clients were not guilty of the charges trumped up against them by the police, but were agreeing to the plea-bargain agreement to avoid a long, stressful and costly trial. Al's side of the courtroom speculated that the Spinellis may have been *told* to bite the bullet on the deal to avoid further and more detailed digging into the business of some of their alleged associates.

Leo the informant faded from view shortly after that, moving to another state and trying to keep his head down. The last Al heard, he was staying relatively honest by selling repossessed cars and had already made some tentative moves toward working with the cops as a confidential informant in the city where he had relocated. I guess maybe he *liked* it. Liked having some blue rub off on him.

A YEAR WENT by before Al heard any more about Tommy Pearl, but it was worth the wait.

A breezy summer night: Tommy parked his new Cadillac in front of his waterfront home on Gull Drive at about eleven o'clock. He had his keys in his hand and was walking toward his front door when he thought he heard someone quietly say his name behind him. He turned, and the first burning slug punched through his shirt and into his chest cavity. His own blood misted in front of his eyes and he began to stumble backward, trying to get away from the hornets that pursued him. Three more bullets tore into his body, and as he fell and lay on the grass a few feet from his car he felt . . . must have felt . . . his assailant approaching, knew what was coming. The last three shots were fired into his head, and then the night grew quiet again as he lay there in the bloodstained grass.

"In case you are wondering," said Al, "my whereabouts on that night are documented. I've got a solid alibi, and all the other cops in my unit will swear to it . . ."

TRAVELIN' MUSIC

AL WANTED TO SHOW ME AROUND. He knew I had seen the underside of Fort Lauderdale as a cop, but most of my work on the streets was as a patrol officer. Al's has been almost exclusively plainclothes or undercover, so the town he knows inside out, especially the nighttime town, is different than the one I fought my battles in. Now he was antsy. Like anyone who is good at their profession, Al would rather be out doing it than sitting around talking about it. Policemen are great storytellers, no doubt, and they can sling it fast and deep when they feel like it, but the ones who really *do* the job, like Al, would rather keep moving.

He picked me up around nine one night and we headed out in his unmarked car. The interior is standard—no buzzers or whistles or anything that looks like a cop car. Al wears a weapon, and keeps a hand-held radio under the seat. The radio was on, the volume muted as we drove. We could talk, but both of us had spent so many years with one ear tuned to that radio that it was easy to monitor the calls and still carry on our own conversation. I was glad to be taken on the tour. I wanted to see some of the locations Al had talked about in the book, and I still had some questions for him about his unique and dangerous job.

127

I had the feeling his answers would come more readily, and with more detail, if we were on the move.

After we were underway, headed for Federal Highway in the north end of Lauderdale, one question had to do with cases that had fallen through. No case in police work is guaranteed, and so far we had only discussed those with a successful conclusion (including the delayed rub-out of Tommy Pearl). Things don't always work out in the undercover cop/hitman business. Real life becomes unraveled around the edges once in a while, and murderers actually carry out their hits . . . leaving an honest-to-god dead person sprawled out behind them as they slink away. No sting, no scam. Just dead folks.

"Did you see the one in the paper today, up in Pompano?," asked Al quietly as he drove. "Man and a woman killed in an apartment, both shot in the head several times. They've already nabbed the two hairballs who did it. They were paid a thousand dollars by some bar owner to hit a guy who owed him some bucks. They go to the place where he used to stay with these two people, he's not there, so they kill *them*, the couple . . . for the thousand dollars." I just shake my head, and as he drives he tells me about one of his that came close.

Al had a part-time informant named James Colt, a fringe member of one of the major syndicate families, who called him on a case after the fact. A prominent and controversial local attorney had been murdered, shot in the back as he walked toward his office. *Now* Colt wanted to tell Al a little story.

Seems Colt had been spending some time in our county facility awaiting bond on a drug charge, and had a cellmate who befriended him. The cellmate was an old guy, angry and spiteful, who was thrown in the slammer because he refused to pay alimony to his ex-wife. Apparently it had been an extremely bitter divorce and the old man hated his ex-wife *and* her attorney:

"Frank Moore was the old man's name, and after he became comfortable with James Colt, and after they had exchanged confidences . . . no doubt Colt telling Moore all about how he was 'connected' and hung around with the real wiseguys and all the bullshit . . . Moore told Colt he wanted to hire him to kill his ex-wife's lawyer. If Colt couldn't do it, maybe he could recommend a real hitman for Moore to hire. The lawyer's name was Bernie Wood, and he was known as a megasleazeball around town anyway, always with his sticky fingers dipped into one thing or another. He also had a reputation for dallying with clients now and then. Old Frank Moore told Colt he'd pay him real good to take out the schmuck lawyer that had made the bucks for his ex-wife. Colt didn't like the sound of it. He gave it a pass, and a little while after that he was released from jail. He said nothing to anyone about the offer and skated out of there.

"The next thing you know, just after Frank Moore gets out of the cell, Bernie Wood goes strolling down his office hallway and gets forcibly intruded on by a couple of slugs, which rip him up inside until he dies, bleeding all over the floor. The shooter walks away, but after a long investigation the homicide guys came up with the old man as the prime suspect. *Then* James Colt calls me with his story, looking for a trade . . . his info and testimony for my help in getting him off the hook on some other beef."

The state took the old man to trial. He did as much to hang himself with his behavior there as all the good evidence and testimony did, and he was convicted and sent away again. But just recently one of the appeals courts decided there was some problem with the way things went during the trial, so it looks like he might get another one. He claimed all along that he didn't do it. Well, *someone* walked up behind lawyer Bernie Wood and killed him, and there just isn't any appeal system under his cold marble headstone.

Ironically, as Al Smith was finishing the Frank Moore story we were driving past an exclusive condominium complex near the Intracoastal Waterway, and I suddenly flashed on a memory. I had been involved in an investigation in one of the condos, one where a burglar had crept into the bedroom and woke the woman sleeping there alone by putting a knife to her throat.

The burglar was dressed like a ninja, with gloves and a hood covering his head and face. The burglar didn't take anything, though, no jewelry or money. And he didn't rape the woman. He just used the knife to cut off her nipples, then left. The woman reported she had just gone through a "bitter" divorce, and so her elderly ex-husband was immediately suspected of hiring someone to do the job. Turned out the "burglar" *was* the ex-husband, who apparently felt the disfigurement was a fair trade for what he had been put through. I particularly remember my feelings as I watched the detectives question him with restraint and patience. I tell you, he would have gotten none from me. I understand the detectives have to use whatever tactics will work to get a damning statement from a suspect, which is probably the reason I was never any good at interviewing suspects.

As we cruised north on Bayview Drive toward Commercial Boulevard, where there are many fine restaurants and busy lounges, we talked about another interesting contract murder that had occurred recently. Some conspirators were looking for a hitman to kill someone, they found a guy who would do it, and the medical examiner got to tag another toe, all familiar stuff . . . but, this one had a familial twist—it was a father and mother act. They wanted their *son* to die, and hired his best friend to do it. The son, drunk and trusting, went for a ride with his buddy, turned to hear something his friend said, and got his head blown off. Left a real mess in his pickup truck. The cops in the town where it happened had things fall into place for them and managed to bag the best friend for the murder.

The best friend knew he was had, and when he saw the serious looks on the cops' faces, and heard the pleasantries they described that waited for him in jail, he decided to better his chances for survival by flipping over on the two doting parents who had hired him for the hit. He fingered the parents of the recently ventilated, and after one or two grunts of surprise from the *new* homicide guys (old homicide guys are not surprised . . . ever), a strong case was made. The parents were convicted of conspiracy to murder, and they and the triggerman all went into "time out" for the rest of their days. Al and I guessed they had a heck of a time selling that truck, too.

We slowed and cruised the parking lots of a few lounges snugged up against the waterway on Commercial. Across from a Benihana restaurant is one of the older, well-established restaurant-lounges in town. It has been popular for years and always seems busy. Al parked across the street so we could watch the valet-serviced driveway. You never know who might be going to dinner with friends. While we waited we discussed more near-misses.

Another one that frayed at the edges and fell apart before the good guys won out was one Al had going with a local artist. This was a guy named Walter Ricketts who not only got his name in the paper because of his artwork but also because he was once seriously injured when his car blew up with him in it. He lived but gimped around at a forty-five-degree angle from then on. He told the investigating detectives that he suspected a young guy named Jones of the bombing—he and Jones had bad blood over some screwedup business deal. Although he insisted he was convinced Jones blew him up, the detectives weren't. They never made a case or arrested anyone for the bombing, and actually kicked around the theory that the artist had rigged up the bomb *himself*.

This lack of prosecution angered the artist, so he approached a young kid who worked part-time around the artist's apartment complex. The kid heard what the artist had to say, looked into Rickett's eyes, and called the cops. Al spoke with him first on the phone, and heard about Ricketts and Jones and the offer of murder for hire, and Al told the kid he'd check things out and get back to him.

"I took a look at what the detectives had on the car bombing, and I delved into the life and times of this Jones. Seems Mr. Jones had a history of narcotics involvement, and the poop from between the lines said that the bad blood between him and the artist Ricketts might have to do with some dirty money. I felt it was a workable case and invited the kid to come into my office and give me a statement. We would work out the details then on how the kid could introduce Al Sanetti, hitman, to Walter Ricketts as the answer to his problem.

"*My* problem then was that at that time the Organized Crime offices were still located at 1300 West Broward, the FLPD head-quarters building. Sure, we were up on the third floor, and we always entered and left through the back doors, but we were mostly an undercover bunch, and it just isn't cool to be hanging around the cop shop when you're supposed to be a bad guy, you know? A little later our offices were moved to their own cosy building. It's better for everybody because the regular-work cops think we're a bunch of fucking weirdos anyway.

"On the day I'm to meet the young kid on the Ricketts case I'm on the second floor, where the cafeteria is, getting a couple of stomach bombs. Department security regs required that we all wear a photo ID pinned to our shirts while we were in the building in case a group of wily terrorists gained a lot of weight, dressed up in polyester suits, cheap clip-on ties and cowboy boots, complained all the time and tried to pass themselves off as cops. So I go trudging up the stairs from the second floor to the third, wearing my wonderful ID badge that proclaims me to be undercover Al, and crash right into one of life's silly moments.

"Walter Ricketts is sitting in the waiting area on the third floor, apparently with an appointment to see a detective about getting some results on his old car-bombing case. We are only a couple of feet away, he takes a good look at me *and* my photo ID, and I open the door to enter the division area only to just about stumble over the young kid from Ricketts's apartment complex who is there to tell me about Ricketts looking for a hitman. Shit on a popsicle stick. Ricketts sees the kid, the kid sees him and goes pale, and we all see each other. There was a flash of recognition . . . or understanding . . . in Ricketts's eyes, and the kid's eyes went real wide as he stood there wondering whether to shit or go blind.

"Either way, the friggin' case was blown. Ricketts laid real low for some time, and the kid from his apartment complex disappeared. He was never seen or heard from again and I *hope* he just got scared and hauled ass.

"Eventually I managed to contact the other guy, Jones, and told him about the bullseye Walter Ricketts was trying to paint on his forehead, and *he* left town. Ricketts is still out there somewhere, and I can only hope that someday he'll paint himself into a corner."

THINGS WERE PRETTY quiet at the lounge we were watching, so Al pulled back out onto Commercial Boulevard and headed west again, back toward Federal Highway. The nighttime traffic was just beginning to build, with most of the dinnergoers finishing up and heading home, leaving the roads clear for the more serious drinkers and party animals to follow. Al was quiet for a few minutes as we rode along, and I guessed his thoughts were following the memories of various cases like the Ricketts one that had taken place here and there along the way . . . just like mine. Through the years a working cop, no matter what his job, will find himself or herself handling altercations, confrontations, theft reports, drunks and other delights in each of the clubs, bars and lounges that are congested in that area of town. It literally comes with the territory, and makes it hard not to glance over at a place as you go by and remember it for that particular time or incident.

Al pointed out a club on his left. "You know that place, The Naked Nymph? I've been in and out of there on a bunch of different stuff . . . even had a bullshit extortion deal in there once . . . what a circus. A girl that danced there, called herself Candy, or Sugar, or some edible thing like that, she got close to a regular customer who told her he could help her invest her overflow of cash she was makin' up on those tabletops. She thought that was a great idea and repaid him by giving him little pieces of herself now and then. Everything was going this guy's way . . . his name was Waldo, his last name . . . until Candy decided she wanted her investments *and* the profits they had made back in her garter. Seems Mr. Waldo had never invested any of the cash but spent it playing a high-roller at other skin bars around town.

"Candy cries her story to a couple of the muscle guys, like Rocky and Bruno . . . I shit you not, they had names like that . . . that hung around the club, supposedly tied in with the owner of the place. They hear the tale of woe, find Waldo and lean on him like a ton of bricks, tellin' him about all the evil shit that's gonna happen to him if he doesn't come up with Candy's twenty-eight thousand dollars within two days.

"Waldo believes these guys, panics and calls the cops. Somehow it got routed to me because OC people were supposedly involved. All we knew was what Waldo told us . . . that these guys were trying to squeeze this money out of him, so we wired him up and sent him back inside the place the next night. Sure as hell, Rocky and Bruno start right in on him, they're gonna break his legs, rip off his head and shit in his neck . . . the usual stuff. They want the money . . . and then they say something about Candy's money that Waldo took.

"So we go in and brace Rocky and Bruno right there in the lounge, bounce 'em off the walls a couple of times, find a couple of guns and bag 'em. Then we have a talk with Candy, get the scoop and go back to Waldo and snatch him too. As a matter of form we had checked him out after his initial contact and found outstanding warrants on his ass for fraud. The only person who didn't go to jail was Candy, and the last time I saw her she was still wailing about all that pissed-away money. Of course, I would guess with the body Candy's got it won't take her long to make up her losses."

I WANTED TO know how Al felt about the dual roles he had to play —cop and bad guy. All undercover officers experience this conflict, and most manage to keep the two from merging, but Al's role as a hired killer was unique, with special attributes and myths attached to it. He shrugged when I first asked him, then was quiet for a few minutes before he began:

"It's real head trip most of the time. Real challenging to me personally because I have to maintain a lot of self-control. Power can be a strong drink, you know, and there's a certain perverse power . . . somehow tied in with fear . . . that comes with being recognized and accepted as a man who will kill for money. Once I'm introduced as a hitman, no matter how that takes place, few people will challenge me. I've walked into places and had the rooms almost clear out because of the way I look and the way these people *perceive* me. If I walked into the same room in my police uniform I wouldn't get a second glance, or maybe there'd be some badass whispers behind my back . . . you know. I'd only be a cop . . . but a *hitman* . . . Al Sanetti goes places, works with people, does things that Al Smith couldn't do. Simple as that. It *is* a struggle to make people buy the facade of Al Sanetti and not lose Al Smith in the process. The hitman role is, you know, intense. To make it work *I* have to believe I'm who I am, understand? If *I'm* sold, maybe I can sell *them*, to do that I have to make Al Smith go away for a while. I can't deny the dark side of it . . . the attraction to the power, the games . . . the women. Women will come on to Al Sanetti like you wouldn't believe. The power thing again, the money, the smell of the dark side, secret stuff, life-and-death games." When he grins over at me now there is no dark side, just a big open face with eyes that can laugh with the memories. "And isn't that the friggin' way with the ladies? When I was a single stud policeman out lookin' to score some nice time with a woman I could never do as well as dumb ol' Al Sanetti sitting there looking dangerous and mysterious. When I was single and had time for it, it was hard going . . . but when I'm working as Sanetti, up to my ass in bad guys on some deal that might blow up in our faces at any time, *that's* when some very fine slice of lady will put her big eyes up against mine, or rather Sanetti's, and suggest a series of bedroom calisthenics guaranteed to knock my socks off.

"But you were asking about playing the roles, right? Like the word I used before . . . facade. Al Sanetti works because people look at me as Sanetti and see what they *want* to see. Sometimes a little window dressing helps, like the gold jewelry, the gun, the hot car, the *attitude.* The way I look doesn't hurt either, right? Let me give you an example of building the image, with some help in blue."

We made a quick U-turn, pulled into a parking lot and Al shut off the engine. He pointed to a small restaurant-bar on the north side of Commercial Boulevard. The sign over the door proclaimed it to be the Apartment Lounge.

"That place came to our attention after a bomb was exploded out in front of it one night. The damage was minimal but the word on the street was that the bomb was set off in retaliation for a cocaine ripoff or deal that fell through. The bombers were Hispanic, Colombian again, or something else, but the recorded owners and a lot of the patrons of the place were home-grown. We decided to get inside and see what was what.

"Right off I met a barmaid named Pat who seemed to be the sparkplug around there as far as knowing everybody. She looked as if she'd made it through a mid-life crisis with a face-lift and a new pair of 88's. I soon learned she dated the owner of the bar but that didn't stop her from coming on to me too. As far as work-related stuff, though, getting introduced around, being included in any action . . . I was getting the cold shoulder. I was a new face in there, and they had a pretty tight group.

"One evening I eased in there when the place was busy and took my usual seat at the bar. Pat came over and started right in with the chatter and I let her have at it. A few minutes later a couple of FLPD uniformed cops came in. They waved a Wanted poster with *my* face on it at Pat and some of the others in there, and then got into the act we had set up. They asked me for some ID, rousted me some, and when I reached for the bag I had carried into the place I got a nightstick pushed into my throat.

They cuffed me right there, then emptied the bag out onto the bar so everybody could get a good look.

"First came a fat bag of cocaine, then my .38 revolver, and then ten thousand dollars in one hundred dollar bills. The room got very quiet, all eyes were on me. When Pat wanted to know if she could hold the cash in a safe place for me I told her I'd need it for bail. That's when one of the patrol cops, loud enough for the gang to hear it, says, 'You think you're gonna get bail on a contract killing?' They were lapping it up.

"The cops dragged me out of there then, and I stayed away for about two weeks. When I did stroll back in there one evening they acted like my ass was gold-plated. I worked that place for about two years after that and came away with good information on shit going on almost every time I went in there for a drink. They bought it, you know? Our little cops-and-robbers act helped them reinforce the image they had already formed about me, or Al Sanetti. Yeah, they *bought* it."

Al started the car again and we drove out of the lot, cruised for a while, listening to the police radio and seeing the sights. We even slid by a couple of convenience stores real slow and checked them out. Old habits. Then we headed south on Federal Highway, and when we passed another nude bar, a big one near Oakland Park Boulevard, Al got a grin on his face again.

"We were talking about girls a few minutes ago. I didn't *always* strike out when I was young and single. Ah . . . I don't know if you want to hear this . . ."

I knew about cops. I knew about *young* cops and I wanted to hear about a young Al. It was, after all, Al's story. Young cops do things that test them, show them what they're made of, and sometimes scare the hell out of them. I knew a little about being single with a limited but uninhibited perspective on things, where short-term goals and immediate gratification are focused on. I knew about young cops chasing pleasures of the flesh as diligently as they hunted down the predators on the streets. Plenty of time and never enough money to burn . . . young cops have that. It's a time of sweat and sweet juices, of magically textured skin and scar tissue, of blood and wine, terror and bliss, duty, pleasure, hunger. It's a headlong, wide-eyed rush into sensation and fulfillment, with never a thought given about price.

So I told Al to tell me the story that made him smile again.

"I was working with Tac Squad on some gig up in this end of town," he said. "We had been at it for several nights, and during that time I kind of got a thing going with the dispatcher that had been on our channel each night. This one was one of those girls . . . like every part of her body was tied direct to her clitoris. I spent the night at her apartment, we had a real fun time, and when I got ready to leave she asked me if I'd ever heard of the G-spot. Well, I thought I'd been around, and I knew we had just had us several hours of good lovemaking, but I wasn't sure if she was messing with me or not. I kept my mouth shut.

"She saw the look on my face, said, 'Uh-huh,' and handed me a small book that she pulled from the nightstand. When she told me a little about it I wanted to tear into that dude right then but she said first I had to read the book, then we'd have to practice. I took the book home, an eager student.

"The next time we managed to get together I was anxious to put what I'd read to the test, and with a little direction from her we topped out on the very first try . . . or maybe it was the second. Who cares . . . all I know is when she had her first G-spot orgasm I thought she was going to rip all the hair off the top of my head and my left ear along with it.

"Afterwards I told her she was the only girl I'd ever dated who came with directions."

WE DROVE ON, and when we were in the big curve near Searstown Al maneuvered around a rental car with four people inside, two of whom appeared to be trying to find "north" on a large road map. Al jerked a thumb over his left shoulder.

"That bar tucked into the corner back there, it used to be called the Saturn Club. The people who owned the place

planned to hit *me* once . . . all over a minor roust. We learned
from an informant that Detroit-mob money was behind the
place. Did some checking and found they had done their usual
trick. Got some struggling businessman who was clean to go
into a partnership with them. They'd put up some cash . . .
usually less than half . . . and help the businessman get
started. The guy gets a liquor license, sets the place up, and as
soon as it begins to turn a profit the mob guys force him out,
and I don't mean gently. The businessman loses his investment
and his time, but he's afraid to make a complaint because he
doesn't want to lose anything else.

"Okay, so we got the word and we went over to take a look.
The parking valets had the public lot blocked off and were
charging people to park their cars. I was with McBride and Stanley. We went around the barriers, parked and even before we got
out of the car one of these hotshots is there in our face telling us
we have to pay him. That turned out to be a one-sided conversation, and after we got to the door the bouncer started in on us.
These guys were such assholes we decided to just work them as
cops . . . no undercover games. We busted the valet for no license and the doorman for having a little coke on him.

"For a couple of weeks after that I made it a point to stay right
on 'em . . . gave them no slack at all. Once I eyeballed one of
the owners in a new Caddy . . . oops, it turned out to be
stolen. I bagged him, and the follow-up on it led us to a local
banker who was making bogus loans to these guys and launder-
ing some of their drug money, all that shit. We had patrol going
in there all the time and checking ID's. We'd pull over people in
cars who'd just left the place . . . kept the pressure on.

"Right after I busted the owner a second time for possession
of a firearm we got the word they were pissed and ready to do
something about their problems. McBride had made friends
with a barmaid who worked at the Saturn. Her boyfriend was
one of the owners but he treated her badly and, besides, she
liked McBride. She told him the two owners were trying to get
permission from the bosses in Detroit to kill *me.* They thought

this would make all the local cops around here chill out and leave them alone. Rocket scientists . . . right? They're gonna do it themselves, with the help of the doorman we popped for the cocaine.

"Sounded like lame bullshit or big talk at first, but then another informant from an old bar out west on the city line told us pretty much the same thing . . . that the Detroit higher-ups were being petitioned by the Saturn Club owners to be allowed to kill a cop in Lauderdale. I personally believed the Detroit brass would have told these assholes to grow up and use their heads for a change, but we had to take action on the info.

"We waited until closing time, when we knew the two owners and the bouncer would be there, and went in for a little talk. You can believe me when I tell you they definitely got the word. The place was sold a short time after that, and the last I heard all the players had left town. One of the owners really was a space cadet, though . . . he got arrested about a year later trying to get aboard the space shuttle armed with a forty-five! No shit."

We drove in silence for a few minutes, through the New River Tunnel and into the southern part of the city. There were a couple of joints on Seventeenth Street Causeway Al wanted to swing by. Traffic was heavy now, and twice we saw either a police unit or EMS running Code-Three to some disaster or other. Al, it seemed, had been brooding about something since he finished his last story.

"Goddamn people who think they can take out a contract on a cop really piss me off. It happens more often than you think, even here in our tropical paradise. What the hell? Do these people actually think that killing some cop that's rousting them or getting too close to some investigation against them is gonna solve their problem? *Any* time a cop goes down we go crazy until we find the bastard that did it. It always amazes me that some of these people out here think they are so smart and so fucking tough that they can put out a contract on a cop and just walk away. Cop is just doin' his job, that's all . . ."

I could feel the intensity of Al's anger. I knew enough to shut up and was glad I did.

"And judges too," Al said abruptly. "This last year one of our best and toughest judges retired, but only a month before he left I nearly made a case on a hit that was forming against *him*. He was one of those judges that made you believe once in a while the system could win one, you know? Didn't take any shit in the courtroom, from the lawyers or the cops or the defendants or anybody. Handed out tough sentences and turned a deaf ear to all the whining about how the guilty party really wasn't a *bad* person, it was just that he was abused as a child and raised by alcoholic pygmies who wouldn't let him join the church choir like he wanted to. This judge was a good one.

"It was another deal where one of my CI's was in a cell with some scuzball this judge had sentenced. Guy told my CI he wanted the judge killed and planned either to do it himself or hire a pro. This was all in another jurisdiction, so by the time my CI got a cop from that town to contact me, the suspect had bonded out. We never could get next to him, and as far as I know the sonofabitch is still out there . . . looking. The judge is retired now, but I still worry about him . . .

"Hell, we even had one supposedly getting ready to come down on a *federal* judge . . . a woman. Some big narcotics smuggler put the word out while he was inside. Offered big bucks to have her killed, specifically wanted her to be raped, then strangled. *He* got out on bond too, then went fugitive and just by luck was later found and captured. He was sentenced to life and another three hundred years, but with as much money as those guys have stashed they can still reach out and touch someone even from their jail cell. Last time I heard, the judge was still alive and kicking."

Suddenly there was a change in the texture of the radio chatter coming from Al's hand-held. An armed-robbery-in-progress call was going out. The target was a pharmacy in the north beach area, and units from the north end of town were being dispatched. Without saying anything Al swung his car around and headed west. We were only one bridge away from the beach, but we were south and we both knew traditionally the bad guys tried to get *off* the beach area and back to the mainland as soon as they could after a hit . . . there was more running room there.

Al drove west on Davie Boulevard, over the bridge (which miraculously wasn't open like it usually is), and onto I-95, northbound. By this time the radio was wild with units in pursuit of a large white older model Cadillac, west on Commercial toward the interstate. We were rocking along doing about eighty, just passing Oakland Park Boulevard, when the pursuing units advised that the suspects had crashed their car and bailed out on foot. A minute or two later an out-of-breath voice informed the dispatcher both suspects were in custody and to call off all the units.

"Score an easy one for the good guys," said Al as we slowed onto the exit ramp for Commercial Boulevard and swung east back toward Federal Highway. "Let's get a drink," he said, which was fine with me, as I realized how dry my throat was and saw that I was clutching the seat belt with both hands.

We parked in the lot in front of a place called Robbin's, about a block from the Intracoastal Waterway on Oakland Park Boulevard. The club had been in business for years, was popular with the yuppie crowd and was known as a meat market where singles went to mingle. Bad guys like nice places too, especially when they have a few bucks in their pockets, and this was one of the clubs often worked by Organized Crime and Narcotics detectives. (It isn't always that the club itself is bad, most often the ownership of the club is legal and removed from any goings-on . . . but it's frequented by people who are actively playing games.)

We found a table on one of the upper levels where we could sit with our backs to the wall, ordered some drinks, and Al proceeded to share a couple of memories of the place.

"Robbin's was a favorite for two heavy-hitter OC types, the Fantisi brothers. They actually owned that big restaurant and lounge just on the other side of the waterway there, near the bridge, but when they were out and about they often came in here. Randy and I were working them pretty heavy for a while. (Randy is the ex-police sergeant who was wounded on duty and had to retire, an ex-partner of Al's.) We were just trying to bust their chops, nothing undercover or anything . . . we were *highly* visible.

"Sometimes these guys get so big and powerful they think they can just do what they want, like nobody can touch them. When that happens sometimes it's good to show them just how vulnerable they are. Take these stupid Fantisi brothers. Couple of real hotshots. Had their fingers in some gambling gigs, lots of narcotics, couple of the clubs, hookers, all that shit. Flaunted it. Fancy cars, wild lifestyle. Had a high-powered attorney on re-tainer who would get all huffy every time any police action was taken against these guys. Randy and I used to follow 'em around at night, right on their butts. Their attorney had actually made a complaint about his clients being harassed . . . can you beat it? After we heard about the complaint we felt it was time to get really personal. Followed 'em into the front parking lot of this place . . . they were driving this really pimped out Mercedes . . . one of the big ones with all the gold accessories. I waited until they slid into a space and then before they got out I pulled in just on the left, and when I did Randy opened his door, *hard.*"

Our drinks came. The waitress was young and pretty, long legs and a great smile. Seemed to me her smile stayed on Al longer than me, but maybe, I tried to convince myself, it was because he was buying. We watched her walk away, then Al went on.

"So *oops*, our car door crashed into theirs, denting theirs and scratching the white paint. We got out and they got out. They wanted to get hot at first, the brother who was driving got him-self all pumped up but . . . gee, we were awfully sorry about it and all. As you know, Randy isn't as big as me but he is one tough boy, works out and has that look, right? The bluster kind of dies down, the two brothers talk for a second, then they shrug it off and come in here.

"We waited until they were at the bar and took the stools right next to them. Loud enough for everybody around to hear us, we started in on their suits. You know how sensitive those guys are about the way they look, right? They might be shitheels but, man, they've got the *threads*. So Randy and I start going on about how it's too bad these clowns had to get their suits from the Cosa Nostra goodwill store and silly stuff like that. They tried to ignore us at first, but we were too loud and one brother got off his stool and turned on Randy when we said something sweet about them looking like homeless pimps. Randy stared the guy down, so the other brother . . . trying to save the situation, I guess . . . he tells the bartender to set us up a couple of drinks, on *him*. When the bartender sets 'em down in front of us Randy and I looked at the drinks, then at the Fantisi brothers. 'Thanks,' we said, then turned the drinks over onto the counter in front of the two scuzbags and walked on out of there.

"Ooops again. Another complaint was filed, and we got our butts chewed out for committing a no-no in a public place. Broke our hearts. The Fantisi brothers, as you know, kind of fell apart that year. We busted them big-time and they went bye-bye after their organization collapsed. Word on the street was that even the bosses of the families up north were tired of the Fantisi bullshit. Randy and I knew how they felt."

We finished our drinks and headed out again, this time just over the bridge to the club on the other side of the waterway Al had mentioned earlier. It was now under new ownership and had been recently renovated. Al told me as we parked in a nearby bank lot that the new owners were connected too but didn't elaborate. He wanted to see if a doorman he knew was working on this night. The doorman had been arrested by Al some months before and Al had cultivated him as another informant. We went inside, and I ordered a couple of drinks as Al waited until a group of people came laughing through the doorway. When they were gone Al stood next to the doorman for a few minutes, talking quietly, then rejoined me.

"That's a pretty nice kid. Got himself swept up in a mid-sized coke deal that was a setup all the way. He's tryin' to get his shit together now. Didn't have anything for me tonight, but I still like to touch base."

We sipped our drinks and watched the action. The place was busy—loud music, some beautiful people, flowing drinks. It was another split-level place, complete with a mirrored dance floor on the ground level that was overlooked by a balcony-bar area. There was a railing around the balcony, and couples were leaning against it, watching the dancers. Al looked up and laughed.

"One night we were out and about, I swear, every place we went for about two hours this guy was *there*, starin' at me. I had never seen him before, didn't know if he was a bad guy, good guy, what the hell. But I knew for sure he was followin' me, you know? I mean, the guy was about as subtle as Randy and I were with the Fantisi brothers. Maybe he worked for them. Either way, I was tired of looking at his face every time I turned around. This place right here was like the fourth or fifth lounge we went into that night. We were looking for some out-of-town jewel thief that was supposed to be here for a hit. We get in here and sure as shit I turn around and here's this same guy again, like three feet away from me, watching everything I do, and trying to hear what I'm sayin'. Maybe he was a private investigator for a lawyer, or some fucking *writer* lookin' for a story." Al looked at me and laughed. "I didn't know. The sonofabitch was bugging me, though, I knew *that*. My partners had already made the guy, too, and were waiting for me to give the word. The normal thing would have been to go to the men's room, or out into the parking lot, and when he came along get in his face and see what was what.

"I guess I didn't feel normal that night. I waited until the guy was right beside me, and I grabbed him. I was standing right up there on that balcony, near that railing. I grabbed the guy, quick, had his neck and his pants before he knew what was what, pushed him over the railing and grabbed his ankles. There he was, the shithead, hanging upside down over the dance floor. Stuff was falling out of his pockets and he was waving his arms around and the people on the dance floor were getting out of the way and everybody was screaming and laughing. Couple of the bouncers came rushing over but my partners headed them off and told them it was a private matter, so they pulled back and just watched. I let the guy hang for about half a minute, then pulled him back over the rail and patted him down. He had no weapon, so I put my face real close to his and told him he was making me nervous following me around, and if I ever saw him again I'd probably have to kill him. He was just nodding his head up and down, his eyes real big. Last I ever saw of that asshole. I never did find out why he was following me, maybe he was gay, maybe he took a shine to me. Maybe I'm just flattering myself." Al looked at me and laughed again, shaking his head.

"I MET A real contract killer once, face to face. I mean a guy who worked for one of the mob families, killed people at their request and was paid for it. I was on assignment to act as a bodyguard for a wiseguy from here who had to go to Philly to meet some guys to set up a big robbery. The wiseguy had been busted and flipped and was working for Florida Department of Law Enforcement as an informant. They needed someone with a face no one in Philadelphia knew, and someone who could play the role of bodyguard to this dude. So I got the call . . .

"The wiseguy gets off the plane first and I'm trailing. He knows the bad guys are sending someone to pick him up for the meeting. He gets off the concourse and into the terminal lobby and waits. I take a position a few feet away at a phone booth, just to see what I can see. The bad guys know the wiseguy will have a bodyguard so I wasn't going to be a surprise or anything. Next thing I know I get a face full of bad breath and it's this guy Gino Grace. I had a file on Grace from our own info on the guy.

Knew he was part of the Philly mob, and knew he occasionally came into South Florida on jobs. He was suspected in probably a half-dozen hits in our area alone. Guy was about five eight or nine, half-bald, potbellied, pocked face. Looked like a guy on a slow track to nowhere. But it was him all right.

"Gino Grace is standing practically on my boots, both hands in his jacket pockets, and asks me if *I'm* the wiseguy he's supposed to meet. I just shook my head and pointed. He gets a big grin on his face and thanks me and walks over to my man. Off we go to the meeting, right in the airport lounge.

"We got out of there, back into the car and drove south on AIA, the beach road. The ocean, calm this particular evening, was on our left, and all the beach hotels and clubs were on our right. Al talked quietly as we drove: "My guy from Florida was acting like a go-between for the two groups, making sure that the wholesale gemstone guy that was targeted was not protected by someone, which would cause embarrassment if he was robbed.

"As far as I know the robbery never came off, and the whole time I was with Gino Grace all he wanted to talk about was the Miami Dolphins and wasn't it a shame they couldn't put a real team around that guy Marino. Within two hours we were on another plane, flying home, and about a year later we got the word that Gino Grace had died of a heart attack after a round of golf."

BY THIS TIME we had traveled past the infamous strip area near East Las Olas Boulevard and AIA and cruised under the overhead walkway that crossed from the beach to Bahia Mar Marina and Hotel. All the charter fishing boats were lined up on our right and at the very end lay the dock where the tourist cruiser *Jungle Queen* tied up. Al got that grin on his face again:

"Got to go back years ago again . . . like on a Saturday, a beauty. Sunny and clear, not too hot, a little breeze and that nice blue sky. I'd just started seeing this legal secretary I'd met when her boss depositioned me on some case. We'd been to the beach, toasted our bods, checked out the tourists and had a nice day. On the way back to her place while I drove my car down Las Olas toward town, she decided to get romantic, leaned across the carseat, unzipped my shorts and put her face in my lap. Zap.

"During the season Las Olas is hard enough to cruise, what with all the out-of-towners changing lanes and rubbernecking and backing into parking spots and all that. This girl was making driving a major problem . . . so I made a quick decision to pull into Collee Hammock Park near the New River so she could take care of the problem that had arisen. Sorry about that, it's corny. But I was young and single, okay? And at that time she was my ideal of a woman, especially since I was short-sighted. She fit my five-B test . . . she was blonde, big boobs, flat belly, blue eyes, nice butt. Does that make me a sexist? Or just a fan? She also had a fun personality and a spirit of adventure about fleshly pleasure. It was a new relationship, and who was I to tell her to go slow? I edged around the log barriers at the street side of the park and pulled up to the river, so close my front bumper was edging over the seawall. Then I leaned back in the seat feeling very good about life, about what was developing, and anticipating the ending—

"At that moment I heard a loud horn and looked up across the front of my car toward the S-turn in the river they call Tarpon Bend. There was the friggin' two-story riverboat . . . the *Jungle Queen* . . . jampacked with tourists from all over the world. I could see passengers moving around or leaning toward the starboard side of the boat, *our* side, and a lot of them had cameras . . . *all* trained on the back of the lady's head in my lap. It looked like the old *Queen* was developing a dangerous list, with all the passengers craning their necks and lenses our way.

"The climactic moment, unstoppable at that point, came and went without the girl being aware of our audience. She sat up with a smile as that old boat wobbled out of sight downriver and said she wasn't unhappy to learn she had not only just made *my* day but had also given a bargeload of vacationers a glimpse of some real Florida wildlife."

Al and I were laughing as we drove west over the Causeway Bridge back toward town. As Al headed toward my house to wrap up the evening I still had a couple of questions for him . . . like what about informants, who *are* these people, how does Al find them . . . how do *they* find Al? He obliged with a brief dissertation:

"Cherokee, I tell you, they come out of the woodwork. Lots of times an informant is your solid citizen who has either seen something or overheard something and knows it's wrong and wants to report it. Most of the time, if the criminal activity is heavy stuff, these citizens will just call in to like CrimeStoppers or whatever. If they have specific info they might be routed to Narcs or OC. Most of the time they want to stay anonymous, and you can't blame them. It's a one-time thing, they give the info . . . a house where dope is being sold, whatever . . . they hang up, and it's up to us to work it. Sometimes a citizen will actually participate in the investigation because he wants to do his duty . . . and also probably because it's exciting to work with the cops, you know?

"Most often, though, informants are people who have gotten into trouble with the law themselves and want to lessen their punishment by trading something to the cops. In the narcotics business these people are the bread-and-butter CI's. You bust a guy for a pound, you tell him it will go easy if he tells you where he bought it. Same old song and dance. You can work your way right up the friggin' ladder that way if things fall into place. Sometimes one player wants to hurt another, so he fingers him to the cops. Sometimes a CI is actually trying to divert attention from himself by giving up someone else. It's a real nasty game, and none of the players are nice people, you know?

"There are professional informants, too. Guys who make their living gathering pieces of info here and there, knowing this player and that player, hanging around the action bars, and then selling that info to the good guys. The state and federal people are famous for paying cold cash for info from a street source. Sometimes the narc units will pay an informant a percentage of the street value of a load if the CI can help them take that load off. *Nobody* likes these types . . . they're weaselly, slinking around. They'll *hold* info on a bad guy if they can't make a buck on it . . . like they'll know a hit's gonna go down but won't tell anybody if they can't make a profit . . . and the hit actually happens! Free enterprise, right?

"Informants often pass on their info to patrol cops that work their areas, or that they see regularly in the same donut shop every morning. Hey, that's why I like to be out and about in the clubs and stuff . . . like that doorman we saw earlier. He knows I'm not interested in little shit but if he hears something having to do with the wiseguys or big narcotics or a hit he'll pass it along. We *cultivate* informants, bring them along, try to be their buddies . . . help them out when they get in a jam. You never know when one of them is gonna lay something in your lap that turns out to be solid gold. It's not pretty but it's necessary.

"If you go out at night, into the bars and clubs, and you mention here or there that you need a certain job done . . . like a contract hit, someone will hear you and pass it on. Maybe that someone will have the connections to put you with a real live fucking scumbag contract murderer . . . and the person you want dead dies. Or maybe that someone will be one of the informants, I'll be tipped and the next person you meet will be Al Sanetti . . . in the flesh. Okay?"

Okay. But how about Al supposedly being undercover all these years but *still* able to make these contract-killing cases? After the first one, I ask, why wasn't his cover blown? Don't these scumbags pass the word? Some of Al's cases have even made the papers—no pictures, of course, but still . . . Al has been working the streets of South Florida for so long every bad guy out there should know him, right?

"Wrong," he said. "You have to remember how transient this

area is. People always coming and going, and that includes the criminal types. Even the Organized Crime groups have personnel changes on account of attrition in the ranks. Sure, if a lounge owner has been around for some years he gets to know who the working cops are, even the undercover types, and if that's the case we try to put fresh faces in the place when we can. As far as some kind of word going out about *me*, I guess it just hasn't happened . . . Hell, you know yourself that the bad guys are just like anybody else when it comes to seeing what they want to see. Randy even busted the same dope dealer *two nights in a row* a few years back out on the beach. Guy was so anxious to sell his stuff he looked right at Randy and got himself busted *again* by the same narc! You also have to remember that I don't just work one or two established crime groups. All kinds of people hire contract killers nowadays, not just OC types. The housewife that hires me probably has never even been in some of these bars or joints around town where somebody might know me as a cop. Same for a stockbroker or some other businessman.

"The biggest thing, though, is like I said . . . *people see what they want to see.* Once they've made up their minds about hiring a gun, they're ready to meet *him.* And in he walks —Al Sanetti. I mean, if they were making a movie about a hitman I'd probably look something like the character that plays one, yeah? You form an image in your mind of this monster who takes money for killing the person you want dead, and that image doesn't look like some guy on the cover of Today's Yuppie. Some guy looks like Dan Quayle, he might have problems passing himself off as a hitman, understand? But me, well, I look like I'm supposed to look."

I wouldn't argue that point with Al.

"I *am* big, and I *am* rough-looking, and we both know about the look that some cops get, a hard look. Street players get it after being in the trenches for a while. If people see me walk into a bar they see the look on my face, in my eyes. It's just there, I don't put it on. They know I'm on one side or the other."

I asked Al for a couple of specifics.

"Well, there was the time the narcs asked me to help them out on a deal. One of their guys was supposed to sell a heavy load of cocaine to some Hispanic buyers out of Miami. Sounds stupid, doesn't it, these guys coming up from *Miami* to buy from us? Anyway, the narcs had the word that the deal was a ripoff all the way. The buyers were just going to blow them away and take the dope. So the narcs asked if I would stand with their guy out front as bodyguard. We'd be covered, of course, but they wanted someone with the look with their boy.

"So when the night came, me and the young narc stood by his car in the middle of this big parking lot over by Sunrise Boulevard and the railroad tracks. We were both locked, cocked and ready, and other guys were hidden around in dumpsters and wrecked cars. Sure enough, here comes the Hispanic bad boys. We have the word they've got automatic weapons, the whole thing. They drive by in their car real slow. Four of 'em in the car. They go by again, all their little heads turned on us, looking hard. Then they make a big circle and come by *again*. This time my young narc waves at 'em and motions them over. They eyeball us real hard, then drive off. We waited around but they never came back. We went to a pay phone and the narc called his CI, who had paged him. The informant said the Latins had called him and said they didn't do the ripoff because they were afraid of the big guy who was with the narc. So, no drug deal, no shoot out, no dead or injured cops, no nothin'. Later there was a lot of joking around in the office about if you wanted to suck some bad guys into a hit, leave Al out of it.

"The other one really pissed me off. I was working at that time with a young guy named Bill Volker. He's a good-looking kid, but man, he is *big*. (I do know Bill Volker, who I call 'Wee Willy'. He's about six-six, two-thirty or so. Works out with weights, eats lots of health foods and looks like a cleaned-up version of the Terminator.) We had some CI out on the beach tell us these two dudes we'd been working had stashed a bunch of guns, money and two pounds of cocaine into the trunk of their car and were headed north that night. We staked out their hotel and sure as hell they left right on schedule. We got a patrol unit to make a traffic stop on them, and when they were off the road and out of their car we made our pitch, told them right out we were looking for guns and dope and wanted to look in their trunk. Now Bill and I are standing there talking to these guys, right? We *ask* them for permission to open their trunk and look inside. No rough stuff, no tough talk. Nice and legal and easygoing. We ask, and they say okay and in we go. Big surprise, there's the guns, the money and the dope, and we bag 'em, nice and sweet.

"Next thing you know we're in court. Their defense attorney wants the case thrown out because he wants the evidence thrown out because he wants the *search* thrown out. He says his clients gave us permission to look in the trunk of the car because they were *intimidated* by us . . . by our size, our badges, and our 'demeanor.' Has us stand before the bench so the judge can get a look at us. The judge *agrees* with him. Says the search was illegal because the defendants were probably intimidated by us into opening their trunk. Illegal search equals illegal evidence equals evidence thrown out equals case dismissed for lack of evidence. Because of the way we *looked*."

BY THIS TIME we had pulled into the driveway of my house. Time to end the evening but we made plans for our next meeting to get back into another of Al's contract-murder cases. Then he added as a sort of wrap-up for the night:

"All this about me being undercover and playing roles—especially contract killer. Maybe I can't *really* explain it. I know I've been a cop long enough, and I've been out there long enough to have an . . . *awareness*. I can play the roles because I *know* those roles. I know about bad guys, about dope dealers and pimps and hustlers and bone-crushers and killers. That, and the way I look, which goes with what people want me to be. They build up an image of what they want in their skull, they see me standing in front of them, and they see what they're looking for. It's not a cop they see . . . hey, people never really see the cop . . . you know? If they did I'd long ago be out of business. Or dead."

O.K. CORRAL

It was not unusual for a long black Lincoln limousine to be slowly cruising the upper-crusty streets of the Coral Ridge section of Fort Lauderdale late on a Sunday night. There are plenty of limos in town carrying high-rollers, high-school prom goers, hotshots and high-society types to nude bars, beach bars and charity bazaars. This residential section in the northeast part of town is convenient to the Galeria Mall and the beaches, and has many expensive homes on the water, with BMWs, Ferraris and Jags tucked into circular drives. The area has the confident aura of established money and good family names.

It was not even unusual for a particular black Lincoln limo to be occupied by four or five men with guns. Fort Lauderdale is known as the white-collar crime capital of the world. It is also known for being one of the major entry points for smuggled narcotics, weapons, aliens and outbound computer technology . . . and with the rest of South Florida as the new murder-rate champion. We have drive-by shootings, traffic-accident shootings, people machine-gunning each other in the streets, people stepping over bodies to reach their fast-food takeout orders, and bad guys so tuned into what the safety-conscious cop is wearing these days that they make sure to stick the barrel of their gun *under* the bullet-proof vest before squeezing the trigger.

There was also nothing out of the ordinary when the limo on

155

this Sunday night made a turn onto a street off Bayview Drive and proceeded slowly through the dark night toward a nice house on the water that was occupied by a convicted drug smuggler. (Bad guys with their new and dirty money buy homes in the area too.) It was business as usual when the limo slowed even more, the windows came down, gun barrels came out and a volley of shots was fired into the front windows of the house, the yard, the shrubbery and the cars parked in the drive. The rapid-fire shook the quiet street with noise and concussion, the limo squealed its rear tires as it sped off, and the quiet warily returned after the last few bell-like tones of falling window glass and the hissing of air out of punctured car tires that ended with a burp and a sigh.

What made *this* little scene unusual, even for Fort Lauderdale, was the fact that the shooters had their lawyer *with* them as they did the deed, and this was the second night in a row they had visited the same beleaguered house . . .

AL FILLED ME in while we were in my office on an early afternoon with a heavy thunderstorm darkening the skies outside and rain coming down hard. He had not one but two dangerous roles this time—bodyguard to protect a man from being killed by a group of people who clearly had every intention of doing just that, and hired killer. This case also had a new twist—this time his reputation had preceded him, he was recognized as Al Sanetti, contract killer, and one of the participants in the deal reacted strongly to that news. It went like this:

"I looked at Jack Long sitting across the booth from me in the Denny's restaurant on North Federal Highway," Al began. "Good coffee and bad company, that's what I had that day. Jack Long was a big guy, powerfully built, a creased face, good teeth and a full head of wavy hair. His hands were big and knuckly, he moved with a solid ease. Looking him over, I figured if I had to tangle with him I'd want to hurt him real fast, finish him hard. Not a man to turn your back on. He wore casual slacks, a white buttondown shirt and some jewelry. You could tell he had money, but it was in his bearing, not the flash. And here was a man who'd taken a bullet in his leg only two days ago. I had a small transmitter tucked into my crotch, down around my balls."

The transcript got it all down:

JACK LONG: You know I'm on probation from a drug smuggling conviction, right? Just grass, from the old days when every-body down here was humping bales of stuff in somewhere. We were all getting rich and nobody was getting hurt until the organized guys came in . . . and then the cocaine, of course.

AL SMITH: I know. You and the others were just pioneer busi-nessmen, not real bad guys, just pirates looking at forty . . . good guys bringing a little ganja for the potheads . . . like the early bootleggers, yeah?

LONG: Hey, you're a cop. I can't blame you if that's how you feel. Fuckin' IRS is who really nailed me anyway, not the DEA or you guys . . .

"We both sipped our coffee, and I took another look around the restaurant dining room. At that moment Long kind of stiff-ened and I saw two guys walk in. One went to a booth a few feet away from us and the other hesitated, looked out the windows, then walked our way. I could see the outline of a gun under his shirt and took a quick look at the one sitting down. He had a gun too. Fucking wonderful. I don't know if the thought crossed my mind that we might have to be running for our lives or what, but before the first guy got to us I asked Long how his leg was feeling. He just made a waving motion with one hand, like it was okay."

Jack Long was a convicted smuggler trying to go straight, at least as he told it, but it seemed he picked some pretty bent people to go straight with. He described to Al a land deal he had gone into with a local attorney in which he had given the attorney twenty-five thousand dollars, cash. Some time went by, things changed in the deal, and he got his money back. Then the attorney began harassing him, demanding the cash again, insisting Long owed it to him. The deal didn't make much sense anyway, and when Al learned that the attorney, Phillip Powers, had a prior drug-smuggling conviction himself and had once fled to Kingston, Jamaica, to avoid prosecution, the whole thing sounded bogus. Long and Powers had some kind of cash deal going, sure, but there was little doubt in Al Smith's mind that the deal was for drugs, not land.

"It didn't make any difference what I thought the money was for, though," Al said. "I was brought in because Jack Long called the police to report he was a victim of an attempted extortion, and was the target of a murder-for-hire conspiracy. And I was assigned to play bodyguard and baby-sit Long through a meeting with the people who wanted to kill him. The brass told me it didn't matter what kind of transaction Long was into with Powers, what was important now was that Long was being forcibly threatened and extorted and would be killed if I didn't cover his ass while he met with the other players in this scuzball deal.

"We learned later that I'd been eyeballed before we really got into this deal. Probably they had somebody watching Long's house, because my very first meeting with him was there. I went alone, in my plain car. Whoever saw me recognized me . . . maybe from one of the bars where I'd gone in and established myself as a player. Whoever recognized me contacted this attorney Phillip Powers and told him that Long had brought in some muscle. Powers was told that Long appeared to be taking this whole thing very seriously, because the muscle who showed up at his house was a guy named Al Sanetti, and Sanetti was usually hired for a very specific job.

"I didn't know it then, of course, but in this case *both* sides believed the other had hired killers on the payroll. It also seems ironic to me that if these guys trying to hammer Long had used their brains they could have gotten the rest of the system, including *me* maybe, to attack Long legally with civil and criminal proceedings. But not these pukes . . . they had to be badasses. I could hardly hide my pleasure as I sat in the Denny's restaurant in the middle of a Monday and listened to a hardass with a gun describe for me what would happen if Long didn't cough up the cash."

Long had told his story earlier. First there came the phone calls from lawyer Phillip Powers demanding forty thousand dollars. Long gave a jumbled explanation on how the twenty-five grew to forty . . . something about interest on the original, and for the lawyer's "troubles" in handling the deal. Long had his money back, the deal was off, and now Powers was calling and threatening him. Long ignored Powers, so the next call he got was from some heavy hitter from up north. He tells Long he's "tied in" with the Teamsters, and the money came from a Teamsters' pension fund of some kind.

Long asked the caller flat out if the Teamsters really had put their money into the original deal. The caller then backed down slightly, telling Long that someone "had access" to some funds, funds that "could be" Teamsters' money. He also said the Teamsters knew nothing about the deal but their money had been used, and now Long had to give it back because the Teamsters had "no sense of humor." Long tells the caller there was no way he was giving the money back and to tell Powers to go to hell. The caller then asked Long if he had ever seen a dog that had been run over by a car . . . "turns into a maimed dog." Long hung up.

Saturday night after the phone calls that black Lincoln limo showed up at Long's fine waterfront home in Coral Ridge. The attorney Phillip Powers got out followed by Fred Toscano, Ray Jersey, Al Carlton and Frank Spatuzzi. Long later told Al that one of these men was the son of a senator from the Northeast and the other was an escapee from a maximum security facility. This attractive gaggle barged into Long's living room before Long realized what was happening. Long rushed into the room demanding an explanation. Powers smiled and told him he had hired these men from a friend "up north." He told Long they were "bill collectors." Long looked them over and told Powers he thought they were "assholes," but Powers, who apparently felt in control of the situation, just told Long to get the cash or "they" would.

At which point Long turned to move quickly up the stairs. Powers apparently saw something in his eyes, because he motioned for Toscano and Jersey to follow Long. They got to him just as he pulled a .12 gauge shotgun out of a hallway closet. They tried to take it away from him but Jack Long is no shrinking violet. Punches were thrown, and then Powers and the other two "collectors" went running out the front door even before Jersey and Toscano came tumbling down the stairs in a heap. They sorted themselves out and followed the others in a disheveled escape to the limo as Jack Long picked himself up and hurried down the stairs with the shotgun.

As the gang of tough guys piled into the limo for their escape, Al Carlton emptied his gun into the front windows and door of the house. One of the slugs, after punching through the wooden door, hit Long in the lower leg and sent him down onto his marble floor in pain and anger.

The limo drove quickly away, and the night got quiet again. A few minutes later two Fort Lauderdale police units arrived at the scene. They had been called by a neighbor who would not identify himself. They cautiously approached the house, looked over the bullet holes and broken glass and rang the doorbell. Jack Long answered the door. He looked pale but was polite to the officers. The shooting? The bullet holes? He was mystified, was sure it was some kind of mistake or a prank. He told the officers he did not want to make any kind of report and there was nothing more he could tell them about it. The two cops did not observe Jack Long's wound. They took a brief statement, which told them nothing, looked at each other dubiously and advised Long to call again if he could shed any more light on the incident, or if he just wanted to talk. Long thanked them and they left. At the end of their shift they filed an accurate, sketchy and skeptical report of what they saw and heard.

Jack Long cleaned up the mess, treated his wound (clean entry and exit, no bone or major nerve or muscle damage), had a stiff drink and began to analyze the situation, trying to gauge just how serious that crazy lawyer was.

"We're in the Denny's restaurant, right?" Al said. "Now the guy gets to our booth, and as he slides in across from me he gives me a sneer and says something about me being the bad bodyguard for Jack Long. That's when he surprised me by telling me 'they' knew who I was . . . I'd been spotted at Long's house and they had a make on me—as Al Sanetti. I had the feeling he was checking me out, trying to see where my loyalty was. Said he'd heard I was a specialist, and if I was, why was I working for Long. I told him I did it for the same reason *he* did, but I did it for more money than *he* was getting, and I did it *better*. That backed him off for a moment.

"He was tall and gangly looking, very pale, with slicked back hair and a white short-sleeved shirt worn with the tails out over blue jeans. He wore a couple of rings on his fingers, a gun on his hip. He was one of the badass hired guns from up north. He was looking at me hard because up until then he only dealt with Jack Long. I was an unknown factor to these guys, other than what they had been told about Al Sanetti.

"I knew I had to play the game with this idiot, but my mind was spinning with the volatile nature of the deal . . . the setup. This guy *and* the other one both had guns and attitudes, and we were in a crowded restaurant in the middle of the day. It could get very messy, fast. I hoped Stanley and McBride were picking up our voices on the wire I had in my crotch when I told the guy from what I had seen so far I was pretty sure Jack Long didn't *need* my help.

"That pissed him off. He told me to fuck myself, to watch my mouth, and maybe I'd live longer. I had the feeling he was trying to convince himself I wasn't going to have him for lunch. Then he looks at Long and tells him, no more bullshit, they have to get the money *today*. He was really twitching, nervous, hyper-like . . . maybe he had done some nose candy to try to increase the size of his balls. Either way, he then moved from the seat across from me in the booth to *my* side, right beside me, but not too close. I knew his gun was on his right side, which was away from me on the outside of the seat, but I felt better having him within my reach. If things fell apart I knew I'd be on his ass like a horny gorilla on a plucked duck. The waitress came over to the table then. I remember she was an older lady, attractive, with a carefully made-up face and hairdo. She asked if we wanted coffee. I don't know if any of us answered her but she poured it all around anyway. Then she must have felt the tension and skedaddled without another word.

"Long watched her walk away, then he calmly turned to the guy and asked him, 'Or what?'. The guy shrugged, put on his wash-and-wear sneer and told us there'd be 'bodies everywhere . . . fucking houses blown down, the whole thing.' Said we didn't know who we were dealing with, that some very serious people were behind the money. I sat there with Jack Long, a convicted drug smuggler, acting as his bodyguard and hitman, and hoped Long remembered how we planned to carry out this game. I also hoped he remembered *he* called *us* for help."

From the transcript taken from restaurant meeting:

MALE VOICE: *(Later identified as Al Carlton)* Forty-two thousand in cash . . . *today*.

JACK LONG: Forty-*two?* Fuck, Powers . . . was saying *forty* yesterday, and even that's a fuckin' ripoff. Why forty-two now?

CARLTON: My friend, Freddy Toscano . . . who you should know is tied in with some *very* tough boys where we come from. He broke his arm falling down your stairs the other night . . . had to take him to the hospital to get it set and all that. The two grand is to compensate him for his injury.

LONG: Fuck you. *(Laughing)*

AL SMITH: You asked me to sit in with you against *these* babies?

CARLTON: You think it's funny, motherfucker? When we left

Long's place the other night *I'm* the one who emptied a full magazine into the front door . . . and I saw him dancin' around in there. I thought I nailed his ass but maybe not. Fuck . . . that was just a little wake-up call. You understand? Don't fuck with us, Jack, or you'll be history . . . the money, man, get us the money and we'll go back to our own town and you'll be finished with Powers.

"I could tell Long was getting pissed, saw his arm and shoulder muscles bunching up, and knew he was about a hair's breadth away from jumping all over Carlton right there in the restaurant. I knew if it started I would probably have to kill Carlton right where he sat, then spin away from the table and take out the other asshole sitting across the aisle from us near the salad bar. This was shaping up to be a *real* clusterfuck."
From transcript:

JACK LONG: *(After letting out long breath)* Fuck it. You think forty-two grand is big money, shithead? Powers has to bring you whores down here to collect that much? I'll tell you what . . . we'll go get the fucking cash right now, and be back here in less than half an hour, okay? You can take it with my fucking blessings . . . give it to Powers and then leave me alone. This shit isn't worth my time, I've got other things going on and your petty crap is giving me a headache. *(Pause)* Just one more little thing for you to think about and pass on . . . my man Al here does for me what you pretend to do for Powers, *understand?*
CARLTON: *(After staring at Al Smith, then back to Jack Long)* This is . . . just business. And why not now? Why do you have to go away and come back? Who you gonna call, the cops?
LONG: No. Ghostbusters, you asshole. Do you *believe* this fucking guy?
　(Pause)
FEMALE VOICE: *(Indistinct, apparently to small child)* No, no,

don't go over there, come back with mommy come back to *our* table . . .

LONG: You think *I'm* gonna bring the fucking cops in on this? And you think I'm driving around with forty grand in my trunk, the way you guys been hounding me?

CARLTON: Forty-*two*—

LONG: Forty-two . . . whatever the fuck. All I want is to be *done* with you and that asshole Powers, okay? I've got a safe-deposit box where I keep emergency cash. The bank isn't far away and I *don't* want a tail. You want the money . . . you just sit here and wait a little while, and we'll be back with it. Then I'll have it in my trunk and you can get it in the parking lot.

Here, Al Carlton stood and looked out the windows into the parking lot as Jack Long and Al Smith moved out from the table and began to turn away.

CARLTON: Wait . . . I got to walk out the doors with you.

LONG: Up your ass, man. You wait here, we bring the money, got it?

CARLTON: You see the one behind me at the other table, I know . . . there's more outside waitin'. The way we got it set up . . . if you turn me down . . . when you walk out those front doors without me they're gonna blow your fuckin' ass away right there in the parking lot, don't give a shit who's out there . . . how many people are around . . . *nothin.* You walk out without me . . . you die, and so does your jackass partner and bodyguard here. Don't make no difference *what* he is.

"We hesitated, and now I really hoped Stanley and McBride were getting all this on the wire. Carlton might have been bluffing . . . we didn't know at that point . . . but if he *wasn't* we were fixing to get outgunned for sure. I was hot by this time, though. I had heard all I wanted to hear from that motherfucker . . . maybe he had all the muscle in the world behind him somewhere, but for a plugged nickel that bastard would have been history. I forced myself to concentrate on the mission. Payback could come later. Me and Long both smiled at the creep, and Long told him, 'After you', with a sweep of his hand.''

They walked out in a small group, and as they headed for Long's car Al tried to scan the crowded parking lot for armed bad guys hunched down in rented cars, and for his partners, who had hopefully already picked out the competition. He saw elderly couples, brightly and ridiculously dressed tourists, gawky groups of teenagers bumping together as they walked across the lot, moms and dads and toddlers . . . but no hitmen, and no cops.

Al and Jack Long then drove out of Denny's in Long's rented Cadillac. Carlton stood in the lot watching them go. His partner from inside the restaurant, later identified as Frank Spatuzzi, had come out behind them and was lounging near the newspaper machines. Not that he could read.

Al and Long had it set up so Don Stanley would follow in his car when they drove off "to the bank" to make sure their tail was clean. Bill McBride would hold his position near the northwest corner of the Denny's lot and wait for their return. Long sat on the passenger side, and as Al drove he reached beneath the seat, pulled out a radio hidden there and called Stanley on the covert channel. He knew McBride should still be able to hear him on the body-wire too:

AL SMITH: You there, Don?

DON STANLEY: Yeah, Al, as far as I could tell there's no tail. You're clean.

SMITH: Okay. We're still gonna go to the bank and my man here will go inside for a minute with the case, then come out and put it into the trunk just in case they got an eyeball there.

STANLEY: Uh . . . listen, Al . . . I'd play it for real. Bill and I saw Powers in his own car when you guys first went inside. He was in the lot for a few minutes, talked with another subject who came out of one of the cars, then left. We haven't seen him since but he's around somewhere.

SMITH: Okay . . . we'll keep our eyes peeled. The two in the restaurant with us are definitely signal-zero [armed].

STANLEY: We copy that *(Laughter)* . . . one other problem here, big guy . . .

SMITH: What's that?

STANLEY: Uh . . . my car's overheating bad. It's running but I don't know for how long.

SMITH: Hey man, I think we're gonna *need* you back at that lot when this goes down . . . we don't know how many of them are waiting.

STANLEY: *(Still laughing)* I *know*, Al. I'm just tellin' ya this car is fixing to take a shit on me . . . I'll stay with you one way or another . . .

I went back to the original reports to see how this mess eventually wound up in Al's lap. The statements show that after a lot of booze and some peroxide and self-examination Jack Long discovered that the bullet wound to his leg was minor and looked like it would be okay if he could keep it from becoming infected. The threatening phone calls kept coming in all that Saturday night, and he came close to calling the police back to his house. He knew the two patrol cops had gone away unconvinced, but he was still trying to "keep the cops out of my little problem."

Powers called Jack Long several times during the day on Sunday, and one or two of the others who identified themselves as collectors. They were abusive and threatening but Long kept telling them to go to hell and hanging up. Then came Sunday night. During the few moments between the hammering volleys of gunfire that blasted into his front yard and house, and the arrival of three or four wailing police units, Jack Long gave some intense thought to his situation.

Al jumped in here to interrupt my study of the case and to add to it from his memory:

"Jack Long told me that any citizen, any businessman, whether he's a convicted drug smuggler or not, on probation or not, doesn't want the kind of attention you get when somebody shoots up your house a couple of times. He said the neighbors start giving you dirty looks and keeping their kids away from your yard, and the fresh-faced young patrol cops and their sergeants start to look at you fish-eyed. He told me he was also almost embarrassed to admit that Phillip Powers and his tough guys might actually manage to kill him with all of their shooting every time they came near the house. So the last time the patrol units were sent to his place he invited them in and told them the basic story. When *I* showed up a couple of hours later he wanted to know if I was some kind of specialist or expert at that stuff.

"Phone calls in the middle of the night, don't you just love 'em? I remember groping for the damned thing and telling whoever was on the other end that 'this better be good.' Then I got to hear all about poor Jack Long and his habit of getting his house all shot up. The patrol supervisors had listened to Long's story and decided this was a case for us supercops in Organized Crime. They got to Captain Garcia at his house, he listened, then passed it on to me. He told me to stick with it to the conclusion . . . to try and set up a meet with the shooters and their boss to make a payoff. Do it and we could nail them on extortion and attempted murder. Swell.

"I could have Stanley and McBride, but that was about it as far as my 'team.' Garcia reminded me that it was the week of the big sweep. A local task force augmented by state and federal groups were gonna take down bad guys connected with various OC figures and operations in South Florida. I was supposed to work on it at least two nights that week. Garcia told me they were committed to it so he couldn't give me any more people. I had to work it with what I had but he wanted me to *work* it, because Long's house had been shot up twice and the neighbors were getting hot about it and the chief was already aware of it and the whole shmear. Garcia also said that our tit would be in the ringer if Long got his ass blown away *after* he asked us for help. So it was me and Stanley and McBride, and a bunch of guys in the Denny's parking lot with guns."

Al went on to tell how he watched as Long went through the charade at the bank, waited as he walked back to the car and climbed in, and headed back to the restaurant, where McBride sat hidden trying to make out who were the bad guys and where they would set up their ambush. Al had to decide if he should just pull the plug because it was untenable, or try at that late moment to get reinforcements in, even if they had to be uniformed patrol guys.

"Don't get me wrong," Al said, "I've got plenty of respect for patrol cops who work those same nasty streets that I do, wearing that badge right out there on their chests for everyone to see. It's just that this deal was going to be hairy any way it went down, and it would need finesse . . . plus invisible cops. My mind held the picture of a movie called *Gunfight at the O.K. Corral*, with the Earp brothers and Doc Holliday facing off against the Clanton Gang in Tombstone. I could almost hear Frankie Laine singing in the background, 'O.K. Corral, O.K. Corral . . .' I tried to make up my own version using Denny's parking lot as I drove back to the place, but it lost something in the translation.

"We'd eyeballed Powers on the scene, and there was no doubt that once we had the collectors in custody we'd be able to convince at least one to puke all over the rest. We could make good charges stick to them all, including the ringleader, but first we had to play out this extortion-payment scenario. The bad guys had to actually receive the money before we could make solid arrests. I knew McBride waited near the lot, and I knew Stanley was behind me somewhere in his ailing car. I didn't like the intended 'victim' one bit, but he sat beside me after asking for help, and the guys in Denny's with the guns seemed to be working themselves up to some crazy violent act and had made it real plain they didn't care who got hurt along the way.

"I remember I gripped the wheel of that rented Caddy, gritted

my teeth and thought we'd just *charge on*. That's kind of my
nature . . . it's hard for me to let go of something when it's
thrown in my face. The rougher somebody wants to play, well,
the rougher I'll play. It's damned hard for me to walk away from
it."

The booming thunderstorm and driving rain that had been
with us for over an hour stopped so suddenly that the instant
quiet made Al and me look up to see what was going on. We
took a break, I made a cup of tea and Al had a soft drink. I went
over my notes while he made a couple of phone calls, one to his
office and one to his house. He told me he was going to have to
pull the plug for that afternoon, but before he left he wanted to
tell me a story as an example of his not being able to let go of
something never mind the odds:

"One year Don Stanley and I bought brand-new matching
TransAms. It was a bigger car then, with engines under the
hood they still measured in cubic inches. We thought we were
the hottest things around town in our stud machines, as our
wives called them. We ended the shift one night and I decided
to cruise by a small restaurant in the north end of town on the
way home. We were going to set up a surveillance on the place
in the morning because it was frequented by OC figures, and I
wanted to see if there was a good vantage point. It was about
2:00 A.M. when I cleared the area and headed home.

"A few blocks away I passed a small convenience store and
saw a car parked on the side of the building with someone behind the wheel. Next thing I see is a guy run out of the place
with something in his hand and dive headfirst into the waiting
car, which then roared away. I caught a glimpse of the store
clerk running out trying to copy down the tag number of the car
as I followed it north on Powerline Road. I got hold of the dispatcher on my hand-held radio and told her I was chasing the
car with two black males in it over the Pompano Beach line.
Then they turned west into a tough section of the county called
Collier City. They made wild high-speed turns up and down
side streets trying to lose me, but there was no way in that

TransAm. Then they tried the more forceful method of getting me to back off. The passenger leaned out the right front window and started shooting at my car with a small-caliber gun. That pissed me off. I fired a couple of rounds back at them so they'd know they were in a fight, but shooting from car to car is never really effective and it can be dangerous to the innocent people in the area. So I stopped firing, but I kept chasing them.

"They made a wild turn right into a block party with about five-hundred people milling around in the streets, dancing and drinking. They jumped out of their car and ran right into the crowd, yelling at the top of their lungs that they were being chased by the cops. Even though I was hot I at least knew better than to drive right into the crowd after them, so I made a quick left turn down a side street. It turned out to be a dead end.

"I turned my car around at the end of the street, and the dispatcher told me there were no nearby sheriff's office units—actually I wasn't too sure of where I was anyway. The crowd then did something that really pissed me off. They moved a couple of cars together to block the road, crowded around and waited to see what I would do. They knew the only way for me to get out of there was to go right past them, *if* I could get through their roadblock.

"Sure, I had my radio, and I knew the dispatcher was still trying to find some backups for me . . . but it was late and I was *hot*. Tell you the truth, later on I thought it was like a scene from *True Grit*, with John Wayne running his horse at the bad guys and shooting and yelling. I pulled my car about two hundred feet from the roadblock, shifted it down into low and put my gun in my left hand. I jammed the gas pedal to the floor and that badass TransAm bucked and roared and left about twenty feet of rubber as I headed right toward the crowd with my gun waving out the window and yelling at the top of my lungs like a real crazy.

"As I bore down on the blockade cars their drivers decided they didn't want any part of what was coming at them and reversed out of there. I drove between them, and the angry crowd parted slightly but began bombing me with rocks and bottles and bullets from at least a couple of guns I saw flashing in the night. Ol' John Wayne did his riding and shootin' in the movies, but this was real, so I didn't fire my gun as I roared through there. Many of their projectiles hit the TransAm, though, tearing holes in the exterior and breaking off pieces of the fiberglass spoilers.

"Other than that I got through it okay, and all I saw in my rearview mirror as I drove away were some wide eyes and open mouths. It took longer to explain the whole deal to Sylvia than it did to get the friggin' car fixed. It also cost more."

A COUPLE OF days later Al picked up the story of Jack Long and the gang that waited for him and Al at the Denny's lot:

"Just as I was tucking the radio back under the seat as we approached the Denny's, Don Stanley came over the air and said his car had just died. Shit. I was pretty sure he was only about a block behind me so I could only hope he could hotfoot it down to Denny's in time for the dance."

"Right," I said, trying to pick up the thread.

"I backed the Caddy into a space along the north edge of the lot," Al charged on. "Almost every space had a car in it and there were still people coming and going. I saw Carlton and Spatuzzi waiting for us near the newspaper machines and two payphones on the wall near the front doors. I stayed behind the wheel with the motor running and saw Carlton give us a small wave, as if to tell us to wait a minute. Spatuzzi got on one of the payphones and made a call. They put their heads together then, watching us and talking, then began walking toward us, slow, looking around the lot, staying a few feet apart.

"I said, 'Here we go' so McBride would pick it up on the wire. I said there were two of them and I'd take them to the back. When I opened the trunk and they took the case, that was the move-in signal. I had no way of knowing if McBride heard me, and still didn't know where Don Stanley was, but this thing was going down . . . one way or the other.''

Have you ever noticed that some people wear socks with *sandals?* No kidding. Usually when we see it in Lauderdale it means the person is Canadian, or a junketing German. I don't know why but it's true. There are other ways to spot normal tourists and regular civilians, and as the two hard guys walked toward the Cadillac Jack Long and Al climbed out, Al scanned the busy lot with his heightened senses, briefly examining each of the men, women and children, skipping over them, hungry for that first . . . *there.* A lean guy, red-faced and hunched over, walking quickly toward them along the back of the cars parked in line with the Caddy. He wore a black T-shirt with some heavy-metal band logo on the front, black jeans, jogging shoes. He walked with one hand in his right-rear pocket. His eyes were focused on Al and Jack Long . . .

"Behind him I saw a movement, low, and hoped it was Bill McBride, who should have exited his car by now, ready to move. I still didn't see Stanley, but a quick glance to my left showed me another one of the lawyer's collectors. He was short and heavyset, wore a loose sweatshirt and gray slacks. He had carefully combed greasy black hair, thick eyebrows and a scowl. He too walked with one hand in his pants pocket, and he came right toward us. At that point Carlton's close to us and says he's got to see the money. He came up beside me on the driver's side of the Caddy. Long moved toward the back of the car, which was up against a chain-link fence that bordered the north edge of the lot. Spatuzzi hung back a little. The other two were still about three car-lengths away. I told him it was in the trunk, in a briefcase . . . forty-two thou in cash. But I held up my hand and stopped him and asked him how we knew he would really take the money to that shithead they worked for. What if they just took the briefcase and ran? Carlton just shook his head. He looked at the others moving in and told me I *didn't* know, but they were hired to do a job and that's what they would do. He said Powers would get his money, they would get paid and they would get out of this sweatbox we called a city. We walked back to the trunk then, I put the key in the lock, the trunk opened slowly and Carlton saw the briefcase. He shouldered past me and grabbed it."

The next few seconds, it seems, were some of those that stretch out real slow and clear, where one hears every word and sees every movement and it stays with one, etched in the mind by the acids of exhilaration and fear.

"Freeze. Police. Everybody freeze."

They all turned to see where the voice came from except Jack Long. He just threw himself onto the ground along the right side of the Cadillac. Al looked to see Bill McBride standing two cars away at the front end of one parked against the fence. He was in a crouch, gun pointed at the one in the heavy-metal T-shirt who had been approaching from the west side of the lot. He was later identified as Ray Jersey, and he turned quickly toward the voice, one hand still in his pocket.

And now the guns were out. Jersey's location and McBride's angle of fire put Al in a bad place, and a silent prayer echoed in his cold bones asking that Jersey not be stupid enough to spark the powder keg they all stood on. As if from a great distance Al heard screaming, and sensed panicked movement . . . but that was all the time he had for the innocents in that moment of time:

"Spatuzzi, who had been near the front of the Caddy, froze in place, and Carlton, beside me with the briefcase, grabbed my arm and crouched down, pulling me with him. He yelled 'shit' into my ear, and then 'it's the fucking *cops*, man!' My gun had already made its way into my hand, and I stuck it hard against the bottom of his nose as I said something along the lines of 'no shit, motherfucker, I'm a cop and you are all mine.' He went near-crosseyed staring at the end of my gun, I grabbed him by the hair and pulled him face down onto the pavement. As Carlton went down Spatuzzi moved toward me. He seemed confused. I didn't see a gun in his hand but swung mine up while Carlton lay stunned. I pointed it right at Spatuzzi's guts and yelled for him to get down, to get on the ground and stay there. His eyes went wide as he dove for the pavement, hands outstretched. I used one hand to frisk Carlton, pulled a gun out of his waistband and stuck it in my pocket. I tried to look over the trunk of the car to see what was happening with the other two and caught a glimpse of movement and color, then ducked down again. I dragged Carlton across the ground to where Spatuzzi lay. I told them that I would kill them both right there in that lot if either of them even farted without me telling them to. I smacked Spatuzzi on the back of the head so his face hit the pavement, then did the same to Carlton. So they'd understand their position.

"Then I heard the gunshot.

"As I turned I could hear McBride yelling for someone to 'freeze' and 'come out of there.' I couldn't see McBride or the heavy-metal T-shirt, Jersey, but off to my left the chunky one with the black greasy hair was scrambling over the chain-link fence, maybe two or three cars away from me. He hit the ground hard and got up to run. Just as I saw the gun in *his* hand I heard Don Stanley's voice, all pissed off, like, 'go ahead you sonofabitch, point that gun or get up to run and I'll blow your ass away.' I remember thinking that definitely was not a PG-13-rated parking lot on that day. I saw Don Stanley then as he jumped onto the hood of a parked car, his face sweaty. He had his gun pointed at the chunky one a few feet away. He yelled at the guy to throw the gun away, throw it to the side. The chunky one was on his knees and threw the gun onto the pavement some six feet away from his right side. As he did, Stanley went over that fence and in one jump was on top of the guy . . . who we later ID'd as Joseph Watts. Watts was yelling 'all right,' and covered his head as Stanley's fists rained down onto him."

Then the screaming of a lot of people entered Al's awareness again. He looked about the lot and saw people kneeling against parked cars, some holding each other, some hugging children to their sides. One elderly couple was crouched over near the newspaper machines, the woman trying to keep the man from running over to the action. Somewhere a small child or woman was crying. Al still did not see McBride . . .

"Then I heard sirens off in the distance and guessed someone from inside the restaurant had dialed 911, but I got my radio from under the front seat of the Caddy anyway. I kept Carlton and Spatuzzi covered as I told the dispatcher we had an emergency, needed backups and that shots had been fired. I gave the location and knew every available unit, marked, detective, K-9, traffic, everybody would be coming our way now. Don Stanley came walking up, leading Watts by the back of the head and belt. Watts's hands were on top of his head and his gun was stuck in Don's belt. Don still held *his* gun in the same hand that had Watts's belt, so Watts was doing *exactly* what he was told. Don wanted to know where Bill was. He had Watts lie down on the pavement beside Spatuzzi and Carlton. I told him to cover them while I went to see what happened to McBride. McBride was really Don's partner, and he showed his respect for me by letting me go. Maybe he didn't trust himself if what he saw was a cop's nightmare—partner down and bleeding.

"I took off to my right down the line of cars to the west. All I could see were people kneeling and hiding beside cars. No heavy-metal T-shirt and no McBride. I kept moving west toward a large lake located at the rear of the Denny's lot. Then I saw them. Jersey had jumped the parking-lot fence with McBride right behind him. He had come to the lake, hesitated, then plunged in. McBride didn't know Jersey had already dropped his weapon into the mud so he had his gun pointed at the small of Jersey's back as he yelled for the guy to freeze. Jersey kept his back to him and kept going deeper into the lake so McBride pointed his gun down toward the mud and grass in the shallow water near his shoes and fired one shot.

"That was the shot we had heard. A geyser of water and grass blew up. Jersey froze and turned around to face Bill. When I got to McBride he had Jersey face down on the grass, patting him down before bringing him over to join the others. McBride's face was set and sweaty, and he told me when I walked up that he'd had a couple of good shots at the puke while he was running through the lot, and he had wanted to waste the guy but the lot was crawling with people. He wanted to know if I couldn't pick a better place for our next shootout. What could I say? I knew exactly how he felt."

A few moments later the lot was filled with police cars and cops running around with their guns drawn and more people screaming and others crowded around the windows of the restaurant looking out to see the action. To them the windows were like large-screen television sets showing cops and robbers in real time. It took a few minutes, but finally things got sorted out. The four collectors were handcuffed and searched and ID'd, then stuffed into patrol units for the ride to jail. One young patrolman was doing his damndest to arrest Jack Long, who was loudly protesting that he was the *victim*. Al got them separated before the young cop could stuff his gun down Long's throat . . .

"I looked around the lot then as most of the backup officers were driving away. All quiet again. The knot of people that had formed to watch was breaking up, and things looked normal inside the restaurant. Just to be sure I asked Carlton before he was driven away if there were any more of his partners inside. I told him to tell me right then and for sure because if I went in there and found one . . . after I killed *that* one I'd come back out and kill him. He told me there were no more, just the four, and Toscano was with Powers. When I asked him where they were he just shook his head, he didn't know. I checked the inside of the restaurant, explained what had happened to the worried and unhappy manager and assured him it had nothing to do with his restaurant."

Fred Toscano was arrested later that day at the airport. The cast on his arm was clean and white. He would admit to nothing, but it didn't help him. There was a strong case on all of them. It turned out Ray Jersey was the prison escapee. He had been serving hard time for robbery and had been a fugitive for a couple of months. That would explain why he was reluctant to come out of the lake.

When they got him into the police station Jersey wanted to be real cooperative. It seemed McBride's warning shot had loosened more than the fugitive's bowels. He told Al about the drug deal and how Long had ripped them off. He added a new twist to the case when he stated that if the cops had allowed Carlton and Spatuzzi to walk away from the Cadillac with the briefcase they were all supposed to open up on Al and Long. It seemed Carlton wanted them dead as an example to others that he wasn't playing around, apparently with the approval of attorney Powers.

"We couldn't find Phillip Powers at his home or office, but he didn't wait to get into an armed confrontation with the police. He turned himself in to our office the next day, *his* attorney at his side. He seemed like a reserved type of guy, bookish even. He made no statement, of course, and went through the booking procedure like an old pro. He didn't know at that point that we already had confessions and statements from the rest of the group, who told us they were to be paid from three to five thousand dollars to get the money from Long. They all made bond except Jersey, the fugitive . . . the senator's son first. We prepared our case against them with a team from the State Attorney's office. Jack Long would be our key witness, along with my testimony, the tapes, confessions and statements.

"We never went to trial, though. Everyone charged pled guilty to *something*. They made deals . . . except for the escapee, who went right back to his former cubbyhole, and they all went away for varying lengths of hard time—even the lawyer. I thought the case should have been called The Clusterfuck, but I guess I'll settle on the O.K. Corral because of all the guns and bad guys and the tonnage of horseshit involved. More than one cop, friends, asked for months afterward why in the hell we went through all of that to cover the ass of a guy like Jack Long, who was one of *them* . . . for sure not one of us or even an innocent citizen. McBride and Stanley would just shrug and roll their eyes and point at me, as if the whole damned thing was *my* fault. That's okay . . . I guess I can take it, even if ol' Don Stanley did stay pissed off for weeks after the dust settled."

It seems Det. Don Stanley's undercover police car that he left on the side of Federal Highway was towed away by some young traffic cop while Don was feeding a knuckle sandwich to a dirtball with a gun in Denny's parking lot.

TARGET BLUE

I WAS OUT AND ABOUT with Al again, but this time we were on a static surveillance. He had received a request from a jurisdiction in northern Florida to watch an address where a man wanted for a double-murder might be hiding. They had information that the man had a former girlfriend who lived in our city and it was felt he might talk her into covering for him. The woman's apartment was located in the north end of town near Federal Highway, and Al backed his car into a busy restaurant lot a few hundred feet away. From there we could easily see the front door to the woman's apartment and her assigned parking space.

I knew Al was getting tired of sitting around my house talking, and this way I was able to spend some time with him as a "cop groupie." I wanted to start the story with a taped transcript of a meeting Al had had with a dope dealer who hired him to fill a contract. Al felt the transcript itself was too dry, didn't paint an in-depth picture of the meeting, so he wanted to augment it with his comments:

MALE VOICE: So you the really bad dude, huh? I ask around, you know, to those Hispanics I do business with, and I get your name. You the man that can do a job for me I'm told.

("He paused, looked me over carefully for the tenth time,

179

then slowly looked all around. It was after two in the morning and we sat in the front seat of a new Cadillac.")

MALE VOICE: But are you bad, white boy? You're like one of those eye*tal*lion guys, aren't you?

("I sighed, like I was bored. He picked his teeth with a gold toothpick he had taken out of a small leather pouch. Four of his teeth had shiny gold caps, and his clothes were understated, tailored and expensive. He looked out at the quiet night again and went on.")

MALE VOICE: So I'm told . . . you is a pro*fess*ional hitman. Twenty-five hundred for a job . . .

AL SMITH: Most of the time . . .

MALE VOICE: *Most* of the time . . . see, the thing is . . . my problems *began* when I dealt direct to a white boy. Did business with him on good faith . . . sold to him like I never do . . . and he turned out to be something *else* . . .

SMITH: I don't need to hear about your problems . . . I just need to hear about the job. Then I'll decide if I can help you.

("His eyes widened, and he turned his head slowly to look me in the face. I guess it was a thing he did as an intimidation tactic. His tough face, those intense angry eyes and his reputation made it effective. He looked at me and I felt a chill. I knew this was a man who would go down hard. He made a careful show of putting the gold toothpick away, making sure I saw the automatic under his left arm as he did. Then he nodded, still looking at me.")

MALE VOICE: Ooh, you must be very sure of yourself to talk to me like that, here in my car with two more cars close by with *my* guys in them . . . here in the fucking *heart* of my part of town.

("I shrugged. I'd cut my teeth as a young patrolman in the northwest section of town. It could be a tough place to work and to live, but I'd learned there were more good people living there than bad, and this hot shit I was talking with was one of the ones who made life miserable for everybody. I shrugged, and thought it was time to make my pitch and slide on out of there.")

SMITH: I meant no offense, I've heard of you on the street, and those who referred me to this job speak highly of you as a man not to be fucked with . . . you have a job for me, fine. Twenty-five hundred is what I get for a garden-variety hit, you understand? If there are difficult circumstances . . . or a special manner in which it is to be done, or if the target is of a special nature, then my price will go up. You . . . as a businessman . . . will understand this.

MALE VOICE: Sure, we'll talk about this like business. When you go talkin' about jackin' up the price you got to remember that you're not the only man out here who'll kill for me . . . or for money. You're a fucking white boy first, and I already don't like that. But there are *others*, white and Latino, who will do this job."

("He looked around again, listening to the night with his total concentration. All the windows in the car were down and I knew he would hear the squeak of a shoe a block away on this night.")

MALE VOICE: And of course there are *brothers* out here who would be glad to please me.

SMITH: Yeah, and you've heard that one about you get what you pay for. You got some important hit you want done, you gonna send one of those bozos you hire outta some bar? And your brothers? Even today a black man would have a hard time walking in and out of a place without being noticed and remembered.

MALE VOICE: Oh, you is so right, Mr. San-*et*-ti . . . that's why even though I'm talkin' to you and thinkin' about others for the job I'm still thinkin' seriously of doing *this* job myself. For the personal satisfaction, dig it?

("I nodded. He had just confirmed one of my greatest worries. A yellow taxi cab came down the street, slowed and turned south at the intersection nearest us. We both

stared at it until its tail lights faded into the night. Then he
went on.")

MALE VOICE: So here it is, my man. I *might* want you to hit
someone for me . . . we'll haggle the price . . . yeah . . .
but what concerns me more is if you've really got the balls
to do the job.

("I waited, looking at his face with a question on mine.")

MALE VOICE: A cop. I want you to kill a motherfucking narc
. . . a paddy little po-liceman.

Scotch and Water . . . that's what they were known as by
other narcs in the South Florida area. Hank MacGregor—tall
and dark blonde with a long face and shaggy hair. His partner
Daniel Waters—lean, slightly smaller than MacGregor and
muscular. Waters was a black man, sleek and usually well-
groomed. They were both in their middle twenties, had less
than five years as police officers and just over six months as
narcs. Waters was single but not often unaccompanied by some
sweet young thing. MacGregor was married to his high school
steady, and she was into a healthy midterm pregnancy.

Both young cops had a penchant for the current look, with
styled hair and the "right" clothes. But when working they had
already developed that effortless flexibility that good narcs pos-
sess. Depending on the street theatre to be acted on that night,
they could look like a pair of ex-fraternity brother yuppies looking for some smooth cocaine for a party, or two street-ragged
players in cheap dirty clothes who had just met on a corner to
score some crack. They had worn tight jeans and body shirts
and held hands while buying Quaaludes in the back room of a
gay bar, and they had pressed on temporary tattoos to go along
with their denims and leathers and motorcycles in order to buy
a stash of crank, or meth, or speed.

Yes, they also went together like scotch and water, this salt-
and-pepper team, one black and one white, which can work or
not work depending on the players. In a world of dope it is not
uncommon to see a white-and-black partnership, some kind of

crossover of cultures formed by the need and the greed. Salt-and-pepper teams were usually not forgotten, though, so they had to watch their backs constantly for that knowing stare, and the hands reaching for guns as some dirtbag said accusingly, "Hey . . . wait . . . I've seen you two before . . ." Not very healthy words for a couple of working narcs.

MacGregor and Waters were both still young and idealistic enough to go after the job with aggressive enthusiasm. They *believed* in their "war on drugs," and they took chances, stretched the envelope and put in the long hours. Waters had a personal thing about the crack dealers. He knew they were a cancer on the young black lives in his town, especially around his old neighborhood. He had grown up in the northwest section of Fort Lauderdale and knew first-hand and personal about crime waves and drug wars. He had grown up watching white police officers trying to slap city-directed band-aids over deep community problems, and he recognized the futility of it. Choosing to be a cop, working those same streets he had been raised on, was bad enough. Being a narc, out there trying to bust the crack monsters, was something else. MacGregor had learned early that all cops bleed the same color blood. He saw Waters as a partner, not as a black cop, and his quiet acceptance of Waters as a man helped bond their relationship. MacGregor just wanted to bust bad guys, what color they were didn't matter to him. Together they went out onto the streets to do what they could to rid the city of the poison, and the cancer.

RUFUS "ROCKMAN" ROCKER was twenty-seven-years-old, over six feet tall, a two-hundred-pound body consisting of muscle, bone and lots of scar tissue. His childhood of poverty and filth told him early on that he would have to take what he wanted, and early on he learned that force and intimidation could gain immediate results. Of course there was the law, an irritating and restricting factor in his apprentice years. He was an experienced burglar and car thief before he got to high school, and he only went there for less than a year as part of a sentencing deal handed down by a juvenile-division judge. At eighteen he had an arrest sheet that included violent armed robberies, more burglaries, a couple of rapes and drug possession.

Rufus Rocker's real education began when he was sentenced to a hard jail for the first time. Prison, and his fellow inmates, opened a whole new world for him, full of possibilities. Rocker was not stupid. He was hungry, and he listened when the experienced career criminals spoke. It didn't faze him that these success stories he listened to came from men behind bars. They had screwed up . . . he knew he wouldn't. He was a model prisoner and got an early release. As soon as he got back on the street he began to set up his little empire.

Drugs were so easy. Rocker wasted no time in getting on the payroll of a distribution operation. He saw that the guys actually selling the drugs on the street level were just day laborers in the trade, going nowhere. He worked as a courier, dropping off the dope, carrying the money back to his boss, passing messages or warnings to the troops. It took him only a couple of months to learn all he could about the group he was with—where they bought, where they sold, where they kept their stash and cash. Then he made his move.

To the cops it was just another drug-related homicide scene. To Rufus Rocker it was an important first step in his upwardly mobile career. Three bodies were found in a small, well-appointed home. The state-of-the-art security system in the house had been deactivated by the insertion of the correct code, and all three occupants of the house—two men and a woman—had been shot in the back of the head, execution style. The word on the street was that Rufus Rocker had come into his own. He had the cash and the connections, and soon had a whole network of street dealers selling his product. The three found dead had been the leaders of the group Rocker had been employed by; they were soon forgotten. The homicide detectives were "pretty sure" Rocker had killed them, but "pretty sure" doesn't cut it in court.

Rocker dealt in crack. The cooked cocaine sold as fast as he could cram it into capsules and send it out. The money came in, loads of dirty small bills. He floated a couple of businesses in the northwest part of town—a carwash, a rib stand, a laundromat. He had legitimate bank accounts and hidden safes stuffed with money. He was careful about his success, though . . . he showed style in a subdued way. He got his teeth fixed, had some nice classy jewelry and a sweet little Mercedes Benz coupe, and a new townhouse filled with all the electronic toys. But he was also cool, he didn't spend hot cash on outrageous and noticeable splurges. Other dealers, doing less volume, took more heat from the cops because of their jive flash and obvious drug-proceeds possessions. Rufus Rocker stayed relatively low, worked his business and tried to keep out of the limelight.

Which is not to say he had no problems. Many of his lower level sales people were users too, always getting jammed up, fighting with each other, trying to rip him off or getting busted. He dealt with them ruthlessly and efficiently, bonding them out if they were caught and convincing them that to talk to the cops about a deal was to die. The ones that tried to rip him off seemed to disappear. Now and then a body with no head and no genitals would be found in a dumpster in Miami or Palm Beach, and the street people would whisper that the Rockman had taken care of some business. He kept his midlevel and security staffs small and handpicked. He kept them loyal through good pay and convincing threats. Most of them were smart enough to recognize a sure thing, and stayed loyal to him within the code of the street.

Al and I were still watching the woman's apartment to see if her former boyfriend, now wanted for a double murder, would show his face. As we waited, Al told me how he first heard about Rufus Rocker and the contract-on-a-cop case:

"I hadn't worked street-level narcotics in a couple of years, I'd moved on to the international groups and then into Organized Crime and Intelligence, but I still liked to hear the stories that came from the cops that did. Most of them were young and still reckless. They fought hard, took chances to get results. One evening I went into our office a little early. I knew we would be surveilling some heavy-duty wiseguy that night and I wanted to study his file. I found a message from a narc sergeant on my desk. He wanted me to call him.

"He gave me some shit about trading in my jeans and boots for silk socks and alligator shoes since I was now going to dinner and all that with the 'olive-squeezers.' I told him he was right, but that I'd still rather be mucking out the stalls in some beaten-down stable. He said something about shit all being the same. Then he got into it. Asked me if I knew about a salt-and-pepper team he had working for him—Scotch and Water. Seems they had busted a real bad guy over in blacktown, some crack dealer with a long history of violence. I told him I didn't know the two young narcs but I'd heard of them.

"He tells me they're a couple of good ones, and they'd been working this dealer for a couple of months. The dealer was supposedly turning himself into the biggest distributor in the area, played real rough, all that. The narc sergeant said he knew I'd think this was small-time compared to all the big multimillion dollar international cases I'd worked—was he being sarcastic?—but this dealer was one of those rotten little bastards that sold to kids. He apparently didn't care if he was a thousand feet from a school or right in the cafeteria. He sold his stuff like popcorn, half his steady customers were high-school age or younger, and he even employed kids as lookouts and couriers. He tells me Scotch and Water were able to get close to this scumbag and busted his ass. The judge didn't know about the guy's background and gave him an easy bond. Now he was back out on the street with a good lawyer, *and* his operation intact.

"I asked the narc sergeant what the problem was. The guy took a fall, they'd get him again and eventually put him away for some hard time. The narc sergeant got kind of quieter then, and told me that this dealer had decided to 'break some of the rules.' Over the phone I could hear the sergeant take a long sip of something, booze or Pepto Bismol, I guessed. Seems the dealer had put the word out on the street that he wanted one of the cops hit that had busted him. He wanted to take out a narc. The sergeant was thoroughly pissed at the idea that this badass was looking for someone to fill a contract on a *cop*. I asked the sergeant the name of the dealer, and he told me it was one Rufus 'Rockman' Rocker.''

From Al's notes made while researching the case from narc-squad reports I learned more of it. MacGregor and Waters had heard a good deal about Rufus Rocker before they decided to try and bust him. Crack cocaine is high-profile stuff, big business on the street, and the inhabitants of all levels of the street talk about it openly. By levels of the street I mean those people who are down and dirty, those that actually work the streets; hookers, thieves, dope dealers and their customers. The next level would be of those legitimate business people who have shops along the sidewalks of the street. Their customers are generally not from the first level but are occasionally victims. Then there are those citizens who must live and work and go to school on and around the street. These people are often victims, and they are in many ways affected by the activities of the first level of street people every day. They cannot escape. The street and its actions flow around them constantly, and like the burbling waters of a stream, the word on what's happening out there is passed from mouth to mouth.

Scotch and Water heard the word about Rufus Rocker. He was just too big, too visible not to go after. Especially when they were told there was *no way* they could bust the Rockman . . . he was too insulated, too smart, too this, too damn that. Scotch and Water looked the thing over, then decided to approach the Rocker problem in the traditional way: get Rocker to sell them some dope, then bust him for it. They did their homework, they put in their time, they leaned (carefully) on the right people, and they got some help from luck . . . and Rocker's own ego.

First they did some surveillance on a popular crack sales area, targeting likely dealers. MacGregor hung back as Waters went in, made a small buy and got out. Each buy was documented, the crack cocaine tested and placed into evidence. Within a week the street dealers in the black section where the action took place were familiar and comfortable with Waters. They sold to him without a thought. During this time both narcs stayed away from Rufus Rocker's townhouse, businesses, hangouts . . . but they kept their ears to the ground to get the street gossip.

Finally, when they judged it was time, MacGregor went with Waters on a buy. The crack dealer didn't even take a second look . . . white people were some of his biggest customers on the corners there, driving in and out in their Audis and Beemers from their side of town. MacGregor went back again and was casually introduced to the dealers, and he asked for more crack, bigger buys. The dealers were happy to oblige. After two weeks the narcs had enough evidence to arrest on warrants at least a dozen crack dealers, but not a shred to link it to Rufus Rocker. It was time for the pressure, and the luck.

Scotch and Water approached a dealer they had a good working relationship with, having bought goodly amounts from him on a regular basis. On this hot busy night they told the dealer, an incredibly tall and skinny man called Balloon, that they wanted to buy a lot of crack, a *whole* lot. He just shook his head when he heard how much, but they pushed him. He tried to back off, telling them he couldn't get that much even if he went to *his* supplier. Well, asked the narcs, then who supplies the *supplier?* Who was the boss of that outfit? Balloon bit his lip, looked all around, then told them to come back later.

They were back in an hour, watching the cars come and go, the dealers standing at the edge of the street waving their ball caps and whistling at the prospective buyers. They moved into the shadows under an old tree with Balloon and spoke in low tones. Balloon's boss wanted to know the story on the white buyer. Waters remained silent as MacGregor made his pitch. He was from the North, he told the crack dealer, and he liked to supply the dealers in his hometown. He usually bought good crack in quantity and took it home with him rather than buying fine coke and processing it down himself. He normally did business with a group of Hispanics in Miami, but they had recently suffered some losses to the cops and gang warfare so he was afraid to go anywhere near them. He sometimes dealt with a supplier in Atlanta, he told Balloon, and Balloon's boss could check his credentials with that guy if he wanted.

Balloon wanted to know the dealer's name in Atlanta, and MacGregor told him on the streets the guy was known as The Saint but his last name was Dobbins and he hung out at a mixed bar called The Stage near the old downtown area. Then Balloon wanted to know how much they intended to spend, and when MacGregor told him he had ten thousand dollars, cash, and could do more if the first deal worked out, Balloon just said, 'You talk pretty big, white boy.'

Rufus Rockman Rocker thought it sounded like a load of bull too, but his interest was piqued. Truth was, he was bored, the summer had been long, too hot and too steady. The dope went out, the money came in, his control over his turf was almost total and that was it. Sure, there were some new groups forming, fringe gangs wanting the action, stealing a piece here and there, waiting for the Rockman to stumble so they could grab his business as he fell. But he was so strong, and had his act together, and he knew he wouldn't stumble.

So now here comes this white boy, steady customer, hangs with a brother, and the street dudes don't smell cop on either of them. Now they wanted to buy heavy, and they still didn't insist on *meeting* him, Rockman, the boss. That was a good sign. Cops would have wanted to deal only with the top dog, but these guys just wanted the dope, and only asked about the boss when the street dealer acted like the deal was too big.

Rockman searched his memory about his trips and business dealings in the Atlanta area, and he did remember the guy called The Saint. Yeah. So he got on the phone, and on the second night of talking to the manager of The Stage Lounge he made contact with Dobbins, The Saint. Over the music and laughter in the background Rocker heard The Saint tell him he knew who *he* was, and did he want to do some business or what? Rocker told him he would, eventually, but first he had this little question about a buyer.

What follows is from a tape transcript but not an FLPD tape:

DOBBINS: What that question be . . . ?

RUFUS ROCKER: White boy with a brother, Mac and Danny they call themselves. Want to buy a goodly amount of product . . . and give me your name as a reference.

DOBBINS: Mac and Danny? Black man very sharp, white boy kind of dumb?

ROCKER: Uh . . . yeah . . .

DOBBINS: . . . but the white boy has the money? He's the one really doin' the business?

ROCKER: Yeah.

DOBBINS: Shit yeah . . . I know those two . . . did some business with them a couple of months ago . . . up here in *my* town. Their money was good, and there was no bull-shit.

ROCKER: No cops?

DOBBINS: Fuck you talkin' about, man? Cops? You think I would have sold to them if they was *cops?* No man. They did all right by me.

ROCKER: Okay, my man. I appreciate your time.

DOBBINS: No problem, blood.

Rufus Rocker hung up the phone thinking that these new buyers might be for real. It would be kind of fun to unload a good load of product for some hard cash for a change. Why should those Hispanics down in Miami have all the easy deals? He let Balloon know the deal was on, and how to set it up.

Scotch and Water couldn't know at that time, and Rufus Rocker couldn't know, just how lucky the cops were with The Saint, Dobbins. Daniel Waters had given Dobbins' name to MacGregor to pass on to Balloon because he had worked a scam in Atlanta some months back while on loan to the Georgia Department of Law Enforcement Drug Task Force. He had been assigned a white partner at that time and made several buys from Dobbins, but was sent back to Fort Lauderdale with a Letter of Commendation for his help before any of the warrants were served in the wide-ranging Georgia investigation.

When Rocker called Dobbins, The Saint had already been busted and leaned on until he agreed to work with the cops in Atlanta. Possibly because of the recent pressures in his life, Dobbins had also begun using his own product, and was consequently whacked-out much of the time. When he found himself on the phone with some dude down in Fort Lauderdale asking about a black-and-white team that wanted to buy dope, he wasn't sure if it was something the cops had told him to cooperate on or not. He really didn't know *what* he was saying when he gave Rocker the green light on Scotch and Water.

But the deal was on, and Balloon told MacGregor to be at the Burger King on Broward Boulevard at nine that night. He told the narc not to worry about who would be there, just to bring the money and he'd get the product. The man MacGregor was to see would be sitting in a light blue rental car. MacGregor was to go to the car and get into the passenger side carrying a paper bag with the money in it. Balloon said Waters could be there too, but he had to sit in the restaurant on the south side, near the windows where he could be seen. Balloon also told them if there was even any smell of cops or a ripoff or anything like that, there would be enough shooting to kill everyone at that hamburger place. Did they understand?

The narcs were busy and short-handed as usual, but they managed to put a small surveillance team into the Burger King parking lot and two inside the restaurant. The team in the lot had a video setup and would monitor the wire worn by MacGregor. He would wear it in his crotch, like Al does, and hope Rocker wasn't one of those who insist he show him his nuts.

They were all in position before nine, and right on the hour Rufus Rocker pulled in and parked on the south side of the lot in a small, light blue rental. By this time Waters, who was sitting inside, had already picked out another car sitting in the corner of the lot in the shadows with three guys in it . . . backup for Rocker. He felt he was being eyeballed by two inside the restaurant as well. He watched as MacGregor stood in front of the doors, looked around and walked slowly to the rental car. As MacGregor got in the tape was rolling:

HANK MACGREGOR: You Balloon's boss?
RUFUS ROCKER: Does it matter? You just sit there and keep your mouth shut now.

Waters and the other surveillance cops watched as Rocker drove the rental car, with MacGregor as his passenger, out of the lot. The car made a right on Broward Boulevard, passed the old burned-out shoestore-that-became-a-church, and was gone. Waters stood and headed for the front doors. The cops in the surveillance van video'd the car driving away, then got on their radios on a covert channel to see if they could get an unmarked chase car to tail the rental. Narcs always know the bad guy isn't going to play a set scenario and that they must stay flexible, but sometimes there just aren't enough people or cars. Before they could act they got lucky again.

Waters saw them first and went back to his seat by the window. The rental car pulled into the lot slowly, having apparently made a circle of the block. Rocker's countersurveillance worked too well. If he had given the cops another ten seconds they would have had the van and at least one other car criss-crossing the side streets looking for him, and he would have made them. As it was, he saw no activity at all, observed the black part of the buying team inside the restaurant where he was supposed to be, and got a no-action signal from *his* covering team in the car parked in the shadows.

From tape transcript:

RUFUS ROCKER: *(Shutting off car engine)* Seems like a peaceful night.

HANK MACGREGOR: Yep.

ROCKER: It will stay quiet if you brought exactly what you said you would . . . the exact amount.

MACGREGOR: Oh, it's all here, no problem. A deal is a deal. Here's the mon—

ROCKER: . . . Shut your mouth. Open the top of the bag. Good, uh-huh. Now close it up.

MACGREGOR: Where's the uh . . . ?

ROCKER: Be cool, brother . . . I got a little speech I got to make first.

(Pause. Sound of breathing and then tearing fabric)

ROCKER: I don't see no hidden *micro*phone, white boy . . . how about a gun?

MACGREGOR: Uh . . . no. Sometimes I carry one in Miami . . . but not tonight.

ROCKER: That's good, because I don't like buyers that carry guns or wear hidden mikes, dig it? Listen here. I'm takin' that bag and I'm gettin' out of the car. I'll leave you the keys—

MACGREGOR: But what about—

ROCKER: I said *listen*. Either key will open the *trunk*, dig it? If I even think you're a fucking cop, or if some dudes come out of their hiding places yelling all kinds of freeze fucking po- lices and all that shit . . . *or* I see your partner there inside make like he's gonna come out with a gun and take this bag away as you drive off with this car . . . If I smell *any* of that shit, my guys waiting in this parking lot will get out of their cars and start shootin' like you've never seen before. They got shotguns and Uzis, brother, and oh my, they *do* like to shoot them. *Understand?*

MACGREGOR: Jesus. I thought those pepper bellies in Miami were gunhappy. Look, I just want to do this deal, make some money, and if everything goes right, do it again . . . in a month or so. Maybe bigger next time.

ROCKER: We'll see about next time, white boy. Just leave the car at Zayre's on the other side of I-95, with the keys under the mat.

Rufus Rocker walked away with a bag full of money. Mac-Gregor waited for a few moments, then started the rental car and drove off, taking care for the first couple of miles to insure he wasn't followed. He then went to a prearranged meeting place, waiting while Waters obtained a judge's signature on a hastily prepared search warrant, and then used the key to open the trunk. The dope was all there, neatly packaged. Later he dropped the car off at the Zayre's lot, and went back to the narc office.

Scotch and Water worked all that night putting their case together. They were sure they had made the right decision at the Burger King. To move in on it like a simple buy-bust would have been very dangerous, Rocker himself had made that clear. There were just too many innocent bystanders around. It could have turned into a real mess. Then there was the dope in the trunk. To bust Rocker right there might be seen as premature by the court, so they let him walk away and got the warrant before looking into the trunk. They knew where to find him, and they set about preparing the arrest warrants they would need to bring him down.

They had photos of him leaving his townhouse that night to go to the meeting. They had him on video and tape in the rental car at the time of the deal. He had told MacGregor, in an oblique way, to look in the trunk for the dope. The money had been carefully marked for later recovery. They packaged the whole deal on paper, got the State Attorney's approval, and a judge signed on the dotted line. They had arrest warrants for Rocker and, under RICO, could seize his car, and maybe even his townhouse after they searched it under warrant.

The Northwest Raiders, a hard-hitting street level narcotics task force, hit Rufus Rocker at six in the morning, three days after he climbed out of the light blue rental car. He was slow in answering the door to his townhouse so they took it down and charged in, finding him crouched near the side of his bed, his face creased from sleep but his eyes wide open . . . awake, aware, angry.

He froze when ordered to do so by half a dozen armed cops, and did not resist when he was handcuffed and made to sit in a corner. Under the bed, near where his hands had been as he crouched there, the officers found a loaded and cocked Mac-10 automatic machine pistol. On the bed they found a very pretty, and very scared, fifteen-year-old runaway from Minnesota.

A search of the house uncovered more weapons, a fair amount of cash, including the bag of money from the deal stuffed apparently untouched on top of a bedroom closet, and a small amount of fine cocaine. It was all seized, and the car was towed even though it was clean. Rocker was allowed to dress, then taken in and booked by MacGregor and Waters on narcotics, weapons and child-delinquency charges. He kept silent throughout, his only emotion showing in his eyes as he stared intently at Hank MacGregor.

Within hours of Rufus Rocker's lawyer posting his bond there was a ripple of excitement tinged equally with glee and dread on the street. News of the Rockman's arrest was interesting enough, his bonding out routine. But what came next put some electricity into the atmosphere.

The word was out that the Rockman was now looking for a hitman.

Rocker's status as a successful street monster *obliged* him to take some kind of action. Just as he had risen over the bodies of his former employers, there were those among his ranks who would jump at a chance to take his place. There were also more outside his ranks waiting, waiting for their time to set up shop on what was once his turf. There was no halfway in the law of his jungle . . . or the law of the street. To stumble, to be ripped off, to be arrested by the narcs . . . these things showed weakness. And any sign of weakness brought on the predators. Rufus Rocker knew the rules, and now he knew he had to *act*. He could not show *any* cracks in his armor.

Of course, not all the street monsters were stupid either. Killing a cop because he busted you would definitely be a macho and effective way of showing everyone how bad you were, but the heat it would surely bring would shut you down anyway. Rocker put out the word that he needed a professional hitman. He sent the word *up* through his suppliers, correctly guessing that the upper-level people would have access to the real thing and not some crackhead street shark looking to make a fast buck.

As we sat in Al's car, still watching the former girlfriend's apartment, he looked at his watch, then began talking about what happened after Rufus Rocker's arrest.

"My life became even more complicated than ever because of Rufus Rocker and his desire to kill his arresting officer. Not only would I be going out to meet with him . . . if he took the bait sent down . . . as the man who would fill the contract on the cop, I was *also* assigned as part of the team that would provide security for Hank MacGregor. Security against *me*, for Christ's sake.

"It turned out they had plenty of security without me, so I could turn most of my attention to being a hitman. MacGregor's pregnant wife, already not too pleased with the world her husband worked in, already scared about the chances he took, already doubting the ability of the department to protect him, was talked into moving from their small house for a couple of weeks as a 'routine precaution.' She went to stay with her mother somewhere in North Florida. Hank drove her up there."

Now, instead of acting, they all had to wait, to react *after* the other guy made the first move. It didn't sit well with any of them. Hank's partner, Daniel Waters, had his hands full trying to keep MacGregor from charging into Rocker's turf for a showdown. Then they got a break.

Rufus Rocker was suffering a temporary cash slump, what with his having to pay a cash bond, his lawyer demanding most of his fee up front (no dummy), and his recent loss of crack cocaine and money to the cops. He had to deal fast and heavy to get himself solvent again, to get himself strong. The lion's share of his street dealers had been busted or were in hiding, but even if they were all out there the income from the nickel-and-dime stuff would be too small, too slow. He needed a big score, now.

And now there was a dude out of Miami. A black Hispanic. He let one of Rocker's mid-level suppliers know he was hungry and wanted to buy. The word that got to Rocker was that the Miami suppliers were spooky because of some federal task force investigations and no one wanted to do a fast deal for a sizable amount. The Miami dude was told to go north to Fort Lauderdale, where the Rockman might be able to do something with him. The Rockman was ready, he *needed* to sell to someone *fast*.

The Miami dude was one Reginald Fuentes, known as Fast Reggie on the street. He dealt mostly in drugs, weapons and girls, and he tried to get along with everyone. He was so busy being popular, and so diversified, that he kept running into cops . . . state, local and federal. It got to the point where even his lawyer told him he was going to go bye-bye for some serious time as a career criminal if he didn't somehow please the cops and the prosecutor. He had charges pending from several different agencies, and he told them all . . . narcs, special agents, deputies . . . that he wanted to "work something out."

Al just shook his head in wonder as he talked about Fast Reggie.

"A friend of mine who works for the Florida Department of Law Enforcement called our office to see if there was some scam we could run with 'his informant.' This guy Fuentes was like a girl engaged to the whole friggin' football team. I took the call, and even while we spoke I could see the possibilities. Rocker needed to work some quick business for cash, he wouldn't even look at a white buyer, and he was too wired now for us to try and connect him with one of our local CI's. This case had started with drugs, and now another drug deal would be needed to allow Rocker to carry on, and the cash from any

new deal would help him finance the planned hit on a cop. Ol'
Fast Reggie might be the answer."

What follows is from tape transcript, fixed terminal to cellular (augmented):

AL SMITH: Twenty-five thousand dollars.
  (Traffic noises, sound of breathing)
RUFUS ROCKER: Man . . . you is some kind of bullshit mother-
  fucker. Twenty-five thou—
SMITH: I told you when we met the first time I'm for real and
  I'll do the right thing on this job. The question is whether
  or not you can afford me, or if you're as big as you say you
  are.
ROCKER: What the fuck you mean by that? I'm the *man* out
  here, hear me? This is . . . my . . . turf, I run it and I can
  afford you *if* you're worth it.
SMITH: Maybe the job's not worth it.
    ("My first obligation was still the safety of my proposed
  target.")
SMITH: *(Continuing)* Maybe trying to hit this guy isn't good
  business. Shit, getting taken down by these guys is just part
  of the whole thing, isn't it? You've been busted before, you
  know it's not a personal thing with the fucking cops . . .
  it's all part of the game.
    ("I had called Rocker's businesses, leaving a message that
  Al wanted to talk, and after two days a woman called with
  a number that turned out to be a cellular portable. It
  sounded like Rocker was driving around with his windows
  down as we talked.")
ROCKER: Look. I don't have time to explain a lot of things to
  you . . . Al. But . . . sure, I've been busted before and I
  know about the game and all that shit. But this motherfucker came right down into *my turf.* The man done played
  me for a fool, fucking bought from me and then came and
  . . . took me outta my *bed.* I can't let that kind of thing go
  unanswered . . . no way.

SMITH: Yeah, I can see why you'd be pissed . . . especially now with the other players out there lookin' at you like it might be time to take what you've got—

ROCKER: Fuck you, man. Nobody's goin' to take over nothin'! And what's it to you anyway? I'm hiring you for a job, not a lecture. And we're talkin' price, okay?

SMITH: Okay, man . . .

ROCKER: Your price is too high, but maybe we can work something out. Call me again tomorrow . . . same time, same number.

(Disconnect)

"Meanwhile, the narcs took charge of Reginald Fuentes," Al said, "but they kept us all advised as to progress. Everyone involved was getting settled in to the long hours. The surveillance on MacGregor's back was tight. Waters reported that if something didn't happen soon his partner was going to go apeshit, and we all knew how he felt. Fortunately our man Reggie worked on the case like he *enjoyed* working with the narcs.

"Rufus Rocker took the bait and agreed to make a heavy sale to Reggie from Miami. He even let Reggie pick the time and place, inside Rocker's turf, of course. On my next contact with Rocker he set up a meet with me for that night. It was all coming together . . . he wanted to meet me *right after* he did his deal with fast Reggie. More than coming together, this thing was coming full circle. Rocker sold drugs for a living, got busted big-time by a local narc, which could drive him right out of business. And now was going to sell *more* drugs not only to stay in business but also to pay for the murder of the narc. All the pieces had to fit, or none of it would fly. We wanted to put Rocker away on the narcotics charges, sure, but in my role as hired killer I needed Rocker to feel cash-heavy enough to afford my expensive hit on the narc that had shamed him. The fact that he'd scheduled his meet with me right after his meet with Reggie would help me with the overt act part of any murder-conspiracy charge. He intended to get the money, and he intended for me to kill for him, and it looked like it might all come together in one tight little ball."

Rufus Rockman Rocker was just a little too hungry and angry on that night. He had become paranoid about his own security and courier people . . . he knew intimately how they could advance their own careers, just as *he* had. So he elected to keep his plans to himself. He didn't even pay attention when the Miami guy picked an alley behind an auto-parts store for the exchange location. It was in the heart of Rocker's territory, and he knew every nook and cranny of it. He knew the best ways in and out, the best places to park, the best dark spots to sit in and watch, all the operational stuff. But he missed something in his then state of anxiety. One block over from the alley was a school. Every good dope dealer knows about the recent laws shaped to hammer anyone selling drugs in close proximity to a school. There were mandatory sentencing parts of the law . . . it was another way for the judges to get tough, and it worked. Rocker should have known, but he was just a little too caught up in catching up. . . .

Al and I were torn away from the Rockman's story now. The woman whose apartment we were staking out in case her ex-boyfriend, wanted for murder, was there, came out and got into her car. Al followed her as she left the side roads and drove out onto the highway. She headed for a drugstore a few miles away, and when she pulled into the lot, got out of her car and went inside, Al sent me in after her. He wanted to know what she purchased. When we came out, and as we followed her back to her apartment, I told Al the woman had gone to the counter with only a few items, mostly female-hygiene products, also a pint of ice cream and a copy of Cosmopolitan magazine. No men's razors or extra toothbrushes or anything like that. It didn't prove he *wasn't* at her apartment, but it didn't point to it either. We took up our earlier point of surveillance after she parked and went back into her apartment. Then Al got back into the Rockman case:

Fast Reggie wore a wire during his meeting for the exchange

with Rocker, but it didn't get much. They stood between their two cars in the alley. The cars were parked nose to nose.

REGINALD FUENTES: Hey, brother, I'm glad to be doin' business with you here in Lauderdale, nice and peaceful.

RUFUS ROCKER: Yeah. You got the money?

FUENTES: Right here in the trunk of my car. Just the amount we agreed on.

ROCKER: What you want is in the trunk of *my* car, dig? Why don't we both take a look, make sure it's cool and then bring it on up and drive away?

FUENTES: Sure. We can visit a few minutes if you want. I'd like to do more business—

ROCKER: Save it. Open the trunk of your car. Mine's open. Take a look, then walk back to your car with the stuff and get out of here. I'll do the same. Believe this, brother, I'm so fucking wired right now that if there's something wrong with the amount in your trunk or if you even *think* about ripping me off I'll blow you out of your fucking shoes and they'll find you with your fucking balls in your throat. Understand?

FUENTES: Shit, man, I'm here to do business, not have you break bad in my face.

With this enlightened exchange, they did the deal. Fuentes got the dope out of Rocker's car, and Rocker got the bag full of marked bills out of the Miami man's rental. They walked around the passenger side of each other's car, watching each other carefully, and climbed behind the wheels of their own cars simultaneously. Fuentes began backing out of the alley first, then turned his car at an angle, threw it into "park" and lay down on the seat. Rocker, himself reversing out of the alley, didn't notice Fuentes's move at first, then slowed as he did. That was when Al pulled into the alley behind Rocker, and the Rockman's car lurched to a stop as it bumped into Al's.

Now the stretched parallel wires of greed and revenge, woven and knotted in their symbiotic motivation, had come to their breaking point. The sale of poison had reaped the proceeds for murder, and Al had to act right now to fulfill the *real* mission of his deadly game. No need or time to play any further.

Rocker's instincts told him what was happening. His hand was already preparing to pull his car into "drive" so he could stomp on the gas pedal and pull away from whatever was behind him. He would accelerate through the alley and smash Fuentes's car out of his way if he had to. But he glanced into his rearview mirror for one split second and saw Al Sanetti getting out of his car. It made him hesitate, confused.

From tape transcript (augmented):

RUFUS ROCKER: What the fuck are you doin' here *now?*
("Rocker said this as I walked quickly up beside the driver's door of his car. His windows were down, as was his habit, and he turned his face to glare at me.")

ROCKER: *(Continuing)*You ain't supposed to get with me for another fifteen minutes, man. And how'd you know . . . ?
("His eyes widened . . . maybe he could hear the sounds of running men coming for him. I was two feet away and saw the look in his eyes change. I'd seen it before. I stuck my gun hard up against his teeth and then into his mouth as I grabbed his throat with my left hand. My face was inches from his as I talked into it.")

AL SMITH: You got to really *freeze* now Rockman. If you *twitch* . . . if I feel the car even *rattle*, I'll take your head right off. Look at me, Rocker. Look into my eyes and *listen*. I'll *kill* you, asshole . . . *understand?*
("Rocker understood . . . and so he lived that night.")

Al and I wrapped up his surveillance on the woman in her apartment, and since there had been no further activity to be seen he drove me back to my house and we sat in my driveway as he finished the dual story of the Rockman-Fast Reggie deal and the Rockman-Al Sanetti hit on a cop.

Even Rufus Rocker's high-powered lawyer couldn't do him much good (and maybe didn't try as hard as before, knowing his client was now out of the money-making business for a while and thus unable to pay for good representation). The charges were too strong, his miscalculations too costly. The bond on the original charges was revoked, the new charges were piled on (including the special caveat about selling near a school), and the judge was advised of all that had transpired since the last time the Rockman had stood before him.

The judge was already unhappy that Rocker had abused the court's trust by continuing his criminal activities while out on bond, and when he saw the Solicitation for Murder charges he really gassed up his gavel. He hammered Rocker with an impossible bond while the former heavy-hitter sat morosely in jail coveralls, studying his manicured nails.

"The court system is never a sure thing," Al said, "but it looked like Rocker would stay in jail until his trial date, and the case against him was so strong he'd probably try to plea out on a deal anyway. The prosecutor assigned to the case also knew about the planned hit on a cop, and promised us Rocker would not get any reduced time deals from him.

"Rocker hadn't even settled into his cell this time before the street erupted for a week of turf wars. Opportunists from inside Rocker's old organization and new guys who had been waiting in the wings charged in to pick over the carcass and set up their new operations. The king is dead . . . long live the king.

"Scotch and Water went back to their world, still tight, still an effective team. I heard later that Hank MacGregor had promised his wife he would transfer out of the narc squad after the baby was born, but some guys find it hard to shed that skin, you know? I went back to Organized Crime, and hoped I would never again be hired to kill a cop."

I stood in my drive as Al drove down the street, his car, and himself, blending into the night.

ULTIMATE REVENGE

AL SMITH HAD JUST COME to my small office from court, and was wearing a suit and tie. He looked very professional, very sharp, but still intimidating. Actually, somehow conventional clothes seemed to intensify his aura of latent physical power, and I was aware again of his formidable presence. He leaned toward a pile of notes and transcripts on the desk next to my typewriter.

"I'm glad we saved this one for last. To me it's like a perfect example of the type of case I specialize in. The deal was very clear-cut and the suspect accepted Al Sanetti and contracted with him to do the job. That, and the . . . I don't know . . . *feelings* I had while we worked the damned thing. I got the case after it got a telephone rejection slip from our big brothers in the FBI."

What follows is from the informal tape transcript (not FLPD tape or transcription):

AGENT SANTIAGO: Federal Bureau of Investigation, Special Agent Santiago.

MALE VOICE: Uh, yes. I want to report a crime . . . I think it's going to be a murder, or at least an aggravated assault.

SANTIAGO: You *think* it's going to be?

MALE VOICE: Yes.

SANTIAGO: Has the crime occurred yet?

MALE VOICE: No, uh, I've been called by someone who wants to hire me to hurt someone else.

SANTIAGO: What is your name, please?

MALE VOICE: Polk, uh, Bob Polk. This guy has called me several times from Orlando and he wants to hire me to hurt some woman up there.

SANTIAGO: All right, Mr. Polk, and where do you live?

POLK: I live in Fort Lauderdale, but this guy is calling me from Orlando, and that's where the victim is.

SANTIAGO: Mr. Polk, to your knowledge, has this person hurt anyone yet?

POLK: Not to my knowledge, no sir, but he's *trying* to hurt them, or he's trying to hire me to do it for him . . . for pay.

SANTIAGO: How did he get your name, Mr. Polk? Why would he call you?

POLK: I don't know. I'm not a hitman or anything like that.

SANTIAGO: Hold on a moment, will you, Mr. Polk?

(Music: Carly Simon)

SANTIAGO: *(Continues)* This is Special Agent Santiago again, Mr. Polk. We won't be able to respond to this report, and I suggest you call your local police authorities and report it to them.

POLK: The FBI won't respond? The local cops are gonna tell me to call the Orlando cops? I thought you guys could handle a case anywhere—

SANTIAGO: Report the phone calls you've been getting to the Fort Lauderdale police, Mr. Polk. I'm sure they have someone there who can help you. Good day.

(End of tape)

Bob Polk fumed a few minutes after his FBI rejection, and then he called the cops. He was bounced around from extension to extension, but finally found himself speaking with Capt. José Garcia, Al's boss. Garcia recognized the jurisdictional problems immediately but he also heard the sincerity and fear in Bob Polk's voice. He determined there was enough about the call to look into it.

"I was just finishing up an afternoon delight that consisted of opening doors and waiting for a bomb to go off," Al said. "One of our local big-time road-developers had received several bomb threats that morning and they were specific enough to get him worried. He too called the cops, and I was dispatched along with the rest of the Bomb Squad. We checked his house first, then spent hours crawling around each of the five cars in his driveway. After a look over, under and around we opened the drivers' doors with a hook attached to a line, then opened the hoods and checked the wiring.

"Nothing went boom, the whole deal was apparently a hoax and I noticed when I got back to the office that my hands didn't shake if I sat on them. Garcia then sent me off to see Bob Polk, and I went happily on my way, enjoying the air that I breathed —it was sweet without a mixture of sweat and gunpowder.

"When I pulled up in front of the Polks' apartment address in central northeast Lauderdale I saw it was in the middle of a seriously low-income neighborhood. Here and there on the corners stood a motley collection of pimps, hookers and crack dealers in hot competition with each other over customers. Garcia had briefed me on the Polks. They were known to be constantly supportive of our department's efforts to bust the bad guys in that area. Polk had even been given a letter of appreciation from the Chief for his help in the past. I went in to meet the concerned citizen.

"First thing Polk wanted to know was if I was some kind of expert at this kind of stuff as he looked over my ID. I told him FLPD did employ a contract killer. Me. He acted like he was hoping to see a smile on my face, didn't see one and told me to make myself comfortable. Then he got into it.

"He began by telling me about the FBI phone call as his wife

—her name was Laurie—brought us iced tea. I told him to start from the beginning as if I hadn't been briefed. So he told me this guy had been calling the house. First couple of times he spoke with Laurie, said he had a special job he wanted Bob Polk to do for him. Polk had Laurie put him off because he figured it was some kind of crank caller, but when the guy kept calling, Polk finally spoke with him. He told Polk he wanted him to hurt or kill somebody . . . throw acid in their faces, bust up their bones, 'do away' with a person. Polk said he felt then that someone's life was being threatened, so he called the feebies, then us.

"I asked him if the caller identified himself, and Polk said the guy's name was 'Art Ball,' or 'Art from Orlando.' The guy told Polk he wanted 'a vendetta' . . . he wanted Polk to 'bust a spine, break some bones, throw acid in a face.' I asked Polk who this guy wanted this stuff done to. Polk said it was some woman with children, but the guy wasn't sure about the kids. He definitely wanted the lady to suffer permanent damage. The guy told Polk it had to be something that could not be fixed by doctors—'forever damage,' he called it. He said the woman would come home to her place around midnight, possibly with another man, and if that happened Polk was to 'take the guy out' so he could then 'take out the woman and make her quiet.'

"Laurie broke in then and said after the guy said that, Polk began to think the guy was truly serious, no crank call. I wanted to know how 'Art from Orlando' had the Polks' phone number, and what made him think Polk did this sort of work. Polk told me that when he lived out West he was a bounty hunter. He worked for bail bondsmen, trying to find people who had skipped out leaving the bondsman holding the bag. Polk insisted he was a law-abiding citizen. He said he'd apprehended people plenty of times but he had never filled a hit contract. He went on about what a good guy and clean citizen he was until I held up a hand and stopped him. I asked again why this guy thought Polk might do this. Polk said the guy told him he'd gotten Polk's name from an acquaintance out West. Polk had passed out a ton of business cards when he was working, and thought maybe 'Art' had come across one. He guessed 'Art' saw the card that said 'bounty hunter' on it and figured Polk did other things too.

"I told them I wanted to hear the tapes that Captain Garcia had said they had made of some of the conversations with this guy. Laurie put the tape in the machine, and the three of us listened in silence. I didn't know Polk, or much about him, but I became a believer after listening to only a few minutes of 'Art from Orlando.' Something in that voice . . . strung out over the long-distance telephone, sounded real to me. Real and bad and twisted. I nodded at Bob and Laurie Polk when the tape ran out."

At that point it didn't matter to Al if the caller had been in Orlando or Anchorage. He was out there, and he fully intended to do those things he was trying to hire Polk for. If it wasn't Polk, or Al, it would be someone else. Al knew, because of the jurisdiction, that this thing could be kicked to the Orlando authorities, but now he had direct contact with the Polks and sensed that would be valuable later when Polk tried to sell Al to 'Art from Orlando.'

"Polk told me," Al said, "that the guy had already made flight arrangements for him to fly up there and meet him. He had set it up so Polk could pick up an Eastern ticket at the Fort Lauderdale airport for the trip to Orlando. I told him we'd go get the ticket together, but he wouldn't be going to Orlando to meet Art Ball . . . Al Sanetti would."

TWO DAYS LATER Al stood on the long concourse near Gate Eleven, in the Orlando International Airport, waiting for the passengers on Eastern Flight #726 from Fort Lauderdale to begin deplaning. He had been in Orlando since before noon, and it was now almost six in the evening. He had an overnight bag and wore a small transmitter in his crotch.

There was a bustle of activity, and the passengers began emerging from the airway door. Grandmothers and uncles and business partners and college buddies and whole families, mom and dad and the kids, hurried out. Because of security (thank you terrorist dirtballs all over the world) there was no one to meet them at the end of the concourse. They looked for the arrow above their heads that pointed toward "Terminal" and "Baggage," and they turned left and began moving in that direction, some in purposeful strides, some in trudging acceptance of a return to a place they didn't want to be, and many in excited awkwardness, especially the young. The families on vacation, faces beaming, marched off toward that wonderful place where the mouse had his kingdom. Al couldn't help smiling as he watched them flow around him, but his smile faded as he joined them.

Al's partner, Bill McBride, was standing at a rental-car counter, casually dressed and speaking with a very pretty girl about something that had her giggling. He had flown to Orlando with Al on the morning flight, but now he appeared to ignore Al as he entered the terminal-lobby area of the airport. Orange County Det. Bill Rawlings, a heavy-set redheaded man in a rumpled lightweight suit, sipped coffee morosely at a cluttered counter. His partner, Det. Steve Ray, a thin, neatly dressed man with wavy brown hair carefully brushed back off his forehead, appeared to be browsing around a paperback-book rack at a newsstand. Al had spoken with Rawlings by phone the night before, briefing him on what they had. He and Ray had met McBride and Al when they deplaned earlier. They had discussed the case, made some working plans and tried to get to know one another by telling bullshit stories about their hometowns, like all cops do.

Detective Rawlings had cross-referenced the phone number "Art from Orlando" had given the Polks, and it turned out to be an extension at a city hall of a small town adjacent to Orlando. That morning he and Ray told Al and McBride they had a tentative identity on Art Ball. He was a clerk of some kind in the city hall, he drove a new black Firebird, and his name was Arthur Baldwin . . .

"Arthur Baldwin waited for me near the exit to the parking area. He gave me a grin and a wave and seemed to be looking me over carefully as I walked up to him. He was in his late thirties, about six feet, slender, maybe one-seventy-five, had real blue eyes and shaggy light brown hair. He wore a cowboy style shirt, jeans and boots, and as I approached he said, 'Hello, Bob.'

"I handed him one of Polk's bounty-hunter cards and asked him if he was Art Ball. He nodded as he took the card, then flipped it over and read what Polk had written on the back. His grin went away, and he had a guarded look as he asked me to wait a minute. I watched as he headed for a bank of pay phones nearby. I didn't see McBride or Detective Ray, and guessed they had already slipped out into the parking lot to get into their unmarked car. Rawlings still sipped his coffee, apparently not paying any attention to me or Baldwin.

"I had prepared the Polks for this phone call, and stood there hoping they wouldn't blow it. Polk was supposed to tell Baldwin that I was his trusted partner, a pro who took these jobs frequently. He, Polk, had been ill for some time so he had sent me in his place. My name was Al Sanetti, Baldwin could trust me and I was just the man for the job he wanted done.

"A couple of minutes later Baldwin hung up the phone and walked back to me. The smile was back in place. He stuck out his hand, called me 'Al Sanetti' and apologized for calling me Bob. He said he was glad I was there, and we walked out into the late afternoon sun. We didn't speak as we headed for his car, which was parked in a taxi lane nearby. He unlocked it, ignored the taxi dispatcher, who was glaring at him, and reached through the car to unlock my side. I threw my overnight bag into the back seat and folded myself into the passenger side. I thought Baldwin's black Firebird looked a lot like my Z-28, but as he drove I looked around at the unfamiliar road and highway signs, the hustle-bustle of boomtown Orlando, the rolling terrain and incredible amount of new construction going on, and reminded myself I was for *sure* not in the friggin' driver's seat.

"Baldwin wanted to know about my association with Bob

Polk, and I told him Bob and I had been involved in the martial arts for years. We had become friends, things evolved to where we began doing specialized work about three years ago and we'd done several deals since then. Baldwin just listened. We drove in silence for a while, then he asked if the Polks had giving me any info on *this* job. As I told him I had just a hazy idea of what the job was I realized that something about him had me spooked. I had a creepy feeling. His voice in the flesh was even more weird than on that tape the Polks had, and it clashed with his average-guy appearance. I felt edgy, and I remember asking myself in his car why the hell I kept doing this fucking job.

"He tells me the target is a woman, and he wants her hurt in a very specific way. She might come home with a guy, and if she does then I have to 'waste him' so I can 'get on with the job on *her*.' The palms of my hands were sweaty, I wondered what the hell was going on. He tells me he'll give me more details on the job as we go but first he wants me to know my pay for his whole gig will be heavy, like seventy or eighty grand. Right then he made a quick move into the center console with his right hand, and my left arm and fist tensed and began to move toward his throat . . . as he pulled out a small wad of cash. He dropped thirty dollars into my open palm and told me it was my plane fare so I'd 'know he was for real.' I took a deep breath and tried to force myself to relax and roll with things.

"He went on to tell me he figured I'd make ten percent of what he got, which he figured to be seven to eight hundred thousand dollars, in a civil suit settlement with one of the big department stores up there. When I looked at him with a puzzled expression he just laughed and kept talking. He'd thought it all out . . . he'd be injured in an accident at the store, they would settle out of court, *and* he'd be in the hospital for his perfect alibi when I did the thing to the woman. As he talked I saw that he was a careful driver, he didn't speed and he always signaled his next move. That, I thought, should make it easier for my guys. He turned off the expressway and slowed onto a side street.

"I asked him what sort of accident did he plan to have with my help. He says about two years ago his eye doctor diagnosed that he was going blind in his left eye. He knew the Driver's License Bureau would revoke his DL because of it and that he wouldn't be able to drive or work. He had thought about it for a long time and decided to put his misfortune to work for him. He had a smug grin on his face as he said, 'So . . . I want you to blind me in one eye . . . with a screwdriver'.

"I pretended to look around like I was enjoying the scenery. I could not let Baldwin know I was trying as hard as I could to keep the roast beef sandwich I ate on the plane from coming back to life and spewing all over the dash of his car. I found I was in a battle with the very character I had created. The thought of plunging a screwdriver into the eye of this sick fuck, although pleasing to Al Sanetti, bothered the shit out of me. Al *Smith* wanted to strain Baldwin through one of the car's vent windows.

"I knew if Baldwin saw that what he was asking bothered the veteran contract killer I was supposed to be, the deal would be blown. So I tried to act unconcerned about the whole thing, like it was a request I had heard often. I guess my anger at him helped me focus on the job. I took a few deep breaths. I looked into the side mirror but didn't see McBride and Ray or Rawlings anywhere in the traffic behind us. I also saw the small sticker in the mirror that read: 'Objects in mirror are closer than they appear', and I wondered who it meant—Smith or Sanetti."

Here is a transcript of a statement taken by Orange County Sheriff's Office, Detective Division:

Q: Do you understand that my name is Det. Steve Ray, and I'm employed by the Orange County Sheriff's Office?
A: Yes.
RAY: Ah, would you state your name please?
A: Connie, um, Constance Matthews.
RAY: Connie, you realize I'm taping this statement, this conversation, and you agree to the taping of it?

MATTHEWS: Yes sir.

RAY: Connie, do you know Arthur Baldwin?

MATTHEWS: Yes, sir, he's my ex-husband.

RAY: Could you tell us about breaking up, your marriage broke up and what happened since that time? Has your husband threatened you at any time?

MATTHEWS: Okay, we were married approximately two years, we split about eight months ago. Art had a lot of pressures he couldn't deal with and it caused a lot of problems in our home. He made threats when he left, like he was gonna take his life, he didn't want to live anymore. He called me constantly, followed me, showed up everywhere . . . that was the first month. The second month he was gonna kill *me*, and he called the house and I changed my number so he called my office and told me I would never live to see a future, and that he would come, eventually somebody would, uh, get me . . .

RAY: Go on.

MATTHEWS: The next month he started going to a psychiatrist so I listened when he called me because I thought I could help him get through some of his problems . . . if I listened maybe he'd get it all out. I felt like I *tried* in our marriage, but maybe I was partly to blame, so I listened. He said the psychiatrist was able to help him with part of his life that he had never been able to deal with, which had caused serious problems in our marriage, and I *won't* discuss that. He seemed to be changing, sending me flowers at work and cards at home. He was drowning me in attention. We tried to get it back together and spent one weekend away and talked a lot, and then we went to a counselor. I still didn't want to live together with him but thought a counselor might help us. But that doctor said, after three sessions, that there was no way we'd be able to put it back together. Art knew then we weren't going to make it, so he started all over again, the threats and the calls. He was begging me and I told him we were stifling each other, and he told me I'd either bury him or he'd bury me. I went to a judge and got a divorce.

RAY: Did that end it?

MATTHEWS: No, sir. He asked to meet me and I parked next to him at a shopping center lot and he threw everything I had ever given him into my car. Then he began yelling at me and telling me he was losing weight because he couldn't eat and that the next picture I got of him would be in his coffin. He said that after he died I'd never be free as long as I live, I'd have to look over my shoulder every time I went anywhere because he would have what he called his 'ultimate revenge.' He said after he dies the money will be used to put a contract against me to either kill me, and everything I had ever worked for . . . my children, my . . . I'm sorry . . .

RAY: It's okay, it's okay.

MATTHEWS: I'm sorry . . .

RAY: Did he ever threaten your children from the first marriage?

MATTHEWS: Yes. He was gonna have my son beaten up, and he tried to hit my daughter once. Mostly the threats were against me, though.

RAY: Did he ever get physical with you?

MATTHEWS: Yes, he choked me once during an argument. He was always accusing me of things. He abused me more mentally.

RAY: Have you ever reported any of this?

MATTHEWS: Well, I didn't really put it on record. I just called and said I was having problems and asked for them to patrol around the house more. I never really filed a report against him.

RAY: Okay. Is there anything else you can think of?

MATTHEWS: Yes . . . he told me there's a fine line between love and hate, and he said, "I only wish I could hate you but I love you." I guess it must have turned back.

"Baldwin was driving slowly now through a parking lot next to a glass building that housed an insurance company, and told me quietly that was where *she* worked. She had the usual nine to five, Monday through Friday schedule. He said he thought he saw her car there, as he slammed on the brakes. It wasn't hers. I winced, but then realized he hadn't noticed the car occupied by what looked like two businessmen that had almost rear-ended us. They had pulled into the lot behind us and weren't prepared for Baldwin's sudden halt. I saw McBride and Steve Ray looking everywhere but at us, and imagined I could actually see the glaring red on Ray's embarrassed face. He was behind the wheel. I still hadn't spotted Rawlings behind us, and thought those Orange County guys had done a pretty good job so far. Baldwin didn't stop talking. I didn't know it then, but they were having problems with the small transmitter I was wearing. They were picking up lots of static, and only parts of understandable conversation":

ARTHUR BALDWIN: Listen, Al, do you know where I can get a nice .9 mm automatic with a silencer? I have another job I want to handle eventually, but that one I'll probably do myself.

AL SMITH: Sure, Art. I can get almost any kind of weapon you want. Tell me about that job, maybe I can help. What is it, a business thing?

BALDWIN: Nah, Al. I'll probably handle it myself after this job you're doing for me.

(Pause. More traffic noise. Subject driving.)

BALDWIN: *(Continues)* I'm gonna go to another place now, and I want you to promise me you won't get nervous.

SMITH: Why would I get nervous?

BALDWIN: First tell me you won't get nervous, 'cause I gotta go by this place for a minute and I don't want you to get uncomfortable.

SMITH: I never get nervous, Art. So where are we going? What's the deal?

BALDWIN: I'm going to go where I work, at City Hall . . . and there are always police cars there because that's where they have the police station in our little town. I don't want you to see the police cars and get nervous.

SMITH: Are you a cop or something, Art?

BALDWIN: *(Laughing)* No. But I do work in records there, and I'm friendly in a roundabout way with some of them.

SMITH: I see . . .

Sure enough, they pulled into the lot behind the small city hall building and Baldwin got out of the car and went in the back door. While he was gone Al spoke softly to the empty car, hoping McBride and Ray and Rawlings were picking it up on the wire. He didn't see them but guessed they were around. Al told the empty car he was waiting for Baldwin to bring him something from inside the city hall and didn't know where they would go next. A few minutes later Baldwin returned and tossed a manila envelope into Al's lap. While Baldwin drove, Al examined the contents. It was a complete profile on one Constance Matthews, forty years old. It had her physical description, home and work address and vehicle make and color. Enough information for Al to find her and do the job. Then Baldwin wanted to know if Al was ready for a drink and some dinner.

From tape transcript (augmented). Location, Bennigan's restaurant, booth near front windows:

ARTHUR BALDWIN: Before we really get started, Al, I want to show you something about me. I don't miss too much that goes on around me.

("The waitress came with the drinks and took our dinner order. My stomach felt like it had been kicked by a pissed-off Shetland pony but I tried to act like I was hungry and ordered a steak.")

BALDWIN: I want you to know why I'm so comfortable with you, Al. And why I know you'll do this job for me. First of all, it's the way you look. I mean . . . sure, you work out and you're a big guy and you've got that black beard and those big hands and all. I mean, you wear those jeans and boots and that tight shirt and you *look* bad, you know? Then there's your eyes, Al. Like, they never stop looking. You're always checking out everything, and you have a real serious look to you.

("Okay . . . could be a hitman . . . could be a cop.")

BALDWIN: And then there's that big heavy gold jewelry you're wearing, Al. It not only tells me you're a player, a with-it guy, but it tells me something else. You really are who you say you are.

SMITH: Oh yeah?

BALDWIN: Sure. Look there . . . "AS" is on your ring. "AS" equals Al Sanetti . . . see?

SMITH: Oh shit. Damn, Art, you're right. I usually don't wear this ring but I was in a hurry for the flight, so I must have forgotten about it.

("He sat back and sipped his drink with a know-it-all look on his face, and I took a gulp of mine, and I waited. He leaned close to me again and went on.")

BALDWIN: Twenty-five hundred for this job, Al. Half up front, the rest when it's done. I know that's just peanuts, and if we can put together the "accident" at the department store, the big money will follow. After the fucking lawyers get through with it.

SMITH: Tell me about *this* job.

BALDWIN: *(Very quietly)* Connie is always whining to me that she wants . . . some peace and quiet . . . all the time, peace and quiet. There are some things worse than death, Al. I want you to blind her, destroy her hearing, rip out her voicebox . . . and cripple her. Paralyze her somehow . . . by breaking her neck or spine, so she'll be aware of what has happened to her but won't be able to move or hear or speak or see . . . ever again.

("Our dinners arrived, and Baldwin dove into his with

great gusto while I tried to remember those old childhood skills required to push the food around on the plate so it looks like you've eaten most of it. He wasn't through yet.")

BALDWIN: Her son is outta the picture. Took off somewhere. Good riddance, he was a stupid dopehead anyway, nothin' but trouble, that kid. There's a fourteen-year-old daughter too, and she might be there. Also maybe Connie will have a boyfriend or a date or something . . .

SMITH: And if there is?

BALDWIN: Waste him.

SMITH: What about the girl?

BALDWIN: She's fourteen . . .

SMITH: What about the girl?

BALDWIN: She's fourteen.

("He looked around the crowded restaurant. The place was filled with couples and families, children, teenagers. He looked back at me and shrugged.")

BALDWIN: If the girl's there . . . do the same to her that you do to the mother. And waste the guy.

Al pushed carefully up against a urinal in the men's room and kept his head turned so he could see the door. He had seen McBride walk into the restaurant, loiter at the bar a moment, then amble back toward the bathrooms. He stood beside Al now, and they spoke in low voices:

AL SMITH: This fucking asshole is one scary dude, Bill.

BILL MCBRIDE: He looks like a fucking punk to me, Al. What's so bad about him?

SMITH: How much of the conversation are you getting over this goddamned wire?

MCBRIDE: That's part of the reason I came in here, Al. The wire is breakin' up *bad* . . . we're gettin' almost nothin', well, it's probably on the tape, and when we clean it up we'll be able to do a readable transcript, *maybe*. But as far as now . . . we can hear you guys talking but we're only getting the words sporadically. Shit . . . I thought I was gonna have a fucking heart attack in that office lot when we climbed up your ass . . . but I guess the punk never even saw us.

SMITH: No . . . he's payin' too much attention impressing me.

MCBRIDE: Yeah. So what's the big deal about this punk? What's so scary?

SMITH: Damn it, Bill, the guy's a stone cold whacko! He sits there looking like a normal person, but inside his mind he's completely *fried*. He wants me to do some weird shit to this woman *and* her kid, and he's got more targets out there he hasn't even told me about yet. The guy just gives me the creeps. I got a feeling he's even more dangerous because he comes *across* as such a regular dude. There's all kinds of twisted snakes and roaches and worms and shit crawling around in his skull . . .

(Pause. Sounds of running water, toilet flushing, door opening and closing)

MCBRIDE: All right, Al. We're still playin' with the wire, and we'll be right behind you all the way, so don't let this pansy bastard worry you.

SMITH: Tell you what I'd like to do, Bill. Save everybody a lot of trouble, and me an ulcer, and that's just wait until we're back in his car and blow his squirrelly head *right off.* Then get back on the airplane with you, go home and forget it.

MCBRIDE: That's my Al.

McBride left the bathroom before Al did, and Al caught a glimpse of him leaving the restaurant as he rejoined Baldwin at their table. Baldwin sat toying with his coffee and checking the addition on the dinner bill. He left some money on the table, and they walked out together:

"Baldwin drove me to a Days Inn," Al said. "He hung around the lobby while I registered for the night, then we walked back outside to his car. He copied down my room and the telephone number of the motel in a little black book. We shook hands and he drove off with a confident wave. I was tired and carried my bag up to my room in no big hurry.

"McBride phoned the room a few minutes later. He was checked in to the same motel but would not come to my room on the off-chance that Baldwin or someone eyeballing for him might come back to see how I was doing. McBride told mc Ray and Rawlings would spend the night at their homes. He had their numbers, and they would meet him at six. I told him some of Baldwin's plans, about the half-payment to come tomorrow and the envelope with the info on the intended victim. McBride felt that even if Baldwin didn't pay me any money up front, with his meeting me, giving me the envelope, showing me the women's workplace, we had enough to nail him right then. He said he'd call me in the morning before the asshole showed up, and he told me not to let the creep ruin my dreams. I took off that screwed-up frigging wire, took the batteries out and put them on the dresser, and examined the wire for any obvious problems. I got some new batteries out of my bag and placed them in the device, hoping that would give it a good kick in the ass."

Al called home after that, spoke with Sylvia for a few moments, then took a long hot shower. He flipped through the television channels, then turned the TV off and went to bed. Before he turned out the light he lay there thinking of the way his feelings had been tossed around by this deal with Baldwin . . . Baldwin sitting there looking out of his twisted fantasy world, intent on using Al to ruin his victim. He apparently wanted Al to inflict on her his sadistic interpretation of "peace and quiet" . . . gouge out her eyes, cut out her voicebox, deafen her, snap her spine . . .

Sitting beside my desk in my office now, Al went on about Baldwin. "The sonofabitch sat there smiling at me and telling me to 'snap her spine' as if the reality of that act was something he had no goddamned idea of. I knew very much about the reality of that act. I was lying there in that goddamned sterile motel room with Baldwin's words crashing around in my head, and it made me remember a terrible time, a horrible time. I don't know, it might be part of the reason I had such a hard time dealing with him. I'll tell you what his words made me remember . . ."

I watched Al work himself up to it . . . first stretching his long legs out, then gathering them under his chair, taking a couple of deep breaths, then letting the air out slowly, crossing his big arms over his chest, then opening them and running his hands down the opposite forearms and finally bunching his fists on top of his knees. He looked out through the wall of glass into my backyard, lush with tropical growth, and began:

"It was a hot and clear Fort Lauderdale evening, about seven o'clock, when my partner and I . . . we were working a plain-clothes robbery detail . . . were sent to a disturbance call because there were no other available units. The disturbance was taking place near Davie Boulevard and Riverland Road. We hauled ass over there.

"As we pulled up I saw a kid, maybe sixteen-years-old, in the middle of the road. He looked scuffed and torn-up some, like he had been in a fight. His hair was sticking up and his eyes looked wild. He stood in the road defying the heavy traffic, making the cars go around him, then screaming at the drivers as they did. A large truck bore down on him as I moved beside the road, trying to get closer. The kid kept on screaming and waving at the truck, almost egging the driver on like he *wanted* to get run down. Out of the corner of my eye I saw a small crowd on the other side of the road, watching the show.

"The truck missed the kid by inches, and the kid swung at the side of it with a glancing blow, screaming obscenities at the driver as the truck sped away. I stepped into the street, held up my badge and ID and told the kid I was a cop and he was under arrest.

"The kid told me to fuck off, then stood in the middle of the road, rigid, screaming some more. I yelled at him again that I was a cop, and then reached out and grabbed the kid's left arm as he began to walk away from me. As soon as I had a grip on his wrist, which was wet with sweat, the kid spun around real fast and threw a wild arching punch at my head with his right fist. I twisted, lunged and pushed my forearm against the kid's neck to force him back and get inside the blow. He kept struggling and we bounced against the police unit and then fell, sort of twisting and writhing down to the pavement of the street.

"Then the kid was very still. His breath came in like ragged gasps as I handcuffed him. I stood up and brushed myself off and told him to get on his feet. His teeth were clenched and he told me he couldn't get up. I told him to get up and walk to jail like a man . . . I was tired of his attitude and thought he was still playing badass games. He got sort of a puzzled look on his face, and then . . . said again that he *couldn't* get up. His neck was broken. He was paralyzed from the neck down."

Al continued the story now, his voice quiet, his face slightly pale. The inevitable lawsuit was filed against the City of Fort Lauderdale and Officer Al Smith on behalf of the kid, and he and his lawyer went away with a million-and-a-half-dollar settlement. Several convincing witnesses came forward in behalf of Al and the city, and there was strong testimony to the effect that the kid was intoxicated on speed or booze, had been fighting and acting in an irrational and reckless manner. Several of the witnesses told about the way the kid had been bullfighting with the passing cars, actually trying to get run over (or appearing to), and several accurately described the brief struggle and Al's actions at that time.

As a cop on the traditional (wrong) end of a civil lawsuit, Al had magnified feelings of frustration with the process. The truth of the incident, the reality, was pushed aside in the interests of expediency and budget. The court and the city focused on the kid's side of the story and his resulting predicament. Al's version of the story, his description of what really happened and his feelings were all ignored. Sure, Al would rather have his hurt feelings than to have to live that kid's life, but the frustration of being a stifled witness to this managing of the truth left its mark on him. Right up to now with Baldwin and his stuff about snapping the spine of his ex-lady love. It brought back acute memories of the kid and Al's mixed feelings about what happened to the kid and to himself.

As a man and as a cop the incident with the kid left Al scarred. Again, *there can be no comparison,* he knows, between the kid's pain and his. But Al did not just walk away whistling a happy tune after the dust settled. He found he had trouble concentrating on the job. He shied away from arrests and hesitated during physical confrontations. Sleep eluded him for months. Most of what he felt was guilt and questions of not *how* it happened but *why.* He knew he worked very hard to go out onto those streets to do the *right* thing . . . so how could this have turned out so wrong? Sylvia hung in there with him when he sought help, including counseling with the pastor of their church. Al clung to his sense of purpose and professionalism, and was especially thankful for Sylvia's strength.

"Sure," he was saying now in my office, "I knew about inflicting pain, about breaking necks. I had an ongoing intimate relationship with all the things that Arthur Baldwin talked about so glibly. I lay in that motel room waiting for the morning, alone with those memories that just don't go away. Not even when you sleep. Anyway, I woke up early, not feeling rested, and it was a good thing I did. I mean woke up early. Because Arthur Baldwin knocked on the motel-room door at six, and when I opened it he stood there with his fucking smile, looking bright and fresh, holding two cups of coffee. I had just finished a shower and was dressed except for my shoes. As he came in juggling the coffee cups the phone rang.

"It was Bill McBride over in his room. He wanted to let me know he had already heard from Rawlings and Ray, but before he could get into it I cut him off and acted like I was talking to the motel manager, some bullshit about my wake-up call being late. While I was talking I could see Baldwin in the mirror behind me looking around the room. I looked down and saw the batteries and the transmitter lying on the desk in front of me. My guts began to knot up, and the only thing I could think to do was pick up the mess and stuff it into my pockets as casually as possible. Baldwin said nothing.

"McBride finally caught on and hung up. I shrugged at Baldwin, told him it was the manager checking the service. Then I sat on the edge of the bed to put my shoes on. Baldwin shrugged too, and sipped his coffee. Couple of minutes later I was ready to ride . . . still with the apparently useless wire stuffed in my pocket. Fuck it . . . I was edgy and a little tight after my ragged night and the early appearance of Arthur Asshole Baldwin. I *really* didn't like the guy. Before we walked out of the room, Baldwin began telling me there was a problem with money. I told him it must be his problem then, and he said it was, that we had made a deal for twenty-five hundred and ten percent of the lawsuit settlement. He knew he had said he'd give me half the twenty-five up front, but it turned out his source for the cash didn't come through so he couldn't have it for me right then. Wanted to know if it would screw us up.

"I let him hang for a long ten-count while I just stared at him. Then I told him our business depended a lot on trust and a person's word. We had made a deal yesterday. He had even given me my plane fare back to Lauderdale . . . big fucking deal . . . and he had given me all the info for the job. I had a target and I knew what needed to be done. I knew Bob Polk had referred me and I trusted him . . . and now I thought he, Baldwin, was a stand-up guy too. I told him I wasn't worried and I knew he'd pay me the half up front when he got it. There were other jobs he wanted to discuss, anyway.

I guess he bought it flat-out. He stayed with me as I checked out of the motel, then we climbed into his car to go to breakfast, and he began talking again like he had a goddamned Gatling-gun jaw."

Here is a transcript of a partial tape of bad quality (augmented):

ARTHUR BALDWIN: There's one little change I want to make, Al, or at least clarify something.

("He talked quietly over his half-finished breakfast plate. My grits had chilled to the consistency of wallpaper paste but I was able to mush them around enough to cover my uneaten eggs. I waited.")

BALDWIN: It's about the neck or the . . . spine part of it.

(Pause)

BALDWIN: *(Continues)* I want you to break her spine, but only so she's paralyzed from the waist down.

AL SMITH: Uh . . . not from the neck down?

BALDWIN: No. From the waist down. I want her to be able to move around *some*, you know?

In my office Al stood, ran his hands hard over his face and began pacing.

"Finally all of my feelings about that piece of shit sonofabitch were beginning to jell . . . like fucking napalm in my guts. That was *it*, I thought, *enough* of this asshole's bullshit. I felt my whole body begin to tighten, my shoulders hunched, my fists balled up, and I wanted to just launch myself over that table. I wanted to punch my fists into his fucking smooth smiling little face and drive him *down*. I wanted to grab his pencil-neck with his stupid little bobbing Adam's apple, pull him out of the booth and kick his perverted ass all the way out of that restaurant and into the parking lot. Knee him in the balls, if he *had* any, then drop the slug into the nearest sewer."

Al looked at me, rolled his shoulders, flexed his fingers and gave me a crooked grin.

"But I didn't. No . . . I'm a cop, right? Right.

"Unaware of how I was feeling about him, Baldwin then hands me a color photo that he pulled out of his shirt pocket. It showed a pleasant looking woman with curly brown hair and a wary look in her eyes. He takes another bite of toast and tells me that was the woman I was to do. He said we'd finish breakfast, then drive over to her apartment so I could get a look at the layout. I had to go to the bathroom again.

"McBride was waiting for me and I told him right off that Baldwin wasn't gonna come up with any more cash right then for the deal. We washed our hands and looked at each other in the mirror as we spoke quietly. McBride seemed to think it didn't matter. We had enough points of the conspiracy with what we had yesterday, and this morning's photo, and the fact that now he was going to take me to the victim's house. He told me they were getting some of the talk on the stupid wire, and said that the Orange County guys also thought we had enough to take the shithead down. I told him I'd get Baldwin to stop at a pay phone after we scoped out the apartment. That's where I'd give them the move-in signal. There were no paper towels in that bathroom, just those idiot hot-air blowers. We dried our hands on toilet paper and when McBride walked out he said he hoped Baldwin would resist. I did too.

"So we did the tour of the apartment complex where Constance Matthews lived, then left the side street and got back on a highway. Baldwin asked me if I thought the setup was okay, could I find a hiding place to wait for her to come home. I told him it was workable. Then, kind of hesitating, licking his lips . . . the whole bit . . . he asked me if he could have the photo of Connie back. He figured I'd be able to recognize her now that I'd seen it, and he felt it was the only thing that directly linked *us* to *her*. I handed it over and told him I liked the way he thought. Then I told him to look for a pay phone . . . I wanted to check on the airlines to see when my flight was. He said he'd make a call too."

In the phone booth, Al took the phone out of its cradle, heard Baldwin drop a quarter in his, and turned his shoulders slightly away from Baldwin. Baldwin turned too, so they were almost back-to-back. This time Al spotted Ray and McBride easily, and then Rawlings. He held the phone receiver level with his chest and pumped it up and down rapidly twice. McBride and Ray left their car at the pumps of the service station that housed the pay phones, and Rawlings pulled his car right up to the phones from the other side of the lot. Baldwin heard the activity behind him, and turned to find himself staring into the barrels of three hand-guns held in the rock-steady grips of three very serious guys who suggested he:

"*Freeze*, dickhead."

"Don't move. We're police officers. You're under arrest."

"Just drop the phone, asshole, just drop the phone . . ."

As they leaned him over the hood of Rawlings's car to pat him down and cuff him they heard him mutter, 'I should have known when I saw those batteries.' Al walked away from him with his back turned. He went to the other car by the pumps, got into the front seat, and waited. McBride would ride with Baldwin to the sheriff's office in Rawlings's car. Al would go with Steve Ray. Baldwin's car would be towed as evidence after it was searched (and the victim-to-be's photo was recovered). Al watched as they drove off, leaving him and Ray waiting for the wrecker. He felt drained.

ARTHUR BALDWIN REFUSED to make any kind of plea-bargain deal, and his lawyer took the case in front of a jury. Again, even though there was good testimony from the victim and the other cops, and plenty of evidence showing the criteria for the conspiracy charges had been met, much of the judicial conflict boiled down to whom the jury would believe—Baldwin or Al.

"I remember that it struck me that when Connie Matthews was there for the early part of the proceedings I couldn't tell if she was more afraid of Baldwin or *me*," Al said. "Then Baldwin's lawyer tried to get cute, telling the court I had blocked the discovery process by deliberately ignoring his request to give a deposition on the case. I pointed out to the judge that the case was over three months old, and the lawyer's request for a deposition had come to me in Fort Lauderdale the evening before the trial when I was getting ready to catch my flight up there. I didn't have to suggest that the lawyer had made a clumsy attempt to delay the proceedings . . . the judge's beautiful fucking scowl showed he knew *exactly* what was going on. The trial went ahead, the prosecutor had his act together, the Orange County guys were squared away, and the jury eventually decided that we didn't just make the whole thing up."

Baldwin was convicted of the charges and sentenced to twelve years in prison. Al went back to work, glad the system had worked but convinced the sentence should have been life . . . just as if Baldwin's plans had actually been carried out. Maybe he'd get psychiatric help in prison, maybe he'd get himself back on track, but Al doubted it. Baldwin was smart enough to manipulate an overcrowded and busy system run by well-intentioned and often naïve counselors. It worried Al that Baldwin would probably serve less than four years, and then he'd be back out in our world, making his plans. Maybe he'd move away from Florida after he got released from jail and live quietly somewhere, sticking long needles into helpless frogs and setting rat traps in small boxes full of white mice.

"About four months after the trial I received a very nice letter from Connie Matthews," Al said. "She thanked me for my work, and I tell you, that letter meant more to me than my making 'officer of the month' for the Baldwin case."

Sometimes it is said about cops who work in vice too long: If you work in the sewer long enough, you'll get some stink on you. Al's special assignments had him cozying up to, and spending time with, some pretty twisted people, and every time he thought he had been shocked enough, or had been hired to do the sickest, evilest thing, some freaky whacko would come along and zap him again. Like the vice cops, Al Sanetti worked in the sewer—a psychological one but just as filthy, just as poisonous. Al Smith fought the motion that he might be getting too comfortable there, and fought to keep clear the separation between Al Sanetti's world and Al Smith's.

I thought some about Al and his job as I reviewed the stories he had shared with me. I had been a cop, had worked those streets, had played some of those games, had worn different skins to blend in with the players. I also knew there were deeper motivations that kept a cop going out there night after night— feelings not easy for a professional like Al to bring out into the open. What's clear is that Al survives those streets and is effective because he believes in what he's doing, he knows what's right and wrong. No faint blue line.

I've felt something of his drive, his not just desire but *need* to help. No speeches. He is a cop, we need *him*. And, like he says, he's still at it.

Al summed it up.

"I've handled more contract murder cases during the time this book was being written . . . there was the doctor down in Miami looking around for a hitman to fill a contract on his wife. A different kind of prescription. No doubt there will be others. I guess hitmen are in demand these days . . . and cops always are. It's an interesting life, being both . . . being a cop hired to kill, and I guess I'll go on with it until Sylvia makes me retire. Or until my luck runs out. I don't think I'll worry about it too much right now, though. There are people out there who want to kill each other . . . and I'm just waiting for the phone to ring so Al Sanetti and I can go help them out."